The Energy Crisis and the Environment

An International Perspective

edited by
Donald R. Kelley

The Energy Crisis and the Environment

An International Perspective

PRAEGER PUBLISHERS
Praeger Special Studies

New York • London • Sydney • Toronto

Library of Congress Cataloging in Publication Data

Main entry under title:

The Energy crisis and the environment.

(Praeger special studies in international politics
and government)
Includes index.
1. Energy policy—Environmental aspects—Addresses,
essays, lectures. I. Kelley, Donald R., 1943-
HD9502.A2E5436 1977 301.31 76-24355
ISBN 0-275-23850-4

PRAEGER PUBLISHERS
PRAEGER SPECIAL STUDIES
383 Madison Avenue, New York, N.Y. 10017, U.S.A.

Published in the United States of America in 1977
by Praeger Publishers,
A Division of Holt, Rinehart and Winston, CBS, Inc.

9   038   98765432

Printed in the United States of America

PREFACE

The life blood of industry and complex consumer economies, for virtually all of the world's industrialized nations, has been the continuing flow of energy from once presumably inexhaustible deposits of coal, oil, and natural gas. Industrial development and the consumption of prodigious amounts of energy have gone hand in hand and have been wedded in the mind of modern industrial man as necessary prerequisites for admission into the world's exclusive club of modern economic giants. That such energy consumption has in the past thoughtlessly disregarded the finite nature of the earth's resources, or that it has occurred for the most part without concern for the environment, have been issues that until recently have occupied the attention of only a handful of conservationists and environmentalists.

All of that has changed within the last decade. The deteriorating state of the environment became an unavoidable reality for most of the world's already industrialized nations in the late 1960s and early 1970s, partially as a consequence of traumatic environmental disasters such as the Santa Barbara oil spill in the United States, the destruction of Europe's waterways from the Rhine to Lake Baikal, and the recognition of bizarre and frightening effects on human health such as Minamata disease in Japan, and also as a consequence of the growing and increasingly sophisticated body of scientific knowledge about the impact of pollution on the ecosphere. As rivers died and the skies of major industrial cities darkened with pollution, environmentalists captured the attention of a growing audience, and in most of the developed nations included in this study, this new awareness translated into stricter environmental legislation.

The realization that real or impending energy shortages also posed a major threat both to industrialized and developing nations struck with traumatic impact just as many countries were beginning to accept environmental constraints. While periodic shortfalls had occurred in the most industrialized states even before 1973, it took the Arab embargo and the OPEC-sponsored price increases that followed, to focus world attention on the extent major industrial powers had become dependent on imported oil. No less important was the impact of such price increases on developing nations, which now had to compete on the world market for scarce and costly fuels. For both, the prospects of higher energy prices and of the potential unavailability of adequate energy supplies at any price raised the specter of difficult reallocations of developmental and consumption priorities.

The impact of the environmental and energy crises was further intensified by the inseparable linkage between the two policy areas. In both technical and political terms, it became virtually impossible to separate the two questions or to avoid at least the appearance that difficult choices must be made between adequate energy supplies and environmental quality. From the technical point of view, energy consumption and environmental protection are really two sides of the same coin. Energy is the key to modern technology and industrial growth, and is also the principal source of modern-day pollution. Moreover, many of the gains in environmental quality that had been made before the energy crisis had been accomplished through changes in energy consumption patterns in industry and densely populated urban areas; this usually meant that high-pollution but less costly and more plentiful fuels such as coal had been phased out in favor of environmentally less destructive but more expensive energy sources such as low-sulphur oil or natural gas. The new situation that prevailed after 1973 inevitably raised the question of whether such conversions had been wise and reopened the question of choosing acceptable trade-off levels between a national energy profile and environmental quality.

The questions of energy consumption and environmental quality are also inexorably linked in the political sense. Vested interests in business and industry, as well as the energy producers and processers themselves, had an important stake in the resolution of the conflict. With a very few remarkable exceptions such as Denmark, business and industry in general resisted stricter pollution controls when the question first arose and now viewed the energy crisis as an opportunity to argue for a rollback of recently passed environmental legislation. The energy producers themselves had an even more immediate stake inasmuch as they became involved in bitter controversies over the development of alternative sources or over their own allegedly self-serving status as energy cartels. Further political sensitivity arose because the questions raised by the energy-environment dilemma easily spilled over into other issues of public concern. Seen in the public mind in terms of the political and economic power of domestic energy cartels, the potential sacrifice of recent gains in environmental quality, the "blackmail" of the industrial states of OPEC nations, the threat to consumer life styles, or the prospect that developmental goals would have to be scaled downward, the whole interlocking set of issues animated a public debate in most of the countries of this study about national life styles and priorities. Moreover, decisions about energy and environmental trade offs were now distinctly political inasmuch as both areas had either historically been under state control or had recently become the subjects of state regulation. Very few of the critical decisions about energy development or the preservation of the environment remained in the hands of private industry or individual consumers; an overlay of direct state control or of governmental policies that attempted to foster desired energy and environmental decisions brought the entire energy-environment question into the forum of public policy making. This politicization was further intensified by the presence of a multitude of governmental agencies with regulatory functions in both areas. The battle over trade offs between energy and the environment was joined not only by private industrial and environmental interests but also by state agencies with frequently overlapping and rarely clearly defined policy mandates and institutional prerogatives that were, in most cases, vigorously asserted or defended.

The purpose of this study is to examine the relationship between energy and environmental policies both as an inquiry into the question of whether the 1973 crisis resulted in substantial rollbacks of environmental protection--subsequent chapters will show surprising results that ran counter to the authors' original estimates--and as an examination of the energy-environment nexus as an important study of the adaptation of political institutions and cultures to new and potentially disruptive issues. What follows is meant to be a political analysis of policy making on energy and environmental questions, with special attention to the conflict among industrial, environmental, and governmental interests in hammering out acceptable trade offs between two important and conflicting priorities. That both issues have assumed crisis dimensions for the most industrialized nations of the study merely intensifies that conflict and contributes an air of frantic concern within which the bureaucratic and public facets of the political process must operate. With this analytic focus in mind, the authors have tried to adhere to a reasonably coherent common framework dealing with (1) the seriousness of the energy-environment dilemma, (2) the extent to which pressures have arisen to weaken environmental protection programs, such as they may be, (3) the response of environmental lobbies and environmental protection agencies at all levels of government, (4) the result, as thus far evident, of the clash between energy-related and environmental forces, and (5) the long-term implications of continued energy shortfalls in terms of possible trade offs between energy and developmental policy on the one hand and the environment on the other.

A word is also in order about the countries selected for inclusion in this study. As the reader will see from the Table of Contents, they run the gamut from industrial superpowers to developing third-world nations. Perhaps even more important in a study of the political dimensions of energy and environmental policies, the great diversity that they represent in terms of forms of government, levels of socioeconomic development, and distinctive political cultures sets the stage for a comparison of the factors that determine a nation's response to energy-related and environmental imperatives. Moreover, the list of countries includes both energy exporters and importers as well as several distinctive national strategies for energy development and environmental protection which stress different technical approaches to both problems or idiosyncratic features such as the nature of domestic energy resources. In short, among the nations of this study one finds a cross section not only of a multitude of social and governmental systems but also of the wide range of energy-related and environmental problems which have come to confront both industrialized and developing nations.

CONTENTS

LIST OF TABLES

The Energy Crisis and the Environment

An International Perspective

THE UNITED STATES: COAL, THE DIRTIEST DECLARATION OF INDEPENDENCE

Walter A. Rosenbaum

> The United States must embark upon a major effort to achieve self-sufficiency in energy, an effort I have called Project Independence.
>
> > Richard M. Nixon
> > Message to Congress
> > January 23, 1974

> Strip mining means just what it says. It strips the people of everything they have.
>
> > Joe Begley
> > Letcher County, Ky.

In late 1973 King Faisal cut the U.S. jugular vein, and it bled oil. Brief but total, the Arab embargo on U.S. oil inspired by the Saudis depleted U.S. imports by 2 million barrels daily. The U.S. public and its officials were shocked into recognizing the widening gap between domestic energy consumption and available resources. The economy was threatened. Washington was particularly chilled by the revelation of national vulnerability to external energy blockades. Federal officials announced an "energy crisis" and preached energy conservation, but it was new energy development they most wanted. Thus was born Project Independence, which, President Nixon promised, could make the nation by 1980 "no longer dependent to any significant extent upon potentially insecure foreign energy supplies."[1]

Project Independence immediately triggered a major conflict between environmentalists and energy developers. Ultimately the U.S. response to the energy crisis will be shaped by the outcome of

1

this conflict, for the environmental movement has become the organizational catalyst for opposition to a massive new U.S. energy
program and the principal political force with which the energy lobby
must reckon in fashioning a new national energy policy.

The project is still mostly rhetoric. Zealous energy developers disagree about the feasibility of U.S. energy "self-sufficiency,"
and the Ford Administration did not fashion an operational energy
program even modestly conforming to the project's prescriptions.
Project Independence, however, has become the rallying point for a
powerful energy coalition embracing the major electric utilities, the
economy's fossil fuel sector, diplomatic and military strategists,
the White House, and numerous legislators with visions of massive
new national energy production. It undoubtedly captures a prevalent
public belief that new energy development is imperative.

Ecologists fear that Project Independence, in some permuta-
tion, will become a pervasive assault on the environment and on
environmentally protective legislation. They warn that the chimera
of energy "self-sufficiency" and the powerful appeal to national security and economic development will be summoned by the energy
sector to emasculate the Clean Air Act, the Federal Water Pollution
Control Act amendments, and other environmental programs. They
worry that the movement will be thrown on the defensive and, while
many do not share Representative Morris Udall's conviction that the
movement "has its back against the wall," they suggest that environ-
mentalism will be in grave trouble if the public is convinced that the
nation faces a choice between energy development and environmental
protection.[2]

From the start of the energy crisis, those concerned about the
U.S. environment have been preoccupied with two strategic issues.
First, will the crisis, and Project Independence especially, affect
current environmental policy? Second, what configuration of political forces will shape future energy development? The answers
must necessarily be tentative, but coal appears to be the resource
concerning which the most environmentally significant decisions will
occur.

COAL AND CRISIS

More than any other energy resource, coal is the fuel that
feeds the conflict between environmentalist and energy developer.
Coal, the nation's most plentiful energy reserve, is an "energy
pariah," the mining technology of which is the most ecologically
damaging of all energy sources. The White House is heavily committed to ambitious new coal production; coal is so prominent that

all White House programs depend on its plentiful availability. Early in 1974 the Federal Energy Administration announced that "all the current scenarios for dealing with the nation's long-range energy needs include coal as one essential element."[3] In early 1975 the president's Energy Message to Congress placed "heaviest new emphasis on coal development";[4] in late 1975 the president elevated coal to "primary reliance" in future energy plans.[5]

The Appeal of Coal

Coal is cheap; coal is abundant. With half the globe's coal reserves, the United States possesses recoverable deposits equal to four times the energy potential of all Arabian oil fields. Conservative estimates suggest that this might fuel U.S. technology for 300 to 800 years. Coal is cheaper to burn than oil or natural gas, and huge low-sulfur reserves from the West could be consumed with greatly reduced risk of violating the new federal air emission standards for sulfur oxides. Although current coal production supplies less than 20 percent of the nation's current energy needs, more than half of its electric power is generated by coal. Industrial demand, particularly for metallurgical coal, is rising.[6]
Coal is the one energy reserve that is immune to foreign blockade and most likely to supplement or supplant diminishing supplies of other fuels. In fact, the U.S. presently exports 10 percent of its yearly production. Nuclear power, once the glittering "energy of the future," will be no significant energy source in this century because the nuclear power industry is beset with technical and economic problems, adding strong disincentives to rapid expansion. Supplies of domestic natural gas, already partially rationed, are unlikely to increase appreciably in the next several decades.[7]

"An Imminent and Inordinate Peril"

The new U.S. coal boom would cut its way across the continent behind the gargantuan shovels of the strip miner. Stripping technology makes coal the environmentally "dirtiest" of all energy to obtain and the issue that incites, more than any other, the opposition to massive new coal development. Critics predict that stripping, without which the nation's coal wealth cannot be efficiently mined, will yield a harvest of devastated land on an unprecedented scale. To the Kentucky legislature, long the indulgent guardian of stripping, it is "an imminent and inordinate peril."

Stripping makes coal unique among the nation's major fuel sources because its extractive costs, in environmental terms, are extremely high and inflicted directly upon the producing jurisdictions. The proponents of stripping seldom deny the immediate, violent ecological metamorphosis it produces. The House Committee on Interior and Insular Affairs offers a bleakly comprehensive summary of its impact, as follows:

> The side-effects of coal mining in the humid areas of the East and mid-West include: acid drainage which has ruined an estimated 11,000 miles of streams; the loss of prime hardwood forests and the destruction of wildlife habitat by strip-mining; the degrading of productive farm land; recurrent landslides; siltation and sedimentation of the river systems; the destructive movement of boulders; and perpetually burning mine waste dumps--these constitute a pervasive and far-reaching ambience. . . . In the Western States and the Northern Great Plains region the discovery of vast reserves of lignite and sub-bituminous coal has inspired plans for the expansion of coal surface mining on a very large scale, thus major adverse impacts to the region's land and people lie ahead. [8]

To obtain the coal envisioned by Project Independence, it would be necessary to strip-mine huge tracts of the unmined Western lands, which hold 70 percent of the nation's strippable coal reserves. The Fort Union Coal Formation, straddling the Powder River, alone contains about 40 percent of these reserves. Estimates suggest that mining the portion of the Formation that lies in the state of Wyoming would profoundly disturb 756,000 acres of farm and grazing land. [9] The Sierra Club predicts that Western stripping could constitute "the most massive industrial development of a rural area within a short period of time that has ever occurred in this country."[10] Compounding the ravages of stripping would be the secondary environmental degradation from the mine-mouth power generating facilities and industrial plants that would be likely to locate near abundant coal supplies.* Proponents of coal development contend that stripped land can

---

*The development of mine-mouth generating plants was seriously considered, and indirectly promoted, by the Ford Administration. For example, Federal Energy Agency Administrator Frank G. Zarb has advocated concentrating energy facilities at a few regional

be "restored" to its former environmental value, that the extent of
prospective land disturbance is exaggerated, that the direct economic
benefits to the states, such as large extraction royalties and increased national economic growth, mitigate the undesirable effects;
in any case, they argue, the country's urgent energy needs compel a
compromise between environmental amenities and energy consumption.

The trade-off calculus of coal resource development is largely
defined as a comparison of economic benefits and environmental costs.
The benefits and costs of new coal production are summarized in
Table 1 (where "primary" items are those whose impact is most immediately felt and "secondary" ones are those more diffuse).

TABLE 1

A Simple Cost-Benefit Calculus for Strip-Mined Coal

Benefits	Costs
Primary	Water Pollution
Heat energy for electric power generation and industrial use	Thermal
	Acid mine drainage
State and federal extraction royalties	Subterranean water-course disruption
Increased employment	Diminished water supplies for agriculture and human use
National security	
Export goods	Grazing, forest, and agriculture land
Secondary	
Petroleum distillates for commercial and industrial use	Air Pollution
	Industrial stack emissions
Economic growth	Auto emissions
Diminished oil and gas consumption	Electric generating emissions
	Increased resource depletion

Note: Primary items have an impact that is felt immediately;
the impact of the secondary items is more diffuse.
Source: Compiled by the author.

---

centers with abundant coal supplies (New York *Times*, December 25,
1975). The North Central Power Study, produced by 35 power companies and the U.S. Department of the Interior, suggested 42 mine-
mouth power plants along the Fort Union Formation, which when
completed would generate 50,000 megawatts of power, consume 210
million tons of coal yearly, and attract perhaps a half million people
to the affected areas of Wyoming, Montana, and North Dakota.

THE NEW POLITICS OF COAL

So long as the environmental degradation of coal mining was considered an economic externality and was not alarmingly overt, as in Appalachian deep-shaft mines, coal development was not a national issue. Except for its involvement in the industry's labor problems, the controlling policy of Washington was distributive and decentralized: it adopted a laissez-faire stance toward mining entrepreneurs and left the regulation of the mines (excluding labor relations) to the indulgent stewardship of the states. In the phrase of David Braybrooke and Charles E. Lindblom, the policy style was "incremental," because policy change, when it occurred, was "through small or incremental moves on particular problems rather than through a comprehensive reform program."[11]

The environmental devastation caused by strip mining forced the disintegration of the economic sector's coal imperium. The new political estate of coal ostensibly resembles a familiar scenario in U.S. politics, in which newly mobilized interests--in this case environmentalists and their allies--force a new debate over policy substance and style, and policy incrementalism is abandoned. Thus the new pluralism assumes one aspect with profound implications for future coal policy, which is that the policy debate is both substantive and structural. Issues concern the acceptable goals for new policy and institutional arrangements for policy implementation.

Two other aspects of the policy struggle, however, distinguish it from the more familiar outcomes in the breakdown of a well-established incremental policy process. First, the simultaneously rapid emergence of stripping technology and strongly mobilized opposition to it during a period of escalating energy demand is moving policy makers toward a "public satisfying-speculative" solution with low prospects of environmental benefit.

Second, there may be no political solution to the current pluralistic conflict over coal development that would have environmentally acceptable consequences. If these latter conclusions are accurate, the nation is likely to endure over the next several decades a cycle of recurring crises between coal development and energy needs in which the environmental and economic alternatives are progressively more severe. Environmentalists will be increasingly isolated from many other major constituents of their present coalition.

THE NEW POLICY PLURALISM

Until the late 1950s, almost all U.S. coal originated in the East, principally in Appalachia. Market forces and the availability of competing fuels largely determined national coal production. Now, in addition to that of the environmentalists, stripping technology has added at least three other major factions in the coal debate.

The States

The coal-ecology debate is shaped in good part by the manner in which the political jurisdictions of the nation overlay the physical distribution of the resource. The nation's federal structure partially distributes the locus of policy-making institutions into a set of 50 state political systems, whose attitude toward coal development is greatly affected by the particular energy-environmental trade-off they confront on the issue.

The states fall into the following three distinct groups in respect to their vulnerability to new coal stripping:

Group 1: Invulnerable.   These states have no strippable coal reserves. They lie primarily in the Northeast, deep South, and Southwest.

Group 2: Moderately Mined. These states, principally in the Midwest and South, are now being moderately to heavily stripped for bituminous coal. Included in this group are Alabama, Arkansas, Kentucky, Tennessee, Virginia, West Virginia, Illinois, Indiana, Michigan, Ohio, and Pennsylvania.

Group 3: Highly Vulnerable. These are mountain and Pacific states where virtually all the nation's currently unstripped reserves, primarily sub-bituminous, now reside. These states include Alaska, California, Washington, Arizona, Colorado, Montana, New Mexico, Utah, Wyoming, Kansas, and Iowa. [12]

Not surprisingly, interstate cleavages over the coal issue tend to divide the states into a developmentally oriented bloc without large strippable coal deposits and a bloc of those actively stripped or facing the imminent prospect of it. The latter group has been the most concerned with regulating and restraining the ambitious coal objectives in Project Independence.

Leaders in the Midwestern and Western states facing an onslaught of extensive stripping have frequently asserted that Project Independence would leave them with little more than a choice between status as an "energy exporter" (if coal mining alone were permitted) or an "energy province" (if mine-mouth electric generating plants proliferate, as the utilities would prefer). The alarm was sounded at the Western Governors' Conference in late 1975, when New Mexico Governor Jerry Apodaca indicted the Ford Administration for its lack of energy conservation. "We do not want to become an [energy] colony for the rest of the nation," he complained. In Montana, which contains half the nation's unmined sub-bituminous coal, the state administration has repeatedly warned Washington that "it will not see itself ripped-off, its land unreclaimed, its life-style disrupted" by stripping.[13] The vigor in this dissent arises from the broad alliance between environmentalists and a coalition of farmers, animal grazers, and foresters supporting it; the anticipated land disturbance and water contamination from stripping is projected as leaving many hundreds of thousands of Western farm and grazing acres, as well as subsurface and surface waters, heavily fouled and irreclaimable.

What tends to isolate the Mountain and Pacific states, with their great apprehension about environmental devastation, from the rest of the states is the differing trade-offs the various state blocs face on the stripping issue. This can be illuminated, I believe, by utilizing selected social indicators to portray the character of these inter- and intrastate differences. Social indicators, as Albert D. Biderman reminds us, are often politically useful because they can refer to conditions that are "social objects and institutional products." That is, they can describe the social conditions that often dictate policy choices to public officials.[14] In Table 2 are the mean values of four indicators describing environmental conditions in the states sensitive to stripping and three measures of economic demand for coal energy.

States without any stripping potential (Group 1) clearly face no trade-off problems between the site damages from stripping and economic gains from enlarged strip coal supplies. Hence they are understandably disposed toward ambitious new coal production. Of more significance is the contrast between the states presently stripped in varying degrees (Group 2) and those facing stripping (Group 3). The natural community of interest that might otherwise create a broad state alliance to control future stripping is considerably weakened, I believe, by the sharp contrast between the coal demand within the states in Group 2 and Group 3. The already stripped states each average more than 5 percent of the nation's current industrial and electric utility demand for strippable coal, whereas the average for the same demand among the Mountain and Pacific states is less than 1 percent per state. In short, states now experiencing strip mining also face heavy pressure for coal development within their jurisdictions, and consequently the equities involved in further coal mining are likely to seem considerably more attractive than appears to be the case among the Pacific and Mountain States. Moreover, it is apparent from Table 2 that the waters in the presently mined states are now heavily polluted and the grazing

lands vulnerable to future contamination are relatively limited. In
both these respects, the situation is quite different west of the Mississippi, where the water quality is comparatively good and grazing
land plentiful; the environmental "cost" in terms of degradated resources would therefore be much greater.

TABLE 2

Mean Values of Environmental and Economic Variables
Associated with States Grouped by
Strip-Mining Potential

	State Group		
	Group 1 No Strip-Mine Potential	Group 2 Presently Strip Mined	Group 3 Prospective Strip Mining
Economic variables			
Population growth	14.9	7.5	16.1
Percent of national industrial coal consumption	.49	5.90	.46
Percent of electric coal consumption	.92	5.30	.64
Ecological variables			
Percent of grazing land	11.1	3.5	21.0
Percent of farm lands	41.3	51.8	52.5
Percent of federal lands	12.4	4.9	39.2
Water pollution index*	2.1	1.2	2.6

*A pollution index was constructed for each state, based upon
the classification of its major streams by the U.S. Environmental
Protection Agency. Under this classification, a "1" would be heavily
polluted waters and a "4" would be almost unpolluted water. Thus,
the higher the score, the better the state's average water quality.

Source: For population growth, grazing land, agricultural land,
and federally owned state lands, see U.S. Department of Commerce,
Bureau of the Census, Statistical Abstract of the United States, 1975;
for industrial and electric utility coal consumption, see U.S. Department of the Interior, U.S. Energy Fact Sheets, 1971 (Washington,
D.C.: Government Printing Office, 1973); for water pollution, see
U.S. Environmental Protection Agency, Office of Water Planning
and Standards, National Water Quality Inventory: 1974 Report to
Congress (Washington, D.C.: Government Printing Office, 1974).

The contrast between the states in Groups 2 and 3 is further illustrated by the statistics in Table 3, which presents the Spearman rank-order correlations between strippable coal reserves among the states in each group and the environmental and economic indicators previously mentioned.

TABLE 3

Spearman Rank-Order Correlations of Strippable
Coal Reserves with Other Economic and
Environmental Variables

| | State Group | | |
	Group 3 High Strip-Mine Potential	Group 2 Presently Strip Mined	U.S. Total
Economic variables			
Population growth	-.573	-.061	
	(.04)	(.42)	n.a.
Percent of industrial coal use	-.569	.168	.411
	(.04)	(.29)	(.001)
Percent of electrical coal use	.396	.506	.461
	(.11)	(.04)	(.001)
Environmental variables			
Percent in grazing land	-.309	-.090	n.a.
	(.09)	(.33)	
Percent in crops	.442	.421	.320
	(.09)	(.08)	(.011)
Water quality	.613	-.244	n.a.
	(.02)	(.21)	

Notes: Significance levels indicated in parentheses.
n.a.: not ascertained.
Source: Compiled by the author.

These correlations, which are useful because of their sensitivity to variations between coal reserves and other social indicators within state groups, portray even stronger contrasts between states now stripped and those anticipating stripping. In general, as strippable reserves increase among the Western states, the industrial coal demand decreases, the water quality improves, and the population growth diminishes; among presently stripped states the demand, both industrial and electric, for strip coal rises with reserves and water quality decreases. Thus, among the Western states the incentives for stripping appear to decrease as coal resources increase, while the incentives increase among presently stripped states. It is understandable that Western state officials should fear a coalition of coalless states and strip-mined ones, together pressing to convert the Western jurisdictions into boiler rooms to supply the nation's energy-hungry multitudes.

The Federal Government

Since the inception of Project Independence, presidents have changed, but the White House dedication to opening the nation's coal fields to pervasive stripping has never wavered. Presidents Nixon and Ford urged, or enacted, the following measures:

1. A request to Congress to amend the Clean Air Act to reduce primary air quality standards for sulfur oxides and to postpone installation of emission controls on industrial and electric generating facilities so that increased coal consumption would be promoted.
2. The Energy Policy and Conservation Act (1975), which grants the president authority to compel electric utilities and large industrial oil consumers to switch to coal.*
3. A request for prohibition of oil heating in new homes.
4. A proposal to concentrate large energy facilities at a few regional centers, largely in the West, rather than to disperse them throughout the country.
5. A proposal, with "proper controls," for the rapid implementation of the coal production goals outlined in Project Independence.
6. A veto of strip-mine regulatory legislation, which these presidents believed would unjustifiably inhibit the profitability of strip mining.

Clearly, when it comes to the gains and losses to be expected from stripping, the view to the coal fields from Pennsylvania Avenue was less ominous than from Helena, Santa Fe, or even Nashville. The imperatives for economic growth, industrial and electric generating energy, and "energy independence" seemed least clouded by

---

*In May 1975 the White House issued orders to nine Midwest utilities to begin such conversion.

other environmental costs in Washington. Moreover, there are international considerations that weigh little, if at all, in the states. Besides the security issue, the White House noted that the U.S. exports 10 percent of its coal production and needs it to offset the increased costs of energy importation. Nationally, the energy-environment trade-off inherent in strip-mine development does not seem so severe as it does to many individual states; and agriculture would not be threatened in its aggregate dimensions nearly so much as particular state agricultural economies might be threatened.

This White House attitude toward new coal production clearly separated it from many of the states on a multitude of coal-related issues. What imparted a particularly threatening aspect to the White House attitude, in the view of many Western observers, was the potentially great unilateral influence it might exercise over strip-mine development through the administration of federal lands. Nearly all of the 193,345 square miles of Western coal deposits are federally owned. Under the Homestead Act, this control embraces the minerals under land already sold to farmers and ranchers and deposits on Indian lands. Washington has already sold, or is considering the sale, of 500 leases covering about 760,000 acres upon which mineral exploration and mining might rapidly evolve.[15] Ostensibly this would be no invitation to an unrestrained environmental onslaught upon Western lands because the Interior Department must approve and regulate any mining operations according to statutory provisions with some environmental safeguards. However, the Western states were very critical of the environmental impact statements prepared by the department prior to issuing the leases, and a suspicion abounded in the West that the department's heart was not in stringent regulations. Besides the mining activities themselves, any power installations on federal land--and the White House favored a multitude of such mine-mouth activities--would also be subject to federal regulation or the lack of it.

The White House, in general, was more enthusiastic about massive new strip mining and more alarmed by alleged dangers in strict regulatory bills than the Congress, and the president and Congress were often adversaries in the coal issue. The White House, though it could not speak for a substantial congressional following, was nonetheless a major force in the coal development issue and one that largely shared the perspective of energy producers and consumers, the last major faction in the current coal debate.

The Energy Lobby

Coal producers and consumers, almost without exception, repeat as a litany the American Electric Power Company's widely

advertised admonition, "We have more coal than the Arabs have oil
so let's dig it." Coal mining companies and electric utilities are
strongly bonded by their economic and technological interdependence.
Half of the country's electric power is generated from coal, and
nearly 60 percent of that is strip mined, and a number of utilities
and mining operations are part of the same, or closely allied, con-
glomerates. Besides vigorously promoting Project Independence's
coal program, this energy coalition has been occupied with lobbying
and public advertising intended to blunt the strictness of the new
strip-mine regulatory programs enacted by Congress but repeatedly
vetoed by Presidents Nixon and Ford.[16] Project Independence has
also given the utilities additional leverage in their struggle to over-
turn the current sulfur oxide standards under the Clean Air Act.

Thus the economy's coal production and consumption sector,
involving all major coal mining companies and the majority of electric utilities, is the most aggressive and unambiguously committed
to major new coal production among all the factions involved in the
current policy debate over coal.

THE ALTERNATIVES

The public debate over coal policy has been so dominated by
substantive issues, which are primarily the question of how much
coal shall be mined and the closely related matter of regulatory
programs for environmental protection, that the structural alternatives that are also implicit in the coal controversy have not been
sufficiently appreciated. Both the substantive and structural features of any new coal policy will have important consequences.

The Structural Issue

The fierce environmental toll necessarily taken by stripping
precludes a return to the common structural solution of past U.S.
resource policy. As Grant McConnell notes, this formula was one
in which the issues were fought between public agencies (usually
federal) and economic sectors committed to resource development;
states and public interest organizations were seldom significant
factors. The conflict resolution was achieved by jurisdictional de-
marcation of authority among the agencies concerned with resources
--each inherited a "turf" and a ration of authority over the resource
involved--and spheres of influence were allocated to the private
resource developers, usually in a manner guaranteeing extensive
latitude for resource exploitation. Logrolling, rather than compromise, was the policy style; agencies with different resource

responsibilities were left relatively free of interference from other bureaucracies.[17]

Environmentalists and their allies among state governments, agriculture, ranchers, and foresters introduce new political elements and viewpoints that must in some manner be accommodated in future resource policy. Two major structural solutions to the new coal pluralism seem possible, the first of which is a national regulatory policy, under which Washington would establish statutory limits on the extent and duration of stripping through the imposition of reclamation requirements on mined land.

The second major structural solution would be a federal self-regulatory program, under which the states would assume primary responsibility for enacting and enforcing regulations. Jurisdictional conflicts between state and federal agencies with coal mining responsibilities would be resolved through adjudication, legislation, or administrative bargaining.

The energy lobby and its environmental protagonists both favor a national regulatory policy, though on very different terms and for different reasons. The energy lobby, resigned to the inevitability of new regulation, fears a patchwork of state controls, different and possibly inconsistent, imposing numerous economic difficulties on national operations. Energy promoters advocate uniform national regulations, albeit less stringent than those Congress has been disposed to pass and the White House to veto. Environmentalists and their allies, drawing upon the bitter lesson of past state stewardship of resources, assert that the states will not, or cannot, offer sufficient resistance to the energy lobby to assure that a strict environmental regulatory program will be imposed on energy producers. Thus an inadvertent consensus has emerged among the adversaries in the coal conflict about the structural solution, although not the substantive features, of proposed policy.

The impasse between White House and Congress led by default to a policy of federal self-regulation, however. As stripping continues to consume 1,000 new acres daily, states threatened with new mining have enacted regulatory measures and presently mined states are ostensibly strengthening long-neglected laws. Twenty-nine states have regulatory programs, and more significantly, the recently enacted laws seem to be more stringent than older ones.

Does it matter, in terms of coal production and environmental preservation, which solution eventually dominates? Persuasive arguments have been made that a program of decentralized, state-based regulation will become a license to strip the U.S. earth, with little regard for environmental consequences or ecological restoration. The past record of state regulation would seem to indicate that high production and negligent environmental protection would be

the cost of such a solution. The conclusions of the House Committee
on Interior and Insular Affairs reflect this apprehension:

> Public confidence in State regulation of surface
> coal mining has frequently been misplaced. . . .
> One factor in the disappointing record of State
> regulation has been the continued rapid expansion
> of the industry relative to the States' capability of
> managing such mines. . . . Political influence is
> another factor in failure of State regulation. Subtle
> or otherwise, it is often used to moderate enforce-
> ment of State laws. In States where the coal indus-
> try dominates the economy as a major source of
> jobs and taxes, powerful leverage is available.[18]

In the light of such findings, it has been customary for scholars
to assert that federal resource management is generally superior to
state oversight. Experience with air and water pollution problems
is customarily cited. There is, however, another side. Once the
impact of strip mining has been experienced, state regulatory programs often improve, sometimes dramatically. In Table 4 is presented a summary of provisions for stripping regulation in 16 states
now intensively stripped or facing the prospect.

It is significant that Illinois, Ohio, West Virginia, Tennessee
and Pennsylvania, where stripping is now extremely prevalent, are
among the group with the most comprehensive and stringent regulatory provisions; conversely, states where stripping has not yet
been significantly experienced, such as Wyoming and Montana, have
relatively lenient laws. There is no reason to assume that federal
officials will necessarily be more strict about stripping than their
state counterparts. A regulatory solution to the environmental consequences of stripping eventually becomes an administrative one;
it can be argued that federal administrators will feel less committed
to regulation than state officials, whose constiuency is directly,
and often quite brutally, exposed to stripping. Moreover, federal
officials may view their responsibility to be to a national constituency
and for a balancing of interests that permits energy developers and
states without any stripping problems a greater voice in their determinations than would figure in state determinations. Finally, as
Theodore Lowi and Joseph L. Sax have argued, the tendency for all
administrators is to exercise their "power to make a deal" and to
avoid making general rules in favor of specific determinations for
individual parties in the administrative process. It may be, in light
of this logic, that no administrative solutions to the regulation of
stripping are likely to produce the degree of controls judged environmentally "safe."[19]

TABLE 4

State Surface–Mining Reclamation Requirements

State	Timing		Future Land Use	Grading/Backfilling			Revegetation		
	Concurrent	Standard		Approximate Original Contour	Terracing	Rolling Topography	Topsoil Saved	Planting Required	Survival Standards
Alabama		x				x		x	x[a]
Colorado		x	x			x		x	
Illinois		x	x		x[b]	x	x	x	x
Indiana	x		x			x		x	
Kentucky	x			x[c]	x[d]			x	
Maryland	x		x	x[c]	x[d]		x	x	x
Montana		x	x			x		x	
North Dakota		x	x			x		x	
Ohio	x		x	x	x[e]		x	x	
Oklahoma	x		x			x		x	
Pennsylvania	x		x	x	x[e]		x	x	
Tennessee	x		x	x[c]	x[f]		x[c]	x	x
Virginia	x		x		x[g]			x	
Washington		x	x			x		x	
West Virginia	x		x	x[c]	x[h]		x[i]	x	x
Wyoming		x				x		x	x

aWhere soil conditions do not inhibit growth.
bGrade to 30 percent on all outslopes over 40 vertical feet.
cArea mining only.
dMaximum slope angle limited to 45°.
eIf approved by administrating agency in conjunction with approved land use, slope angle limited to 35°.
fSlope angle of highwall and outslope limited to 35°.
gReduce highwall to maximum extent possible, no slope angle limitations.
hSlope angle limited to 32° for highwall and outslope.
iIn acid-producing areas only.

Source: U.S. Department of the Interior, Study of Strip and Surface Mining in Appalachia: An Interim Report to the Appalachian Regional Commission (Washington, D.C.: Government Printing Office, 1966).

In any event, once the structural decision has been made, the substantive policy issue turns largely upon the nature of the regulations.

Reclamation or Restoration?

The volume of coal to be mined in the United States will depend in good part upon the degree of environmental protection imposed on stripping through regulations.[20] Questions of this sort focus upon a few crucial issues, as follows:

The gradient of land at which stripping will be prohibited. The steeper the hills upon which mining is permitted, the more coal can be recovered. Environmentalists want gradients set low; miners prefer higher limits on gradients.

"Concurrent" or "Standard" land restoration. Under concurrent restoration, land removed from coal seams must be replaced as the mining occurs; "standard" practice would permit replacement at much later intervals.

The degree of contour restoration. Very stringent regulations would require miners to restore the land to its original contours; less demanding laws would tolerate fills, which preserve some terracing or simply allow surface depressions to be eliminated. Environmentalists favor total, or almost total, contour restoration.

The extent of demonstrated revegetation. The most rigorous environmental standards would require that all land removed for mining "cuts" be restored with the topsoil in its original place and that the replaced land be able to support ecologically useful vegetation for a stated period. Unless miners can demonstrate an ability to meet both requirements, ecologists insist that mining be prevented.

While options exist in achieving any of these major goals and arguments arise within the contending factions about which options are preferable, these four issues are pivotal in the energy-environmental conflict over coal. Environmentalists often assert that only land capable of "restoration," that is, land capable of rehabilitation to a state closely resembling its original condition, should be mined. They often insist, therefore, that it must be mined concurrently, only on low gradients, with almost total contour restoration and with vegetation standards. Mining operators have asserted that total restoration is often impossible and that "reclamation," which is essentially the refilling and replanting of mining cuts, is a more reasonable standard. Indeed, they have argued that restoration would mean a severe constriction of future coal production.

PROGNOSIS: A CRISIS CYCLE?

Some tentative conclusions about the future direction of U.S. energy policy are implicit in this discussion. First, it seems evident that no national coalition exists that has the capacity to restrain the imminent escalation of coal production, with a strip-mining boom to follow. We have seen that the potentially powerful solidarity among the coal-producing states facing the environmental ravages of stripping is weakened by countervailing needs for industrial and electricity-generating coal among many of them. The nation's unwavering determination to have additional energy and the influential coalition of interests promoting the energy boom (including the coalless states) virtually assure that future U.S. energy policy will seek, even if it does not attain, the coal objectives of Project Independence. This, the most environmentally significant aspect of the "energy crisis," means that the only major ecological issue appears to be the extent to which the ravages of stripping can be contained and rectified.

Second, while structural and substantive decisions concerning coal policy may, as I have noted, moderate the environmental degradation of stripping, another possibility is that a combination of current policy styles and technology in the coal area may produce no environmentally satisfactory solution to the energy-ecology trade-off in stripping. This in turn might well lead to the conclusion that the prospect of a future series of crises, each posing harsher, less abundant alternatives between energy and environmental preservation, is inevitable. Let is examine, briefly, these ideas.

The Problems of Speculative Argumentation

In his study of federal air pollution policy, Charles O. Jones describes a policy style adopted by Washington to deal with demands for more rigorous air pollution regulation; this style, which he calls "speculative argumentation," is the rejection of an incremental policy approach in favor of new policies involving large change and low understanding of policy consequences. This approach is precipitated by circumstances akin to those attending the current coal controversy, (1) an expansion in the number of participants in policy development without "a proportionate increase in aggregate knowledge" of policy implications; (2) "active competition among elected officials to produce and be credited with strong legislation"; and (3) "constant monitoring of policy development by the media."[21] The deficiency in such a solution, suggests Jones, is that policy is legitimated before the organizational or technical means for satisfactory implementation are created.

Public demonstrations and opinion polls project a
clear message to decision-makers: "Do something
dramatic about pollution. " Denied the process of
filtering demands through those affected by regulation and of moderating policy choices in light of
existing knowledge and capabilities, policy-makers
are left to speculate as intelligently as they could,
both about what would satisfy the public and whether
the policy devised could in fact be enforced. [22]

In the case of stripping, the problem may lie in the dubious
efficacy of restoration technology, that is, in the control procedures
themselves. If true, this poses a very different, and more difficult,
enforcement problem than air pollution control. In the latter case,
Jones argues that "speculative" policies may be rescued from im-
potence by vigilant, sustained public pressure upon regulatory bodies.
But what is the value of mobilization in the interest of regulation if
the tools of control themselves are inadequate?

The Technology Problem

Environmentalists, who are often too quick to predict malevo-
lence in a new technology, may not be quick enough in grasping the
inadequacies of restoration and reclamation procedures for stripping. The most fundamentally disturbing aspect of stripping is the
possibility that restoration of stripped land may be almost physically
impossible and reclamation but a cosmetic concealment of irreversible ecological losses.
"The potential for rehabilitation of any surface mined land, "
noted a 1973 study by the National Academy of Sciences, "is critically
site specific. "[23] Referring particularly to the Western lands now
destined for stripping, the academy warned that the combination of
low rainfall and/or high evapotranspiration rates poses a "difficult
problem, " as follows:

Revegetation of these areas can probably be accomplished only with major, sustained inputs of water,
fertilizer, and management. Range seeding ex-
periments have had only limited success. . . .
Rehabilitation of the drier sites may occur naturally on a time scale that is unacceptable to
society, because it may take decades, or even
centuries, for natural succession to reach stable
conditions. [24]

The House Committee on Interior and Insular Affairs, after review-ing the Academy study and other materials on revegetation of stripped land, concluded that "the possibility for permanently de-spoiling thousands of acres of productive agricultural lands is very real indeed." As for restoration of lands already stripped, the evidence gives little encouragement to believe that major ecological reinvigoration is possible. Such restoration as has been accom-plished appears mostly on level or gently sloping terrain; strip-mine "benches" cut into steeper slopes more characteristic of the newly mined reserves are seldom restored or even reclaimed. Thus, most recent congressional studies of strip-land rehabilitation, many of which include detailed scientific evaluations by experts, do not provide compelling evidence that land already stripped is, or can in fact be, restored to ecological health.

It is of course conceivable that a technological breakthrough, or truly rigorous reclamation laws, might increase the prospects for land restoration or confine stripping to that (relatively modest) portion of current coal reserves where soil, climate, and topography permit reasonably effective restoration. At the moment, however, the prospect that most of the land currently vulnerable to stripping will be ecologically protected seems rather remote.

Impasse and Crisis

Governmental decision making in the pluralist U.S. society has, for a multitude of reasons, sought policy solutions to group conflict that provide all major participants with some reward; the tendency is to find that common policy denominator that will permit sufficient group support to generate majorities in Congress and strong backing to the White House for its policy choices. Adopting a regulatory approach for resolving the conflict between energy promoters and environmentalists has this to recommend it: appar-ently something is given to everybody; but if, as we have suggested, the regulatory approach is an act of faith tied to a very unproven technology, the subsequent failure of the technology is likely to in-tensify the polarization of energy proponents and environmental interests as the environmental toll of stripping and U.S. consump-tion of coal simultaneously grow. The prospect would then appear to be a growing crisis, generated by increasingly difficult options between energy and ecology. Options will become less plentiful and the costs of choice greater.

It is not at all fanciful to predict a time, perhaps only a few decades hence, when public officials will have to choose between coal production with little environmental restoration, or else

environmental protection only at the cost of greatly diminished coal
production. It is, in effect, the option environmentalists fear:
energy or ecology. If the past be a lesson for the future, the likely
consequence of such a policy dichotomy would be a national option
for energy. In short, as coal production increases, the prospects
of environmental protection decrease. It is this which may ultimately make the coal program likely to emerge in the late twentieth
century the "dirtiest" of all recent declarations of public purpose.

NOTES

1. Project Independence was officially declared by President
Nixon in a November 7, 1973, address to the nation. The president's commitment to "energy self-sufficiency" was mentioned in
his Energy Message to Congress on January 23, 1974. The detailed
program known as "Project Independence" was created by a federal
task force and announced by Federal Energy Administrator John C.
Sawhill on November 12, 1974. The report did not urge increased
coal production but explored its possibilities; it did assert the potential for doubling U.S. coal production in a decade. However, the
Ford administration generally assumed that production, as explored
in the project, was desirable and possible. Thus President Ford
embraced part of this program on October 8, 1974, when he declared
a national goal of eliminating all oil-fired power production by 1980,
a step that would dramatically increase coal use.

2. New York Times, January 10, 1974.

3. New York Times, January 14, 1974.

4. New York Times, October 21, 1974.

5. New York Times, March 24, 1975.

6. The figures cited are drawn from Congressional Quar-
terly, Inc., Continuing Energy Crisis in America (Washington, D.C.:
Congressional Quarterly Service, 1975), pp. 2-12, 75-82; Dennis W.
Ducsik, ed., Power, Pollution and Public Policy (Cambridge: MIT
Press, 1971); the New York Times, February 18, 1974, June 16,
1974, and October 21, 1974; and Federal Energy Administration,
Project Independence: Final Task Force Report (Washington, D.C.:
Government Printing Office, 1974), Text and Appendix.

7. The demise of nuclear energy as an imminent substitute
for coal, oil, and natural gas is discussed in the New York Times,
November 11, 1975. It is also explored in a number of recent congressional documents, including U.S. Congress, House, Committee
on Banking and Currency, Oil Imports and Energy Security: An
Analysis of the Current Situation and Future Prospects (September
1974); and U.S. Congress, Joint Economic Committee, A Reappraisal
of U.S. Energy Policy, March 8, 1974.

8. U.S. Congress, House, Committee on Interior and Insular Affairs, Surface Mining Control and Reclamation Act of 1974: Report, May 30, 1974, House Report 93-1072, p. 57.

9. New York Times, April 11, 1974.

10. New York Times, March 24, 1975.

11. David Braybrooke and Charles E. Lindblom, A Strategy of Decision (New York: The Free Press, 1963), p. 71. On coal policy generally, see David Howard Davis, Energy Politics (New York: St. Martin's, 1974), Chapter 2.

12. This grouping is based upon estimates of strippable bituminous and sub-bituminous coal reserves provided by the U.S. Department of the Interior, Bureau of Mines, to the House Committee on Interior and Insular Affairs and cited in U.S. Congress, House, Committee on Interior and Insular Affairs, op. cit., pp. 54-55. States with no strippable reserves are included in Group 1. The states in Group 2 are those that the committee reports to have land disturbed by coal surface mining in excess of 5 percent of their estimated reserves. See ibid., p. 56.

13. The Western Governors' Conference is cited in New York Times, September 24, 1975; the Montana quote is from New York Times, August 14, 1974.

14. Albert D. Biderman, "Social Indicators and Goals," in Social Indicators, ed. Raymon H. Bauer (Cambridge: MIT Press, 1966), p. 145.

15. The implications of federal land ownership are fully explored in Congressional Quarterly, Inc., Energy Crisis in America (Washington, D.C.: Congressional Quarterly Service, 1973), pp. 27-37; see also the New York Times, January 25, 1975.

16. The energy lobby's position on stripping is discussed in the New York Times, October 21, 1974. Major oil companies, through ownership of mining operations, control approximately 30 percent of domestic coal reserves and 20 percent of domestic coal production capacity. See Congressional Quarterly, Inc., Energy Crisis in America, op. cit., pp. 28-41.

17. Grant McConnell, Private Power and American Democracy (New York: Vintage, 1968), p. 244.

18. U.S. Congress, House, Committee on Interior and Insular Affairs, op. cit., p. 61.

19. See Joseph L. Sax, Defending the Environment (New York: Alfred A. Knopf, 1971); and Theodore Lowi, The End of Liberalism (New York: Norton, 1973), for thoughtful examinations of the weaknesses in administrative regulation of economic sectors.

20. The problems associated with differing regulatory procedures are usefully summarized in U.S. Department of the Interior, Study of Strip and Surface Mining in Appalachia: An Interim

Report to the Appalachian Regional Commission (Washington, D.C.:
Government Printing Office, 1966); U.S. Congress, House of Representatives, Committee on Interior and Insular Affairs, op. cit.

    21. Charles O. Jones, "Speculative Argumentation in the
Federal Air Pollution Policy-Making," Journal of Politics 36, no. 2
(May 1974): 454-55.

    22. Ibid., p. 463.

    23. Quoted in U.S. Congress, House, Committee on Interior
and Insular Affairs, op. cit., p. 57.

    24. Ibid.

2

THE UNITED STATES:
NUCLEAR ENERGY
David Howard Davis

Nuclear energy evokes an aura that is quintessentially Ameri-
can--powerful, modern, technical, and potentially risky. Do the
politics of this most recently developed fuel match its technology?
Are its politics uniquely American or are they applicable world wide?
To what extent is this issue American and to what extent is it nuclear?

The political importance of nuclear power far outweighs its
present energy contribution. The 1976 National Energy Outlook reported that the atom contributed 2 percent of the nation's total energy
and 6 percent of its electricity.[1] Only recently has it come to supply more energy than firewood. The atom's contribution to pollution
is harder to assess, for few can agree upon a definition, let alone a
measurement, of the damage to the environment by nuclear plants.

ENVIRONMENTAL DANGERS

Nuclear pollution strikes more directly than does pollution
from coal or oil. The foremost fear is not that it despoils the landscape or kills fish and birds, but that it kills people. Radioactivity
causes both somatic and genetic damage. Somatic damage can be
immediate or long-term. In 1961 three workmen died from accidental exposure at the AEC's Idaho Falls testing station.[2] Less intense
doses produce several weeks of radiation sickness. The symptoms
include vomiting, malaise, and hair loss. The illness is not inevitably fatal. Low doses of radiation increase the risk of cancers
occurring decades after the accidental overexposure. Genetic damage is, of course, long-term. Children of irradiated parents may
be miscarried or born with congenital defects. The grim legacy may
not devolve for years. The babies and toddlers exposed to gamma

rays from the Climax Mine tailings in Grand Junction, Colorado, during the 1950s and 1960s are just reaching childbearing age.[3] Like genetic defects from other sources, those from radioactivity will not necessarily appear in the first generation but may be carried recessively to a second or third generation.

The dangers of nuclear power range from literally explosive accidents to subtle contamination. The most dramatic would be a reactor meltdown, in which the atomic pile heats up uncontrollably to 5000 degrees Fahrenheit, causing a steam explosion of the water coolant, bursting the steel vessel and concrete containment. Even the comparatively mild 1957 explosion of Britain's Windscale reactor released a radioactive cloud that blew across England and northern Europe. Much worse accidents are possible.

As a result of his experience during the volcanic eruption at the Icelandic island of Heimaey in 1973, physicist Sterling Colgate hypothesized a hitherto unanticipated risk: dynamic self-mixing. A reactor meltdown would trigger a mechanical (not nuclear) chain reaction that would explode with a force equal to 19 tons of TNT. This would occur virtually instantly, long before any safety measures could go into effect.[4]

Accidents are not the sole risk. The routine operation of nuclear power generates radioactive pollution. Mining uranium imperils the miners, processing plant workers, and local residents. Unless exposure is carefully controlled, these groups suffer a high risk of cancer. Although the industry controls and monitors its workers' exposure, even the best designed plant emits some radiation. Living in the vicinity; using a river downstream; or drinking milk or eating fish, which concentrate the radioactive material, all expose the unknowing public to the dangers. While a nuclear industry worker voluntarily accepts the risk, members of the public do not. Unlike air and water pollution, radioactivity does not necessarily disappear after a time. Some forms are extremely long lived. Plutonium will persist for thousands of years. No permanent disposal technique is known. At present all nuclear waste is in "temporary" storage. To avoid the risks inherent in transportation, most spent uranium fuel is simply kept at the reactor site where it was used.

The 1974 publication of the AEC's Reactor Safety Study,[5] under the supervision of Norman C. Rasmussen of the Massachusetts Institute of Technology, marked a shift in assessing the dangers of nuclear power. Prior environmental objections had centered on the routine low-level emissions. Thermal pollution and plant siting had been secondary issues. The AEC regulations setting the radiation level at five millerems per year (compared to 100 millerems from natural sources) satisfied nuclear power critics.

The willingness of the AEC to comply with the National Environmental Policy Act (NEPA) after the Calvert Cliffs law suit resolved the other major objections.

While environmental problems of routine operation diminished, the Rasmussen Report brought the dangers of an accidental explosion to widespread attention. The report reassuringly set the odds against a meltdown ending in a major explosion at one in 5 billion, but other scientists calculated the risk to be much greater. Even those who accepted the Rasmussen Report noted that the one in 5 billion odds were misleading since they applied to one person for one plant for one year. By the year 2000, several hundred plants were scheduled to be on stream. Critics disputed the report's calculations of the likelihood of accidents and the possibility of evacuating people living within a 20- to 40-mile radius of the plant. For example, an explosion at the Zion, Illinois, nuclear plant might require evacuation of the city of Chicago. [6]

The federal government insures against catastrophic disasters under the provisions of the Price-Anderson Act, first passed in 1957. The Price-Anderson Act, however, limits liability to $560 million, clearly not enough to replace a small town, let alone Chicago. A serious accident would be more likely to inflict damage amounting to over $10 billion. Notwithstanding the paltry liability limit of $560 million, in December 1975 Congress passed, and President Ford signed, Public Law 94-197, extending the Price-Anderson Act until 1987.

The act's unrealistically low insurance liability, along with two other nuclear power problems--meltdowns and waste disposal-- stirred California environmentalists to propose a strict safety law be put to the voters. [7] California, like a few other states, provides for an "initiative." A new law may be proposed and then voted on in a popular election. If passed, it becomes a public law just like those passed by the state legislature and signed by the governor. This proposed law was known as Proposition 15, numbered according to its place on that day's ballot. Thus on June 8, 1976, millions of Golden State voters went to the polls to decide whether nuclear safety standards were satisfactory or should be made more stringent. By 3.6 million to 1.8 million, they disapproved the proposed law.

The ominous set of environmental dangers, ranging from a reactor explosion to routine low-level emissions, stirred public concern well before the so-called energy crisis of 1973. Apprehension, even alarmism, is a tradition among nuclear scientists. This began as concern with the military side of nuclear energy. The awesome power of the atomic bomb caused the very men who invented it to question the application of their handiwork. The scientists' concern for the public welfare made an easy transition from weaponry to reactors. In the late 1960s the nuclear community debated how many babies would die of nuclear radiation: 400,000 or 400 or only a few? Proposed reactors at Calvert Cliffs, Maryland, and on Lake Cayuga, New York, stirred angry outcries from local citizens who feared nuclear and thermal pollution. Acrimony climaxed at AEC hearings about the Shoreham reactor on the north shore of Long Island. Opponents effectively organized a coalition (the Lloyd Harbor Study Group), including a Nobel laureate and a number of experts from the AEC's nearby Brookhaven laboratory. Under withering citizen attack, the Long Island Lighting Company (LILCO) offered major concessions to assure safety and environmental protection. For the intervenors, however, even these were not enough. They argued that the plant should not be built at all. The result was that the AEC hearing panel disregarded the environmentalists' extreme demands and granted LILCO the license to proceed with construction. [8]

The marginal profitability of reactors has proved a greater impediment to nuclear energy than has environmental protection. Though proclaimed as virtually inexhaustible sources of cheap electricity, reactors have rarely generated a profit. Until the mid-1960s, all installations were government-subsidized in their operation, to say nothing about research and development costs. This was usually accomplished by congressional designation of the facilities as demonstration.

The plant at Oyster Creek, New Jersey was the first plant built without an AEC operating subsidy. Until the 1973 oil boycott it was unprofitable. The quadrupling petroleum costs that year made it marginally competitive, and yet even at high prices, oil was still more profitable in a number of circumstances. Kerosene-fueled jet turbines could generate the extra electricity needed for the peak evening hours, then be turned off. Since electricity cannot be stored, the more flexible turbines proved economical despite the high cost of fuel. Nuclear power was good for base but not for peak loads. The low operating cost did not compensate for the extremely high capital cost.

Coal plants enjoyed an advantage over nuclear plants insofar as they were able to externalize their costs. Air pollution is the most obvious externalization. In reaction to the OPEC oil embargo, the federal government adopted a policy of reconverting oil and natural gas fueled plants back to coal. Many of these plants had only recently shifted away from coal to reduce pollution.

Besides air pollution at the generating plant, the coal industry externalizes its costs at the mine. Strip mines are inadequately restored. Miners suffer from black lung disease. The right of coal producers to disable their workers is so firmly established that the federal government willingly subsidizes the practice. Under the provisions of the Coal Mine Health and Safety Act, the federal government provides medical care and pays disability benefits to afflicted miners, although other industries assume their fair share through state workman's compensation programs.

Not even the uranium mining industry enjoys such a subsidy. The Colorado miners afflicted with lung cancer from inhaling radon "daughters" gained no AEC compensation. On the other hand, the nuclear industry has a far superior industrial safety record. Only a handful have died in the nuclear power industry, while 90,000 coal miners have died in accidents since 1907.

The external costs of the atom are more uncertain. The chief unknown is the long-term danger. While few die of radiation sickness, how many are more likely to develop cancer? How many will transmit defective genes? Because the industry is only a quarter of a century old, no one knows.

TECHNOLOGICAL FACTORS

This chapter began by asking which was the greater determinant of U.S. nuclear energy policy, its political setting or its technology. In truth, both factors push in the same direction, giving a political style that is especially, though not uniquely, American. The complex technology of nuclear fuel demands an advanced scientific and industrial infrastructure. Coincidentally (and with some notable exceptions), the developed nations tend to be representative democracies. Hence the technical and political explanations are parallel.

Expertise is the factor that is most clearly technical. The uninformed layman must defer to the expert, and since the technology is arcane, policy formulation usually has been the exclusive province of the scientist and the engineer. Secrecy derived from the military side of the process has reinforced the experts' monopoly. In the late 1940s knowledge was so closely held that even the AEC commissioners and the Joint Committee on Atomic Energy (JCAE) members abdicated their policy-setting role to the scientists through the establishment of the General Advisory Council (GAC), headed by J. Robert Oppenheimer.

Nuclear expertise has occasionally yielded to outside attack. Sometimes laymen acquire sufficient information to challenge the scientific establishment. Admiral Lewis Strauss, a Republican appointed to the AEC by President Truman, reduced the influence of the GAC scientists by exposing a number of specific instances of lax management. During the mid-1950s, Democratic senators forced the AEC to speed development of electric power generation, with

special advantages to public (that is, government-owned) utility companies and rural consumers. Lay involvement increased during the
1960s and 1970s. The environmental impact statements required by
the National Environmental Policy Act gave ordinary citizens a chan-
nel of access. It became commonplace for nonexperts to offer their
opinions. For example, even the National Council of Churches has
gone on record warning against the dangers of nuclear power.

More often, however, the debate was expert against expert,
rather than expert against layman. The issue of how many babies
would die from radiation pitted two of the AEC's own scientists, John
Gofman and Arthur Tamplin of the Lawrence Livermore laboratory,
against the agency's headquarters.[9] In January 1976 three nuclear
engineers resigned their positions at the General Electric Company's
Nuclear Energy Division at San Jose, California, to protest industry
and government disregard of nuclear safety and to campaign full time
in favor of Proposition 15.[10] The chief critics of the Shoreham, Long
Island, reactor were nuclear scientists, a number from the AEC's
Brookhaven laboratory. Others, however, while scientists, were
not nuclear physicists. A prominent opponent, Nobel laureate James
Watson, was a biochemist. In her analysis of this pivotal controversy, Carol Spader argues that the scientists abandoned the mores
of science in favor of the adversarial system of courtroom debate.[11]
Consciously or unconsciously, the scientists prostituted their calling. They exploited their reputations to browbeat laymen. This
abuse of science was largely successful in convincing the hearing
board and the public. Under this "science" offensive, the Long
Island Lighting Company offered major concessions to increase plant
safety. Spader found, however, that though the Lloyd Harbor Study
Group scientists outscored LILCO in the hearings, they were unable
to consolidate their victory. Rather than accept the offer to increase
plant safety, their response was to demand that construction be
stopped entirely. Consequently LILCO prevailed.

The need for expertise (real or perceived) to participate effectively in policy formulation is not the only consequence of the fact
that nuclear energy is highly technical. The complex technology
means that only the most industrially advanced nations can autono-
mously support a nuclear power industry. Underdeveloped nations
can only have nuclear energy as clients of scientifically powerful
exporters. The U.S. export role gives a political dimension to what
would otherwise be a strictly economic transaction. The United
States desires to exert strict controls over the importers' operation
of the reactor. While this is chiefly intended to guarantee against
military malfeasance, environmental protection is also a factor.
Possibly a nuclear accident could be so big that it would spread
radioactive fallout that would endanger the United States itself.

More likely it would only pollute the importing country and those in the region, but the United States would suffer the political fallout. Propagandists could accuse the United States of recklessly, even intentionally, endangering foreign peoples and their progeny. Racism and genocide would be implied.

Nevertheless, the U.S. nuclear monopoly ended long ago. India built its "peaceful nuclear device," exploded in May 1974 from fuel from a Canadian-sponsored reactor. Thus the United States frequently exports reactors without adequate safeguards against military diversion or environmental pollution. Lacking a monopoly, the United States tends to restrict exports only when a military danger presents itself. Environmental safeguards receive a low priority. The perils of exporting nuclear reactors differentiate this from other energy sources. The millions of tons of coal shipped abroad present no long-term environmental or military risks to the United States; and neither does petroleum endanger the OPEC countries for more than the few weeks until it is consumed. Nuclear energy is different because the primary commodity exported is technology, not fuel. Once a reactor is built and in operation, embargoing the long-lasting fuel is of little use. The high level of technology means that a small number of countries control the total market. There is an oligopoly, though not a monopoly. Thus the United States enjoys hegemony. Since the Indian explosion, the noncommunist reactor exporters have been more willing to establish international supervision, through the International Atomic Energy Agency of the United Nations.

The uncertain technology of nuclear energy precludes a calculus of pollution. How can one determine the cost-benefit ratio when the costs are disputed? The benefits are clear and highly favorable to nuclear power. The output is solely electricity, a completely clean and highly efficient form of energy. It is the environmental price that defies calculation. Fossil fuel generating plants produce measurable amounts of air pollution. Natural gas is the cleanest; coal, the dirtiest. Air pollution can be controlled through low-sulfur coal or oil or by stack scrubbers. Society has many years of experience with the costs of fossil fuel pollution; in contrast, nuclear fuel is so new that the industry still has its spent fuel in temporary storage. No agreement exists about the dangerousness of radioactivity. Recent studies indicate greater danger than was previously assumed. On the other hand, careful supervision of the nuclear industry may be overprotecting the public from nuclear dangers. Only a handful have suffered death or illness from reactor radiation, compared with the thousands, perhaps millions, who have suffered from coal. Though environmentally less polluting and despoiling, oil and gas have claimed their victims too. What, indeed, is the trade-off between nuclear and fossil fuels?

Hydroelectricity is usually portrayed as the cleanest and safest power source, but it too has an environmental cost in terms of scenic valleys flooded, farmers dispossessed, water lost, and salinization. What if Californians could trade a nuclear plant for the restoration of the flooded Hetch Hetchy, a Sierra valley John Muir considered even more exquisite than its sister, Yosemite? What if Long Islanders could trade the Shorham plant for an end to oil spilled from ships and for smog-free air? What if the United States could trade the risk of a nuclear meltdown for the risk of war to control Middle Eastern oil fields?

Indeed, choices such as these are made constantly. Three recent cases exemplify three ways in which the government decides. The 1976 California initiative submitted the decision to popular vote. The Shorham hearings were decided by a quasi-judicial system. The AEC-sponsored Rasmussen Report set forth the issue for the scientific community to decide.

The merits of the three methods--voting, adjudication, and scientific--for deciding the technical problem need to be evaluated in terms of (1) presentation of the facts, (2) weighing of the facts, (3) alternatives considered, (4) implementation of the decision, and (5) correctness of the decision.

In comparison with hearings and scientific evaluation, the facts suffer the most in a popular vote. The average Californians, lacking training as nuclear engineers, unable to understand most of the relevant information they received, garnered what they could from the mass media, but television and even newspapers could supply only superficial knowledge. The major protagonists, Project Survival and the Pacific Gas and Electric Company, presented contrasting information through advertising and mailings, but this was generally simplistic and often irrelevant to the questions of safety versus energy.

The legalistic form of the Shorham hearings was more effective in bringing out the facts. Expert witnesses presented detailed information to a knowledgeable panel of AEC experts. As a by-product, LILCO, the environmentalists, the press, and concerned citizens received detailed and specific information. Like a trial at law, the hearing was adversarial. The proponents marshalled all the facts favorable to licensing the plant, and the opponents marshalled all facts to the contrary. Having made the strongest case possible, each side criticized the other's case and rebutted the criticism of its adversary. As in a court, the adversarial hearings were designed to elicit the maximum information.

The scientific debate engendered by the Rasmussen Report had the similar goal of setting forth all information, critiquing it, and rebutting the critique. Whereas legal debate formally has two sides, scientific debate is supposedly multifaceted. Scientific debate is less intense, insofar as it transpires via publication over a period of months or years rather than being a face-to-face oral argument concluded within a few days or weeks.

While the common technical subject matter of the three cases would suggest a common presentation of information, in fact the commonality was more that of an adversarial style. Proposition 15, being a yes or no choice, generated two coalitions, one for and one against. The Rasmussen Report spawned a counter report, the Report to the American Physical Society by the Study Group on Light Water Reactor Safety.[12] The APS report rebutted the Rasmussen Report point by point, thus imitating the adversarial system of a court trial. As discussed previously, the Shorham hearings were highly polarized. In sum, the legalistic Shorham hearings and the scientific Rasmussen Report and its critique were both effective in bringing out the relevant facts. Because of the simplifications required for a mass audience, the Proposition 15 debate failed to bring the facts to bear except in the most superficial manner.

After having presented the facts, however satisfactorily, how effective was each of the three decision-making methods in evaluating the information? Again, the initiative proved least effective. Being ignorant of nuclear physics, the average California voter tended to decide either on the basis of a superficial understanding of the issues or on some other basis. Both sides used scare tactics, predicting either a radioactive doom or an energy shortfall.

The well-informed participants of the Shorham controversy did little better. Those nuclear physicists, Nobel laureates, and highly educated citizens also resorted to hyperbole and doomsaying. The technical testimony had little effect on either side. The non-technical impact of the intensity of the opposition, however, did influence LILCO to offer concessions. While not persuaded that it would enhance safety, the power company was nevertheless willing to pour more concrete in order to secure permission to continue construction.

The less intense, scientific decision-making mode proved best for weighing the facts presented. The juxtaposition of the Rasmussen and the APS reports showed broad areas of agreement, whereas the explicitly adversarial Shorham hearing procedure emphasized the disagreements. Of course, Shorham was a specific, present problem, whereas the Rasmussen Report dealt with hypothetical, potential problems; yet Proposition 15 also dealt with a hypothetical, potential problem, and it generated intense feelings and uninformed evaluation of the issue.

Neither the California initiative nor the Shorham hearings fostered consideration of the alternatives. Nuclear power generates pollution as well as electricity. People run the risk of cancer, genetic damage, and radiation sickness. Fossil fuels also pollute, however. Lung cancer and emphysema are correlated with air pollution. Recent evidence points to hitherto unsuspected connections of cancer and genetic damage with industry. Burning coal, oil, and natural gas have already increased the level of carbon dioxide in the atmosphere 10 percent and will further increase it by 10 to 20 percent by the year 2000.[13] Changing the world's climate might decrease agricultural production. The 1973 OPEC oil embargo grew out of the Israeli-Arab war, and demands for oil might touch off another war. President Ford and Secretary of State Kissinger crassly implied this threat on several occasions in the fall of 1974.[14] An oil war would probably cost more American lives than a reactor meltdown. The yes or no choices of Proposition 15 and Shorham precluded consideration of the alternative risks of disease, starvation, and war induced by fossil fuels. While not specifically considered in the Rasmussen Report, the more leisurely scientific decision-making mode brought forth these issues.

The facts and the alternatives having been presented and evaluated, how do the three decision-making methods succeed in implementing the decision? Here the popular initiative excels. Had the people voted favorably, Proposition 15 would have been self-executing. The law, however, would not have been so straightforward as it might have seemed. Its specific provisions did not require an immediate halt to nuclear plant construction but called for a halt (1) if the federal government did not remove the $560 million liability limitation of the Price-Anderson Act, (2) if evacuation plans were not published, and (3 and 4) if the state legislature in 1981 determined that safety system testing and radioactive waste disposal were inadequate. Thus what appeared at first to be self-executing was actually conditional.

The legalistic decision-making method of the Shorham hearings produced dual methods of implementation. The official mode was the decision of the AEC panel sitting in judgment. After hearing the testimony and deliberating upon it, the panel allowed LILCO to proceed. The intrinsic purpose of the hearings was to make a rather specific determination. Such a procedure was usually routine. Safe plants got their licenses. Unsafe ones were required to be made safe. Shorham was exceptional in the elevation of a licensing hearing into a major forum for debating the wisdom of all nuclear power plants. The unofficial aspect of implementation was the bargaining between LILCO and the environmentalists. Just as most lawsuits are settled out of court, energy-environmental conflicts are also negotiable. LILCO offered to make significant design changes to reduce radioactive emissions and thermal pollution. Thus implementation of the decision derived from the informal as well as the formal process.

As exemplified in the Rasmussen Report and the ensuing debate, the scientific decision-making mode is ineffective in implementing its conclusions. Whereas Proposition 15 was (at least supposedly) self-executing and the Shoram hearings gave a prompt
resolution, the Rasmussen Report led to further debate. Though the
consensus was greater, the results were fewer. The maturity of the
conflict would seem to account for this. The Rasmussen Report
dealt with a remote, vague issue, while the Shoram hearings dealt
with an immediate, specific one. In fact, this explanation is correct
but backwards. The AEC scheduled the Shoram hearings because
the plant was moving toward completion. In turn the intervenors
were able to wring out concessions for the same reason. LILCO
could not afford delay. On the other hand, the Rasmussen Report
and the California initiative dealt with a disaster that could happen
any day. Although the chances are small, a nuclear reactor could
explode at any time. Windscale did in 1957. Detroit Edison's Fermi
reactor almost did in 1966, and the TVA's Brown's Ferry reactor
almost did in 1975.

The final concern in analyzing the three decision-making procedures is the correctness of the decision. By its nature this is impossible to judge, since if the correct decision were apparent, there
would be no controversy. It is the delicate balance between the two
opposing sides that determines the specific narrow choice that must
be made. Easy decisions do not get on the ballot or generate pro-
tracted hearings or cause scientific controversy. It would be foolish
to equate the knowledge of the decision makers--the voters, the AEC
officials, or the scientists--with the correctness of the outcome.
The key is not who decides but who sets the agenda. The California
voters were confronted with a choice just as intractable as the choice
faced by Norman C. Rasmussen.

POLITICAL FACTORS

Thus far this chapter has considered the nuclear problem in
an essentially technical fashion. Nuclear energy has been political
only insofar as it endangers and/or benefits the whole population.
The questions have been, how should the technical decision be made?
What are the consequences of allowing laymen to decide technical
issues? How do decision-making procedures like voting and adjudication borrowed from the political sphere affect the correctness of
the technical decision. Nuclear energy also has political characteristics less tied to its technology. These relate to government
structure and public attitudes.

To a degree unmatched by any other industry, nuclear energy was conceived, dominated, and encompassed by a single government agency, the Atomic Energy Commission. The commission literally invented the form at its Idaho Falls test center. To quote the graffito the jubilant AEC scientists scrawled on the laboratory wall at the time, "Electricity was first generated here from atomic energy on December 20, 1951."

Congress had established the AEC in 1946 as a civilian successor to the Army's Manhattan Project. Awed, perhaps overawed, with the novelty of the atom, the Atomic Energy Act of 1946 created two novel institutions. First was the AEC, which had the status of an independent commission, direct links to Congress, and a separate personnel system. Second was the Congressional Joint Committee on Atomic Energy (JCAE). This was the only permanent joint committee with full legislative power. Its close ties to the agency are explicitly written into the law. The 1954 rewriting of the Atomic Energy Act left these two institutions unaffected.

Criticism of the privileged status of the AEC and the JCAE did not bring organizational changes until January 1975, and even then the reorganization was more cosmetic than substantive. The theme of the criticisms was that the AEC-JCAE was a closed system. The act charged the AEC with both regulating and promoting nuclear power. The latter mission overruled the former.

The Energy Reorganization Act signed October 11, 1974, remedied the AEC's regulation-promotion conflict. The law established an independent Nuclear Regulatory Commission. The rest of the AEC's functions went to the new Energy Research and Development Agency (ERDA). The AEC supplied 84 percent of the budget and 85 percent of the personnel. Indeed, Congress was so concerned that ERDA would merely be a new name for the AEC that it demanded that the administrator of the new agency not be identified with nuclear energy and included a number of specific provisions in the act that would assure that ERDA's nonnuclear 15 percent not be overwhelmed.

Congressional insistence that the ERDA head not be identified with nuclear energy was not necessarily an improvement for environmentalists. The last two chairmen of the commission both were appointed because of their concern for environmental protection. The last, Dixy Lee Ray, was a marine biologist. President Nixon appointed her first as a regular commissioner before elevating her to the chairmanship because she was an ecologist. Her predecessor as chairman, James Schlesinger, though an economist by profession, was an amateur ornithologist who emphasized environmental protection.

Nixon's two ecologically oriented chairmen contrast with Kennedy's appointee, Glenn T. Seaborg, who was a nuclear physicist

who staunchly advocated nuclear power. He championed the fast
breeder plutonium reactor as the second generation planned to come
on stream in the 1980s. Unlike the light water uranium reactors
currently used, the fast breeder produces plutonium, an extremely
lethal substance difficult to dispose of. Seaborg's critics accused
him of promoting this technique because he personally had discovered plutonium, hence vaingloriously sought its use.

In 1972 the AEC and the Environmental Protection Agency
clashed on the issue of jurisdiction over nuclear pollution. Reorganization Plan Number 3 of 1970, which established the EPA, transferred responsibility for regulating radiation pollution from the AEC
to the EPA. Hence the EPA began preparing detailed regulations.
When the regulations were ready for publication in the Federal Register, the AEC demanded that they not be issued because the subject
was within the AEC's jurisdiction. The dispute escalated to President Nixon, who ordered Roy Ash, the Office of Management and
Budget Director, to sit in judgment. Ash decided in favor of the
AEC. The EPA regulations were not issued, but neither were any
from the AEC. The conflict preceded the 1973 oil boycott, and its
concerns centered on agency jurisdiction, indicating that it was not
an issue-oriented battle over energy or the environment but an ordinary bureaucratic "turf fight."

While the congressional and bureaucratic structure is one form
of almost purely political, as opposed to technical, impact on nuclear
policy, public attitudes are another. As a review of the three cases
discussed previously will illustrate, policy formulation is judged by
its legitimacy as well as by its technical outcome.

American norms stress democratic participation and due
process. The California initiative was quintessentially democratic.
The procedure is a legacy of the early twentieth-century reformers,
who saw it as a guarantee of the will of the people against corrupt
machines like those in the East. California is unusual, though not
unique, in having established and maintained this form of direct
democracy.

In their elaborate and formal trappings of due process, the
Shoreham hearings also had a high degree of legitimacy. In fact,
this might be a basis of criticism. The correct adherence to legal
form superseded the fair consideration of the issues. LILCO, with
its years of experience and its battery of lawyers, supposedly enjoyed an advantage over the naive Long Island citizens dedicated to
protecting their environment but ignorant of the labyrinths of the law.
David challenged Goliath. Democracy challenged legalism. In this
case such a characterization would be inaccurate. The environmentalists were themselves knowledgeable in physics, AEC procedures,
and publicity. They hired skilled lawyers and imported expert

witnesses. Such procedural sophistication is, however, rare.
Nuclear opponents displayed it in the Calvert Cliffs and Lake Cayuga
hearings, but in few other instances. Shorham marked a high point
for environmental intervenors. Some say it marked a victory. Although LILCO got its license, it and other power companies reduced
the level of radioactive emissions to 5 percent of the natural background level. This made the emissions so low they were negligible.

The Rasmussen Report was weakest in terms of legitimacy.
It was sponsored by an official government agency responsible to the
president, the commissioners of which were confirmed by the Senate,
and it considered a broad range of evidence; this gave it a basic procedural correctness. The arcane subject matter and the inevitable
dependence on experts made it remote and possibly suspect, however.
The decision process was far from democratic. Confronted by it,
the average citizen felt alienated. The report told him that he might
die, contract cancer, or have malformed children because of nuclear
accident. The Rasmussen Report lacked the legitimacy conferred by
popular participation, as in the case of California Proposition 15,
or by due process, as in the Shorham case.

Like legitimacy, patriotism is a public attitude that influences
nuclear energy policy with little regard for technical considerations.
Since their invention, nuclear reactors have been entangled with
U.S. defense. World War II spawned the nuclear age. The first
reactors were built for Navy submarines, and even today ERDA is
responsible for both weaponry and reactors. All of these factors
confuse patriotism with promotion of nuclear generated electricity.
Beginning as anti-Nazism and anti-imperialism, pronuclear attitudes
shifted to anticommunism in the 1950s. To challenge the wisdom of
developing nuclear power bordered on treason.

Faith in science reinforced these attitudes. Nuclear energy
was the most modern, which implied that it must be the best. It
radiated prestige along with gamma rays. Cities and businesses
sought nuclear plants for this purpose, sometimes even when they
were economically inefficient. The environmental risks were be-
littled.

Popular support for nuclear power also derived from the New
Deal promotion of hydroelectric projects. What dams were in the
1930s, reactors were in the 1950s and 1960s. Indeed, many of the
same political struggles were repeated. The 1954 Atomic Energy
Act revision copied language from the TVA legislation. Democratic
senators supported a government role echoing that in hydroelectric
projects. The symbolism was parallel. To build a nuclear plant
was good in itself, since it proved the excellence of the U.S. system.
The American devotion to nuclear power as a symbol of cultural
superiority both rivaled and replicated the Soviet dedication to

hydroelectric giantism. It had elements of a competitive sport, like the two superpowers' rivalry at the Olympic games or in the space race.

CONCLUSIONS

Technical factors outweigh political factors in determining nuclear energy policy. Nuclear politics may be distinctly American, but much of this quality derives from the high U.S. technological level rather than from U.S. political characteristics. The Shorham hearings exemplify the situation. The effectiveness of the citizen intervenors derived from their scientific expertise more than from their political expertise. Indeed, their chief weakness was their lack of the political skills of bargaining, logrolling, and compromising.

The Californians' consideration of and vote on Proposition 15 was more a product of particular political institutions. The popular initiative is not a widespread decision-making mode, but it is neither uniquely nor universally American. Other countries utilize the initiative, and within the United States only a few states do so. The scientific debate, and presumed eventual resolution, of the safety problems that the Rasmussen Report began is not exclusively an American procedure. Such policy making can transpire anywhere that scientists are free and informed; yet again the United States has more scientists and access to more information. On the other hand, in relation to other branches of science, nuclear physics is more closed. The military applications of nuclear weaponry impose secrecy not found in biology, chemistry, and the other physical sciences.

Hence U.S. nuclear policy making is not so much unique as archetypical. It shares its characteristics with other countries that are technologically advanced and politically open. In the noncommunist world these two features go together. Canada, Britain, Scandinavia, West Germany, France, and a few other countries combine the two attributes and hence may be expected to have similar nuclear politics. The communist bloc is obviously different. The Soviet Union is a technologically advanced but closed society. Surely the voters of the Ukraine would not go to the polls to approve or disapprove nuclear plants like the voters of California, but what of a scientific debate over safety like that the Rasmussen Report engendered? Can the scientific process work, let alone flourish, unless there is some freedom of discussion? Even if the Soviet Union is willing to tolerate higher levels of pollution than Western nations, it cannot risk a catastrophic nuclear reactor explosion.

Conceptualizing the various countries in terms of a hierarchy rather than a matrix aids in understanding the place of the United States vis-a-vis other countries. The arrangement is one dimensional rather than two dimensional. The United States and a few other politically open and technologically advanced countries confront the problems and resolve them, years ahead of other countries. These lagging countries then adapt the policies of the leading countries as appropriate. The world aviation industry furnishes a model. The U.S. Federal Aviation Administration evaluates and then certifies new airplanes as safe. Other countries then accept the FAA certification. The United Kingdom is one of the few noncommunist countries that independently evaluates aircraft, and when the United Kingdom approves a new British airplane, the FAA accepts its certification. Similarly, the worldwide nuclear power industry follows the lead of the United States and a few other leaders in the atomic hierarchy.

The 103-nation International Atomic Energy Agency (IAEA) is the institutional manifestation of this hierarchy. The United States and a few other nuclear reactor producers use this functional agency of the United Nations to enforce their policies on the nonproducers. The reactor producers' source of strength is their oligopoly of nuclear technology. Their source of weakness is their disunity. The IAEA is no unified cartel like OPEC. If one producer refuses to sell a reactor, another will usually oblige. In recent years, however, the Indian bomb, instability in the Middle East, and global terrorism have awakened the nuclear nations to the grave dangers of their disunity. More cooperation to block weapon proliferation is apparent. Better control of environmental risks is the by-product.

On balance, American nuclear energy policy proves to be more nuclear than American. Technological factors explain more than political factors. Although the lessons of the U.S. nuclear situation are not applicable everywhere, they are applicable to other industrialized and democratic countries.

NOTES

1. Federal Energy Administration, 1976 National Energy Outlook, pp. xxii, 241.

2. Sheldon Novik, The Careless Atom (Ann Arbor: University of Michigan Press, 1969), pp. 5-10.

3. Peter Metzger, The Atomic Establishment (New York: Simon and Schuster, 1972), pp. 115-44.

4. Kevin P. Shea, "An Explosive Reactor Possibility," Environment 18, no. 1 (January-February 1976): 6-11.

5. U.S. Atomic Energy Commission, Reactor Safety Study WASH-1400 (the Rasmussen Report) (Washington, D.C.: Government Printing Office, 1974).

6. David Dinsmore Comey, "Do Not Go Gentle Into That Radiation Zone," Bulletin of the Atomic Scientists, November 1975, pp. 45-47.

7. "California as Nuclear Bellwether," Science News 109 (May 22, 1976): 324; John P. Holdren, "The Nuclear Controversy," Bulletin of the Atomic Scientists, March 1976, p. 22.

8. U.S. Atomic Energy Commission, Division of Licensing and Regulation, Long Island Lighting Company, Docket No. 50-322, 1970.

9. David Howard Davis, Energy Politics (New York: St. Martin's, 1974), pp. 159-61.

10. U.S. Congress, Joint Committee on Atomic Energy, Investigation of Charges Relating to Nuclear Reactor Safety, 94th Cong., 2nd sess., 1976, pp. 1-89.

11. Carol Spader, "The Roles of Scientists at Public Hearings" (Ed.D. diss., Rutgers University, 1975).

12. Reviews of Modern Physics 14, Supplement 1 (1975).

13. Frank von Hippel, "A Perspective on the Debate," Bulletin of the Atomic Scientists, September 1975, p. 38.

14. General Services Administration, National Archives, Presidential Documents, vol. 10, 1974, pp. 1164, 1182-84.

3

THE SOVIET UNION:
THE SELF-MADE
ENERGY CRISIS
Donald R. Kelley

Like any major industrial nation, the Soviet Union has found that its future well-being is inevitably tied to the availability of adequate energy supplies. While it has not experienced the trauma felt in the West, as OPEC-sponsored embargoes and price increases have threatened to play havoc with the consumer life styles and national solvency of the United States, Japan, and many European nations, it has begun to feel the bite of an energy crisis of its own.

There is indeed a paradox in the energy situation facing the USSR, and like most apparent contradictions, it has produced frequently confusing and conflicting policies and priorities. Compared with the world's other major industrial nations, the USSR is rich in fossil fuel reserves. Nevertheless, energy shortfalls are a growing reality to be faced by its planners and political leaders alike, largely because existing reserves or alternative technologies have not been developed quickly enough to meet current needs. In this case the problem is largely self-made; no devil theory can lay it at the door of a producer's cartel; nor can it be blamed on the collusion and greed of private oil corporations.

BACKGROUND

Any assessment of the interplay of energy and environmental policy in the Soviet Union must be read against the background of that nation's past performance. Three interlocking strands of policy have shaped energy and environmental affairs over the last several decades. These are (1) the growing crisis in obtaining adequate oil supplies, based in large measure on earlier decisions to convert major industrial and domestic users from coal to oil or gas;

(2) the present level of commitment to environmental protection; and (3) the institutional and political milieu in which energy and environmental policies are made.

Of critical importance in comprehending Soviet energy policy is the fact that since the mid-1960s the USSR has been approaching a potentially dangerous energy shortage that is largely of its own making. The problem stems not from the waste of private consumers with high performance autos or energy-eating appliances but rather from the near-depletion of the oil and gas reserves that had fueled the early industrialization of Russia's European sector. While planners have placed their long-term bets on the timely development of West Siberian oil and gas reserves and the mining of extensive coal deposits in the East, delays have been experienced, and it will be years before increased deliveries will meet the demand for energy in the industrialized Western sectors of the nation, to say nothing of the growing energy requirements of the new industrial centers east of the Urals. Construction delays and as yet unresolved technical problems associated with the extraction of oil and gas under Siberian conditions, plus the need to siphon off large capital investments into the development of the extractive industries and transportation networks, have made the development of these resources a gamble against time and the elements.[1]

It is also important to understand the close relationship between past energy policy and even modest improvements in environmental quality. On the whole, the relationship is probably much closer than it would be in a more developed and technologically sophisticated economy such as the United States. In the latter case, improvements in air quality have been achieved not only through controls over the industrial and domestic utilization of dirty fuels but also through programs to limit the serious problem of auto exhausts and to develop sophisticated pollution-abatement technology to process industrial and domestic wastes. In the Soviet case, primary emphasis has been placed on the creation of centralized heating facilities to provide heat and hot water in cities and on the conversion of domestic and industrial power consumers from coal to oil or natural gas, especially in urban areas. In both cases the primary motivation has been efficiency and the modernization of industry; purely environmental payoffs were a fortunate by-product. Far less reliance has been placed on the control of auto pollution, which promises to become a growing problem as the number of private and fleet vehicles increases, and on the development of sophisticated emission-control technology. Rather, the emphasis has been on the control of major sources of air pollution by improvements in the quality of the fuel consumed.

In the short run this was both a sensible and successful strategy. When it was begun in the late 1950s and early 1960s, Soviet planners were as yet unconcerned about the continued availability of low-cost, high-quality fuels; moreover, it was technically easier to deal with a limited number of the more toxic sources of air pollution. Once conversions were completed or sections of the cities brought within the central heating networks, little additional vigilance was required. There was little need to rely on the construction of pollution-control facilities or the development of more sophisticated abatement technology, which has never been a strong skill among Soviet scientists and technicians or a high priority among Soviet planners and construction officials. It was also a successful policy to cleanse the air, especially in high priority areas, for which the top leaders provided the necessary investment capital for conversions and the political backing for relocating particularly offensive factories outside the cities. Marshall I. Goldman has grapically described the improvement of air quality in Moscow, although even Soviet officials admit to continued violations of pollution norms, and other important urban areas have shown similar gains. [2] In the long run, however, this strategy may well backfire if the growing shortage and higher cost of clean fuel force reconversion back to coal or lower grade oil. As we will note in detail below, initial steps in this direction have already been taken, and top planning officials and resource consumption experts have begun once again to praise the virtues of cheap (and relatively dirty) coal.

A final background comment must also be made about the political setting in which environmental and energy policies are made. For decades Soviet planners and industrialists have been singularly devoted to the notion that continued rapid economic growth is the panacea for the nation's problems. Growth--and even the "giantism" of the Stalin era--became synonymous with political legitimacy and the protection of the homeland against foreign threats, and that growth meant not only ever-higher production quotas in heavy industry but also prodigious expansion of the energy industry. Every Soviet school child, and every Russian-speaking tourist who has seen the slogan-bearing power station on the Moscow River across from the Kremlin, knows that electrification and communism were symbolically combined early in the Soviet experience. In contrast, concern about the environment has been a very low priority item, except in some exceptional cases, such as the Soviet capital, and unique natural resources, such as Lake Baikal. [3] In this setting it is difficult for political leaders and industrialists alike to accept the notion that either energy shortages or environmental constraints could limit future growth. [4] It seems likely, given past performance, that a higher priority will inevitably be attached to dealing with impending energy shortfalls than will be given to the heightened threat to the environment. The problem is compounded in political terms by the distribution of power and authority within the Communist Party and the state bureaucracy. Longstanding vested interests in both quarters have closely identified with the rapid growth of industry and with the energy extraction and processing industries; in contrast, spokesmen for the environment are less well placed within the institutional pecking order. When the time comes to argue the virtues of a clean atmosphere against the desire to burn high-polluting fuel or to develop new energy resources with little concern for their environmental consequences, the advocates of the latter will unquestionably speak with a stronger voice.[5]

THE ENERGY SCENE

In their public comments, Soviet officials radiate optimism about the abundant fuel supplies of their nation. According to their own estimates, the USSR holds 57 percent of the world's coal reserves, 45 percent of its natural gas, 37 percent of its crude-oil-bearing areas, 12 percent of its potential hydroelectric power, 46 percent of its oil shale, and 60 percent of its peat.[6] Recently accelerated exploration programs have ostensibly found even larger reserves, especially in West Siberia and other remote regions outside of the European sector.[7] Soviet leaders laud their development of nuclear power and their lead in the development of breeder reactors, and pride is expressed in the experimental development of solar, tidal, and geothermal energy.[8] New attention has also been focused on the further development of hydroelectric generating capacity. Western analysts have frequently shared this optimism and even spoken enviously of the Soviet ability to reap windfall profits from oil and gas exports.[9] On the whole, energy shortages in the West, and the adjustments that have been made necessary by increased prices and conservation programs, have led most outside observers to overlook the fact that Soviet specialists themselves have acknowledged that the nation faces an energy crisis of its own.

Two factors have accelerated the emergence of the crisis. The first has been a shift in the pattern of consumption away from coal, wood, and peat toward oil and natural gas. In 1960, oil and gas contributed only 26 and 8 percent of the nation's power, respectively. According to Soviet predictions published before the impact of the energy crisis in the West, by 1980 oil was to contribute well over 40 percent, and natural gas 25 percent. In contrast, the share provided by the buring of coal has constantly been on the decline.[10] While such conversions were originally motivated by the desire to

modernize industry and to reduce reliance on diminishing reserves
of coal in European Russia, they also played an important role in
the improvement of air quality, as we have noted.

For industry as a whole, and for the numerous heat and power
stations and domestic boilers that have been converted, the important point is that the fuel demands in the European sector will be
relatively inflexible in the short run, especially in industry. Considerable investment capital for reconversions and other adjustments would be needed to shift back to coal, at a time when Soviet
planners would prefer to place their bets on the rapid development
of the oil and gas deposits in West Siberia. To the extent that these
reserves prove to be less reliable than originally thought or that
construction and technological problems impede their development
--and there is growing concern on both points--energy officials are
placed in the bind of having shifted the energy balance in a flush of
premature and unfounded optimism. The current five-year plan,
however, does establish new priorities in terms of the future development of the nation's energy balance (see the section below on
long-term developments).

The second factor that has accelerated the coming of the
Soviet fuel crisis is the slower-than-anticipated development of the
extensive fuel reserves of the East, especially the oil and gas deposits of West Siberia and the North. The major short-term problem is the supply of adequate fuel to the industries and urban areas
of the European sector and the Urals, which are both areas in which
the most extensive conversion to higher grade fuels was accomplished in the 1960s. Taken together, these two regions account for
more than 75 percent of domestic fuel consumption. Unfortunately,
local energy supplies have not been adequate to the need since the
middle of the 1960s. The region contains only approximately 12
percent of potential energy reserves, and the more accessible local
fuels are being depleted or had been thought to be prohibitively expensive to exploit. Moreover, only limited new reserves have
been located by geological survey teams; nor have the existing extractive industries extensively modernized their technology in order
to draw the maximum reserves from each mine or well. One Soviet estimate indicated that the 1970 local energy shortfall for the
European and Urals sectors was approximately 15 percent of the
total Soviet fuel consumption and that this deficit would multiply
rapidly in the near future, doubling about every five years. By
1973, serious fuel shortages were being reported openly by the
media in industrial regions such as Sverdlovsk, Cheliabibsk, and
Perm. Soviet officials have admitted that repeated localized crises
are likely.[11]

These serious shortfalls have compelled Soviet authorities to undertake emergency short-term programs to provide adequate fuel for deficit areas and to rethink their long-term commitment to the greater utilization of oil and gas for domestic and industrial purposes. In the short run, Soviet experts have admitted that sufficient quantities of West Siberian gas cannot be produced or piped westward rapidly enough to meet the demand, and the prospects for relying on expanded production by the Komi fields are similarly pessimistic.

The situation with respect to oil is not very different. Delays and construction difficulties have been commonplace in the development of the West Siberian fields, and even if production were rapidly increased, serious shortcomings in the transportation and pipeline network would make it difficult to move adequate supplies to the deficit areas. Moreover, present plans call for a large portion of these extensive reserves to be consumed in the East itself by an expanding network of local industries.

The rapid exploitation of the large coal deposits of the East is also fraught with difficulties, although they will become an important part of the long-term solution. The technical problems of extracting this coal, even through extensive strip mining under primitive conditions, and the costs of transporting it westward or burning it locally in large thermal power stations and then transmitting the electric power to deficit regions through an extensive (and, at present, largely nonexistent) grid network, make it unlikely that this option will provide energy relief in the short run.

The further development of nuclear and hydroelectric generating capacity is also in the cards, but this will be of little importance in the immediate future. The only short-term solutions lie in increased imports of fuel from the Middle East, particularly gas from Iran and Afghanistan, and in a shift toward the use of cheaper-grade local coal in European Russia and the Urals, which could presumably provide the time necessary to bring other resources into production and to develop alternative sources. In the former case, fuel imports have constantly increased, especially to provide needed energy in the European deficit region. It is likely that such increases will continue, despite the paradoxical fact that the USSR is also simultaneously exporting other fossil fuels in return for hard currency or through barter of resource-sharing arrangements in order to obtain sophisticated technology.[12]

To compound the difficulties and uncertainties facing the officials of the Soviet energy industry, doubts have begun to arise about the ability of the West Siberian and other non-European reserves to meet long-term future needs. Two problems have surfaced in recent years to cast a shadow of pessimism over this once-lauded

storehouse of fossil fuels. The significance of these doubts is readily apparent when it is noted that West Siberia alone was expected to
provide between 75 to 80 percent of the increase in oil production
for the 1970s as a whole, with similar optimistic assessments initially offered about the production of natural gas. [13]

The first problem is simply that the reserves themselves may
be considerably smaller than originally thought. While there is no
question that large reserves of crude oil, gas, and coal exist, there
is doubt that the initial Soviet estimates accurately reflected the
actual holdings. Through an act of statistical sleight of hand in the
late 1960s, the definitions of "proven" and "probable" reserves in
Soviet estimates were altered to combine both categories, giving an
inflated and undoubtedly overly optimistic figure that includes not
only those reserves that have been verified through exploration but
also those that are thought in theory to exist. Moreover, Western
geologists are skeptical of the geological theories advanced by their
Soviet counterparts to justify these inflated estimates. Simply put,
it appears that scientific theory may once again be undergoing considerable "stretching" in order to provide the optimistic assessments pleasing to the ears of higher authorities. [14]

The second problem concerns both the anticipated costs of developing the West Siberian reserves and the technical difficulties
involved in exploiting them. Although the official version holds that
the development of these reserves will be less costly than the further exploitation of the Volga-Urals fields or the development of
alternative power sources, some economists and energy experts
have estimated that actual costs will far exceed these optimistic
projections. Regardless of the accuracy of the original estimates,
it remains clear that enormous investments must be poured into the
development of the gas and oil fields themselves and into the development of transportation and pipeline networks. In addition, the
integrated development of associated industries and urban settle-
ments in the East will require even greater outlays of investment
capital in an economy chronically short of it. Either exceptionally
high priority must be given to the development of these new energy
resources, or foreign sources of investment capital must be found.
In the former case, although the Brezhnev regime seems firmly
committed to this scheme, it remains true that allocations for West
Siberian development must inevitably be obtained at the expense of
other investment priorities, a fact likely to produce bitter ministerial and regional competition. Attempts to obtain developmental
capital from abroad are also fraught with difficulties, as we will
note in the discussion of trade prospects below.

Technical difficulties and construction delays have also re-
tarded the development of new energy-producing areas. The problem

is not only that the richest reserves are in remote and inhospitable areas--for example, West Siberia's most promising gas deposits are within 200 kilometers of the Arctic Circle--but also that Soviet extractive technology may not be up to the task of drilling deep wells under permafrost conditions. While the major oil deposits are further to the south, conditions are still unfavorable. Not only do technical problems in reaching the deposits of crude oil remain, but construction problems and difficulties in building transportation and pipeline networks in the swampy taiga have caused considerable concern among Soviet officials intent on pressing the new reserves rapidly into service. Evidence is mounting that a host of construction delays has placed the entire project years behind the original timetable, with the frustrating result that completed wells must sometimes produce below capacity because other elements of what was to be an integrated network are still under construction. While top leaders have repeatedly called upon the relevant ministries to accelerate their efforts, the harsh conditions of West Siberia and the technical problems of the oil and gas industries themselves will undoubtedly remain unyielding to rhetoric alone.[15] As one Western observer has put it, the Soviets have undertaken a "desperate gamble" in the development of the energy reserves in Siberia, one that may, at least in the short run, exact a severe cost.[16]

Having recognized the problem facing their nation, Soviet leaders have instituted both short- and long-term programs to provide adequate energy supplies. In the short run, energy shortfalls will be alleviated through imports, conservation programs, and the utilization of low-grade coal in the European sector and the Urals. The long-term solutions include a fundamental shift of energy policy in the coming years to place less reliance on oil and gas, especially in nonindustrial uses, and to stress instead the development of nuclear and hydroelectric power and the greater utilization of the nation's vast coal supplies, particularly those in the East.

SHORT-TERM PROGRAMS

One way of dealing with the short-term problem of an energy shortfall in the European sector and the technological problems of developing Siberian resources is simply to enter the international energy and technology markets to obtain the needed resources. Since 1967 the USSR has imported Middle Eastern oil in increasing quantities for domestic consumption or for reexport at higher prices in hard currency markets. These resources have been obtained preferably through technology and fuel barter arrangements with less developed nations (in this case, the USSR exports the technology

in return for the fuel) or more recently through hard currency purchases, although the latter are becoming more costly because of
OPEC-sponsored price increases. The USSR could also easily
purchase the technology necessary to develop additional resources
from the West by exporting fossil fuels to earn hard currency, although that would compound domestic problems.

Faced with the sudden increase in oil prices following the 1973
embargo, the USSR made windfall profits through the sale of Soviet
oil to European and American consumers, apparently in part by
making up the domestic deficit through imports from the Arab producers themselves, although the Soviet leaders did honor their less
profitable export commitments to Eastern Europe.

The long-term decision of how to handle this perplexing paradox has not been an easy one for the Soviet authorities, and policy in
this area has become a confusing mixture of short-run compromises.
On the question of importing fossil fuels in the short run, it is likely
that the USSR will have to increase purchases abroad even though
the market has turned unfavorable, with some Arab nations now demanding world prices in hard currency rather than barter arrangements.

A more confusing picture exists concerning fuel exports.
Sales to the soft-currency areas of Eastern Europe are slated to decline rapidly in the coming years, even given the obvious political
factors and the fact that the USSR has been the major energy supplier for years. This change was already in the cards as early as
the late 1960s. Of greater interest are the growing sales of fuel to
West European nations and the consideration of bilateral projects
with other countries for the development of Siberian resources.
Sales to West Europe have increased rapidly since 1967, facilitated
by a growing grid of pipelines running westward from Soviet production areas to European consumers. Such sales have earned the USSR
much-needed hard currency and have paved the way for access to
superior Western technology. However, there is growing concern
among Soviet energy experts about the wisdom of these exports,
and officials have put both present and prospective importers on
notice that deliveries in the future are likely to fall considerably
short of previous expectations.

Political considerations have also entered into the picture,
especially in relation to the United States and Japan. Soviet officials briefly considered and then dropped a plan to sell oil directly
to the United States because of opposition from Arab producers; in
the long run, the Soviet Union may be primarily concerned with
preserving its access to Middle East oil regardless of the price.
Once highly touted plans for U.S. technical assistance to the USSR
to facilitate the sale of liquefied natural gas to the United States have

apparently been put on the shelf because of political difficulties over
the linking of U.S. trade and Soviet emigration policy and because
of lower than anticipated offers of investment capital from potential
consumers.

Plans to invite Japanese participation in the development of
Siberian resources have also been called into question. The problems in this case are both technical and political. On the technical
side, continued concern over the size of the Siberian fuel reserves
has prompted Japanese caution. This issue has arisen before, and
the Japanese have pulled back on the brink of similar deals in the
past. Tokyo has been stung before by revision downward of the
amount of fuel that the USSR was willing to export to them even under favorable conditions.

In political terms, Soviet-Japanese relations have recently
cooled to the extent that the latter has improved its ties with Peking,
further reducing the likelihood that long-term cooperation on a
sensitive issue such as energy development will be a high priority
item for the Kremlin.[17]

In environmental terms, importing the needed gas or oil would
certainly entail the least threat to air quality; presumably, high-
grade fuel could be imported in sufficient quantity to prevent the
environmentally hazardous reconversion of large enterprises and
urban areas to lower-grade coal, although the USSR would have to
compete in the open world market. However, continued reliance on
imported fuel would place the Soviet economy at the mercy of OPEC
price policy, a prospect that Soviet leaders would view with the
gravest concern. There are also economic and political problems
associated with the utilization of extensive foreign investment and
joint development programs. In this case, the primary reservation
is the fear of foreign penetration and influence over what are regarded to be important national resources. The traditional Russian
fear of opening Russia, and especially any aspect of its economy,
to foreign scrutiny and influence, plus the growing concern about
exporting sizeable quantities of fossil fuels at a time when they are
needed at home, will undoubtedly limit their willingness to enter
into sweeping agreements such as those originally envisaged with
the Japanese.

Probably the most attractive short-term option open to Soviet
policy makers is a combination of strengthened conservation efforts
to cut the loss or waste of fuel and the more extensive utilization
of lower-grade fuels, with immediate attention focused on the further exploitation of coal mined in the Urals or the European sector
from deposits that were once thought to be too close to exhaustion,
too expensive, or too poor in quality for further production.

Soviet leaders have increased their conservation efforts in the last few years, although it is true that token conservation programs were on the books long before. The tone of the official pronouncements has sharpened considerably, chiding both wasteful industrial consumers and the extractive industries. Criticism has been directed toward factories and other consumers that waste fuel in production or in heating and lighting their enterprises, although there is nothing to indicate that the potential penalties, which include forced fuel reductions or outright cutoffs, have been systematically applied. It is also directed toward the extractive industries, which have characteristically left second-grade deposits in the ground or have permitted high losses in transit.

There are strong economic reasons why neither industry nor mining and drilling interests have been careful stewards of the nation's fossil fuels. Concerning industry, the primary indicator of success or failure has always been the ability to meet planned production goals or to maximize the profit indicators for the enterprise. Little attention has been given to energy consumption so long as the basic goals were met, and there has been little interest in spending always-scarce capital on "unproductive" items, such as insulation.

The problem for the mining industry has also been caused by the system of financial incentives. As Marshall I. Goldman has pointed out, the cost structure for the individual mine or other extractive enterprise is not related to the real scarcity value of the resource itself. Even the recent increases in fuel prices and additional user costs imposed on the mining and drilling enterprises are unlikely to have much impact unless far greater priority is attached to them.[18]

The most promising suggestion for alleviating the energy shortage in the European sector, at least in the short run, is the greater utilization of local coal and other low-grade fuels, although this option carries with it a threat both to air quality and to the mining areas themselves because of the destructive impact of extractive operations. Official plans to increase the consumption of low-quality European and Urals coal and other low-grade fuels first came to light with the publication in July 1974 of an article by Mikhail Pervukhin in the journal Planovoe Khoziaistvo (Planned Economy). A member of the collegium of the State Planning Committee (GOSPLAN), Pervukhin began his comments by citing Lenin's insistence that low-grade local fuels be utilized whenever possible. Noting that the lignite of the Moscow basin and the Urals and the extensive peat and oil shale deposits found elsewhere in the European sector were of little use to industry or transportation, he argued that they were ideal for consumption in thermal power stations. He criticized recently constructed generating plants that used oil or gas and lauded instead the operation of older elements of the system that for years had consumed nothing but low-grade Moscow or Urals coal. While he accepted the argument that some thermal power stations had turned to oil or gas because of the slow development of the coal industry in the last ten years, Pervukhin urged greater utilization of low-grade coal, noting that gas and petroleum products "must first and foremost be used in industry as valuable raw materials or as a precious fuel that makes it possible to employ highly efficient technological processes."[19]

The call to rely more heavily on low-grade coal for the generation of electrical power was echoed a few months later during a meeting of the Soviet Academy of Sciences devoted to a discussion of the energy industry. The principal advocate of the measure was V. A. Kirillin, a member of the academy and the chairman of the influential State Committee on Science and Technology. Kirillin returned to the same theme in the January 1975 issue of Kommunist, the party's theoretical journal.[20]

Two things are significant about the timing and the source of these policy recommendation. On the question of timing, it is important to remember that the Soviet leadership was involved in what appears to have been a heated debate on the priorities to be set forth by the tenth five-year plan, the basic guidelines of which were issued late in 1975. In this setting, the question of energy supplies was undoubtedly an important point of discussion, and it would therefore not be unusual to find forums like Academy of Science symposia or important journals such as Planovoe Khoziaistvo and Kommunist used as sounding boards for various points of view. The second important point is to note the range of institutional backing that had evidently lined up behind the shift to coal as early as the beginning of 1975. Two important institutions, GOSPLAN and the State Committee on Science and Technology, expressed public support for this shift in patterns of energy consumption.

The draft basic guidelines of the tenth five-year plan, for 1976-80, reflected the priorities articulated by Pervukhin and Kirillin, although they did not make the argument for coal with quite the force of the earlier pronouncements or spell out any clear long-term solution. Issued in December 1975, the draft called in general terms for "the wider use of cheap solid fuel in the production of electric power," although accelerated development of oil and gas reserves, nuclear power, and hydroelectric generating capacity was also promised.[21]

A new and potentially significant dimension was added to the discussion shortly after the publication of the draft guidelines by the intervention of the Tula Province party secretary to demand increased mechanization of his region's mining industry and greater

utilization of low-grade Moscow basin coal, both of which had allegedly suffered because scientists and designers had become "en-
grossed" with the question of environmental protection.

The importance of this development is political rather than
technical. As any student of Soviet politics knows, local and regional party and state officials are constantly involved in competitive efforts to increase investments in and the industrial might of
their bailiwicks. Leaving the technical merits of the argument
aside, the Tula party chief undoubtedly saw an opportunity to exploit
a local natural resource and to strengthen a local industry, the importance of which had been on the decline. Thus a national energy
problem became an important local opportunity.*

Months later, similar comments were heard from the chairman
of the Ukrainian Republic Council of Ministers, who lauded the further development and modernization of his region's coal industry.
While it is as yet too early to know whether other regional officials
in similar coal-producing areas will pick up the issue, their past
record of aggressive regionalism would suggest that such actions
are a strong possibility if the shift to lower-grade coal can be translated into increased local prerogatives. What is politically important is that the secretaries in the European and Urals industrial
provinces, which would be likely to benefit from such changes, are
already individuals of considerable political clout, whose advocacy
of the program would carry political weight in Moscow. [22]

LONG-TERM DEVELOPMENTS

The long-term solution to the Soviet energy dilemma was
spelled out in further detail by Premier Aleksei Kosygin in his report on the economy to the Twenty-Fifth Party Congress, which
began in late February 1976. Taken as a whole, it represents both
a continuation of existing programs to develop technologically
sophisticated power sources such as nuclear power and also a return to the development of hydroelectric generating capacity and the
nation's abundant coal supplies. The most striking alteration of the
nation's energy balance comes in the reduced priority attached to

---

*It must be noted that the enthusiasm of the Tula party secre-
tary was not universally shared even within his own region; a few
months later the chairman of a local collective farm pointed out that
valuable crop land had been converted into a "lunar landscape" by
local miners and called for greater attention to restoration projects.
(See Pravda, March 4, 1976, p. 2.)

the utilization of oil and gas as basic fuels. While certain important urban areas or industrial processes will continue to burn these fuels, increasingly they will be channeled into industry as raw materials.[23]

The further development of the coal industry is perhaps the most environmentally important aspect of the energy program. Taking a long-term perspective on the nation's energy needs, the Kosygin report addressed itself more to the question of the future utilization of the coal reserves of the East, which are to be mined primarily through open-cut operations. Emphasis will be placed on the construction of large thermal generating stations that burn coal and the conversion of existing oil-burning generating facilities in the Urals and Volga regions. As the Eastern deposits are mined, stress will be placed on the construction of large generating facilities in those areas and the development of an extensive network of power transmission lines.

Both the short-term emphasis on older low-grade coal deposits in the European sector and the eventual utilization of coal from the East will present several threats to the environment. The first is the obvious impact on air quality, which, as I have noted, has in the Soviet case been closely tied to the quality of fuel consumed. In the short run the use of lower-grade European deposits does represent the greatest threat to air quality, although it should be noted that Soviet officials have not called for extensive conversions in industry as a whole; the focus has rather been on thermal generating stations. In the past these have more often than not been built directly in the urban areas they serve. Moreover, since they are not listed as "productive" enterprises (in the sense that industry is productive), they have been exempt from certain pollution controls.

The extent to which their utilization of lower-grade coal will have a deleterious impact on air quality will depend on two factors. The first is the willingness of Soviet authorities to continue to burn gas or oil in certain high-priority urban areas such as Moscow. The prospects of this are probably favorable, since Moscow and Leningrad have been regarded as pollution abatement showcases in recent years.

The second factor is the ability of Soviet technicians to improve their own pollution abatement technology. In the past the record has not been good. The state agency responsible both for research in this area and for the manufacture of pollution control devices has been poorly funded and is always far behind in its deliveries. The quality of the devices is generally poor, and they are frequently operated by unconcerned and unskilled personnel. It is unlikely that there will be significant improvement in this area unless greater concern is shown at the highest levels.[24]

In the long run the use of non-European coal reserves and the creation of a more extensive grid network may reduce the total pollution load in the already industrialized regions that are to receive this power, although the development of industry in the East itself will eventually consume an increasing share of this electricity and localized pollution problems in the new industrial centers are inevitable.

The second threat comes from the environmental impact of the mining industry itself, particularly strip mining and the other open-cut operations that have become commonplace in the USSR. Pollution from both shaft and open-cut mining operations has long been a problem in heavily industrialized regions. Added environmental peril comes from the Soviet intention to accelerate the use of strip mining wherever possible. Even before the recent reemphasis on coal, mining officials predicted that strip mining would become the principal method of extraction in the 1980s, and it is certain that increased utilization of coal will accelerate that timetable. Kosygin estimated that 60 percent of the increased coal production during the new five-year plan would come from open pit operations.

In the past, little attention has been given to the extensive damage wrought by strip mining or to the restoration of the land once production stopped, although Soviet officials are now more aware of the need to protect fertile farm land. The problem was the system of financial incentives at work within the mining industry; no adequate fee was charged for the use of mining sites, and the allocations per hectare for restoration were never adequate to the task. As a result, strip-mining sites were often simply abandoned unless local officials could bring pressure on the mining industry. [25]

The Kosygin report also called for accelerated development of nuclear and hydroelectrical generating capacity. According to his projections, the share of the national energy balance contributed by these two sources would increase from 22 percent in 1976 to almost 40 percent by 1980. Special attention is to be devoted to the construction of additional nuclear generating capacity in the European sector as a primary element of the solution of that region's chronic energy shortfall.

Initial development of Soviet nuclear facilities began in the mid-1950s, but construction was slow throughout the next decade. By 1973 the USSR had an installed nuclear generating capacity of only 2,770 megawatts, which represented only about 1.4 percent of its total electric generating capacity. Soviet scientists have also stressed the development of breeder reactors, which produce more fuel than they consume. While most Western experts acknowledge that the USSR is ahead of other nations in breeder technology, many

problems remain in the Soviet program. The first breeder reactor
was completed and submitted to testing in November 1972. Apparently breakdowns have been frequent, and the reactor has been able
to function at only 30 percent of its rated capacity. While other
breeders are under construction, they do not seem promising as a
short-term solution. Moreover, the costs of nuclear-generated
electrical power are relatively high, thus undoubtedly increasing the
tendency of Soviet authorities to look to other sources.[26]

The rapid development of Soviet nuclear power also represents
a threat to the environment, both in terms of the pollution generated
by functioning reactors and the dangers associated with accidental
discharges of radiation and the disposal of radioactive wastes. On
the whole, Soviet authorities seem unconcerned with these problems,
and there has been no effective pressure from the scientific community or citizens' groups to challenge the official optimism that reactor and disposal technologies are adequate. Examinations by Western technicians, however, offer a much less sanguine picture.
Soviet burner reactors lack secondary back-up cooling systems,
thus increasing the chances of accidents, and outside observers
who have viewed the safeguards used on breeder reactors have com-
mented that much of the technological lead acquired by the USSR
seems to have been purchased by ignoring potential difficulties.
There are also indications that the Soviet reactors have presented
many of the technical problems that have plagued their counterparts
elsewhere and that there have been a few minor accidents or near-
misses on more serious malfunctions, although data are hard to
verify on the latter point. The "solution" to the problem of nuclear
wastes has been simply to dump them into the Black Sea, apparently
with some localized impact on the fishing industry, or to bury them
in underground chambers. According to the exiled dissident scientist Zhores Medvedev, improper underground storage procedures
resulted in a vault rupture in 1958 near the town of Blagoveschensk
in the Urals, which produced a nuclear cloud that drifted several
hundred miles. While Soviet scientists now speak of using improved
vaults, the Western experience with similar programs suggests that
a serious threat will continue to exist.[27]

Certainly less danger to the environment would result from
more extensive exploitation of other, more esoteric, power sources,
such as solar, tidal, and geothermal energy. Soviet scientists have
begun experimental programs in each of these areas. Solar energy
has been tapped to run experimental stations; tidal power has been
harnessed in a small way in several generating stations in the North;
and geothermal energy has been used to heat whole villages in the
Caucasus. Despite successes, however, these remain essentially
experimental programs, and advocates of the development of such

esoteric sources have been quick to point out that there has been
opposition from existing energy-related government agencies to
their further development. While additional investment will be
channeled into their development in the coming years, Soviet officials are quick to admit that they will play no immediate role in
solving the energy crisis. [28]

Greater importance is also being attached to the further development of hydroelectric energy. Because it possesses approximately 12 percent of the world's useable water power resources,
the USSR is potentially in an advantageous position in this respect.
Many difficulties will haunt the development of this resource, however. To begin with, only 18 percent of the nation's total hydroelectric capacity is located in the European sector, and the most promising sites have already been developed. Additional sites exist on
the rivers of the North and Siberia, such as the Yenisei and Angara,
but their development will be slow-paced and costly. In addition,
electrical power produced in these remote regions will require an
extensive transmission grid to bring it to industrial and domestic
consumers, the development of which will also be expensive and
time consuming. [29]

The development of hydroelectric potential also entails a related environmental cost because of the loss of land and the mineral
riches that may underlie it. Large-scale hydroelectric projects inevitably entail the flooding of adjacent lands, whose value as fertile
crop land or in minerals production is lost. In the past little attention has been given to the evaluation of the land's alternative value
before flooding has occurred, and vast tracts of forests and potentially productive farm land have been lost. The problem will be
especially acute in the European sector, where the best hydroelectric sites have already been developed and crop land is at a premium.
Recently passed agricultural statutes assert that land is to be evaluated primarily through its potential use in food production, and
they establish a complicated set of nonscarcity prices and guidelines by which alternative uses may be evaluated. Nevertheless,
there is little prospect that this will have any more than marginal
impact unless local party officials intervene on behalf of the farming
interests. The further development of the hydroelectric potential
of the East will certainly be less costly in arable land, but it will
involve destruction of valuable forests and probable flooding of
mineral-rich lands. No one can accurately gauge the value of lost
resources, especially in terms of the latter, but Soviet officials
have become sufficiently concerned with similar losses brought
about by watershed management and irrigation schemes that some
massive projects that were once a part of the Soviet plan to "re-
make" nature have been scaled downward or dropped. [30]

POLITICS OF ENERGY AND THE ENVIRONMENT

Thus far the new energy program has elicited virtually no public criticism from state environmental protection agencies or from other groups in the society that are historically concerned with environmental quality. The only criticism to be heard has come from agricultural sources concerned with the loss of farm land rather than with more clearly defined pollution-abatement issues. This is hardly surprising in the Soviet context, especially when the apparent outlines of the new policy have been formalized so recently. Students of the successes and the failures of pro-environmental forces in the Soviet Union have noted that on environmental questions the policy-making process is dominated by industrial and energy-related interests and is frequently closed to environmentalists and conservationists.

This is not to say that Soviet officials do not recognize that a link exists between energy and environmental policy. To the contrary, knowledge of the interrelationship is a frequent topic at scientific meetings. The Academy of Sciences session on energy policy at which Kirillin spoke also included a lengthy review of the environmental impact of the further development of the energy industry. Its author, M. A. Styrikovich, called for increased care in coping with potential difficulties and for more research on pollution-control technology. Other commentators have also noted the importance of limiting the environmental impact of new schemes to tap non-European reserves of oil and coal, and there are at least some cases on record in which local concern has prompted officials to take additional steps to protect the environment. One such instance occurred in 1974 when officials of the Tomsk Geological Administration forced the developers of a large petrochemical complex to take additional precautions to protect underground water supplies from contamination.

The overall importance of such cases should not be exaggerated, however. Common to all protagonists is the assumption that environmental protection and energy development are not fundamentally opposed goals. There is a widely held sense of optimism that the environmental consequences of the utilization of the nation's energy reserves can be handled easily through some sort of technological solution or simply written off as inconsequential. This optimism about man's technical ability to manipulate and maintain the environment is a widely held view even among those most seriously concerned about pollution. It therefore contributes to an atmosphere of overall confidence that reduces the likelihood of direct and bitter confrontations between environmental and energy interests.[31]

On the whole, it is unlikely that greater short-term reliance on low-grade European and Urals coal or the long-range development of the coal reserves of the East, of nuclear energy, and of hydroelectric power will cause a serious conflict between the advocates of environmental quality and national planners. The only serious prospects for such conflict are linked to ministerial competition over the control of some scarce resources, such as arable land or timber, as has been noted above. Several factors militate against the emergence of a purely environment-energy conflict at the present time.

The first of these is the lower priority that has been attached to problems of air pollution or the potential dangers associated with nuclear and hydroelectric power. With the exception of a few showcase cities, the greatest stress and largest investments have been put into water-pollution control, which has always been regarded as a more serious problem. It should be remembered that the improvement of air quality associated with the conversion to oil and gas was largely a secondary benefit; the motivation behind the conversion was to modernize industry, and environmental concerns were clearly secondary. If anything is seen as a primary threat to air quality in Soviet cities, it is the rapidly growing number of automobiles, not the conversion of thermal power stations back to coal. Higher priority has also been attached to improvements in water pollution abatement technology. Only a serious deterioration of air quality would be likely to change this priority, an unlikely development unless conversions back to coal are extended across the board in major industries.

Both nuclear energy and hydroelectric power are seen as minimal risks to the environment. Soviet technicians are supremely confident of their reactors, and if their optimistic assessments prove correct--and if they are lucky--a spreading network of nuclear generating stations will provide relatively pollution-free power, barring accidents and assuming that disposal problems can be solved. In any event, there is little prospect for the emergence of an antinuclear lobby such as exists in other nations. Both the exceptional secrecy that has surrounded nuclear development and, perhaps more importantly, the acceptance by the educated public and the man in the street of the argument that nuclear power is safe diminish the likelihood of serious opposition.

Slightly different dynamics are at work regarding the perceived threat of hydroelectric power. In this case, secondary cost in terms of losses in land, timber, and minerals are going to measure only as distant concerns to urban and industrial consumers. As we have noted, the only direct opposition will come from those most immediately concerned with these losses. The greatest complaints are likely to come from agricultural interests in high-priority farming areas, forestry officials, and spokesmen of the mining industry.

In terms of assessing the likely opposition to the more immediate pollution threat, one must bear in mind the weakness of the state environmental protection agencies and the tendency of Soviet pollution-abatement law to place responsibility for control programs into the hands of the producer agencies themselves. In the former case, both the Sanitary Epidemiological Service of the USSR Ministry of Public Health and the Hydrometeorological Service have environmental responsibilities. The first is charged with monitoring emissions and enforcing protection measures. In practice it has little formal power or political influence. It can impose only modest and ineffective fines, and although it has the authority to close offending enterprises, it is a power seldom used. Its greatest impact has been felt in those cases in which local party and government officials have backed cleanup programs, as in the Soviet capital; its role in routine pollution-abatement programs in nonpriority areas is much more modest. Moreover, the service is also required to spread its never adequate staff over a wide range of other public health tasks. The Hydrometeorological Service plays an even less direct role in monitoring overall pollution levels and suggesting guidelines. As we have noted, the tendency to place important responsibilities in the hands of the industries and individual enterprises themselves also diminishes the effectiveness of abatement programs. The obviously higher priority attached to the fulfillment of the plan causes abatement regulations to be overlooked, and the capital budgeted for emission-control devices is frequently diverted by factory and ministry personnel to more "productive" purposes.[32]

Another factor that reduces the likelihood of a direct confrontation between the nation's energy program and protection of the environment is the limited role that semiofficial environmental groups can play in the USSR. Unlike their counterparts in the United States and elsewhere, such groups cannot form freely and create interlocking networks at the national and local level. The few existing groups are largely closed out of the policy-making process because of their low position in the ministerial pecking order and are unable to gain access to higher leaders except under exceptional circumstances. The most important of these are the All-Russian Society for the Conservation of Nature and its republic and local counterparts throughout the USSR. While their total membership is large, an estimated 19 million in the RSFSR alone, most members are inactive or only marginally involved in the education programs of the society. The All-Russian Society has not played an aggressive role in environmental affairs, even on exceptional issues like Lake Baikal, and has tended to limit its concerns to conservationist and wildlife issues rather than pollution abatement.[33]

Of potentially greater importance is the possibility that an informal, ad hoc alliance of environmentalists might form in opposition to some aspect of the new energy program, as happened when industrial development threatened Lake Baikal. If we take the Baikal case as a prototype, it is likely that such a group would involve leading scientists, writers, and members of the academic community. The key to their success in the Baikal case was their ability to build an ad hoc institutional base around various research institutes, the USSR Academy of Sciences, and the academic community and then to mobilize a much larger elite audience through repeated criticism in sympathetic media, such as Literaturnaia Gazeta and Komsomol'skaia Pravda. This provided the stage for a lengthy battle against the Ministry of Timber, Paper, and Woodworking and other industrial interests. One of the keys to assembling and sustaining the coalition was the truly unique nature of the natural resource being threatened. For a similar strategy to be successful in this case, it would probably be necessary for a cause celebre, such as the air quality of Moscow or Leningrad or a serious nuclear accident, to emerge as the focus of a national debate. A serious deterioration of air quality in other industrial centers or less traumatic events in the development of nuclear or hydroelectric power would probably not be sufficient to mobilize such a coalition or create a large, favorably disposed audience, although local protests might be expected.[34]

NOTES

1. The best general works are Marianna Slocum, "Soviet Energy: An Internal Assessment," Technology Review, October–November 1974, pp. 17–23; J. H. Chesshire and C. Huggett, "Primary Energy Production in the Soviet Union: Problems and Prospects," Energy Policy 3, no. 3 (1975): 223–41; John P. Hardt, "West Siberia: The Quest for Energy," Problems of Communism 22, no. 3 (1973): 25–36; and Iain F. Elliot, The Soviet Energy Balance: Natural Gas, Other Fossil Fuels, and Alternative Power Sources (New York: Praeger, 1974).

2. For a general discussion of air quality in Moscow, see Marshall I. Goldman, The Spoils of Progress: Environmental Pollution in the Soviet Union (Cambridge: MIT Press, 1972), pp. 121–36; and David E. Powell, "Politics and the Urban Environment: The City of Moscow" (Paper presented at the meeting of the American Political Science Association, Chicago, September 1976).

3. Goldman, op. cit., pp. 177–210; John Kramer, "The Politics of Conservation and Pollution in the USSR" (Ph.D. diss., University of Virginia, 1973), pp. 162–80; and Donald R. Kelley, "Environmental Policy Making in the USSR: The Role of Industrial and Environmental Interest Groups," Soviet Studies 28, no. 3 (1976): 570–89.

        4. Donald R. Kelley, "Economic Growth and Environmental Quality in the USSR: Soviet Reaction to The Limits to Growth," Canadian Slavonic Papers, forthcoming.

        5. For a discussion of the impact of environmental lobbies and industrial interests, see Kramer, op. cit., pp. 18-28; Kelley, "Environmental Policy"; and Donald R. Kelley, Kenneth R. Stunkel, and Richard R. Wescott, The Economic Superpowers and the Environment: The United States, the Soviet Union, and Japan (San Francisco: W. H. Freeman, 1976), pp. 166-72.

        6. Chesshire and Huggett, op. cit., p. 224.

        7. The most extensive discussion of reserves is contained in Elliot, op. cit., pp. 18-36, 75-81, 132-35, 183-89, 198-203, although the comments in Marianna Slocum, op. cit., on the accuracy of these estimates should be carefully read.

        8. Phillip R. Pryde and Lucy T. Pryde, "Soviet Nuclear Power," Environment 16, no. 3 (1974): 26-34; and Elliot, op. cit., pp. 111-31.

        9. Marshall I. Goldman, "Russia Finds an Unexpected Ace in Oil," New York Times, April 28, 1974, p. B4; and Marshall I. Goldman, Detente and Dollars: Doing Business with the Russians (New York: Basic Books, 1975), pp. 79-123.

        10. U.S., Department of the Interior, Bureau of Mines, Minerals Yearbook, vol. 3 (Washington, D.C.: Government Printing Office, 1969), p. 749, and (1970), p. 799; Elliot, op. cit., p. 13; Hardt, op. cit., p. 26.

        11. Slocum, op. cit., p. 25; and Pravda, March 7, 1976, pp. 2-8.

        12. Slocum, op. cit., p. 26.

        13. Hardt, op. cit., p. 26.

        14. Ibid., p. 27; and Slocum, op. cit., pp. 20-23.

        15. Hardt, op. cit., pp. 28-30.

        16. Robert Campbell, comments before U.S. Congress, Joint Economic Committee, Subcommittee on Economic Priorities, published in Changing National Priorities (Washington D.C.: Government Printing Office, 1970).

        17. Chesshire and Huggett, op. cit., pp. 233-34; Hardt, op. cit.; Slocum, op. cit.; Goldman, "Russia Finds," op. cit., and Detente, op. cit., pp. 79-123; Arthur W. Wright, "The Soviet Union in World Energy Markets," in The Energy Question: An International Failure of Policy, ed. Edward W. Erickson and Leonard Waverman (Toronto: University of Toronto Press, 1974), vol. 1, pp. 85-100.

        18. Slocum, op. cit., pp. 26-28; John Kramer, "Prices and the Conservation of Natural Resources in the Soviet Union," Soviet Studies 24, no. 3 (1973): 364-73; Goldman, Spoils, op. cit., pp. 43-76. For evidence of a recent concern with fuel waste and

conservation programs, see the New York Times, November 28,
1973, p. 8; December 26, 1973, p. 49, January 14, 1974, p. 21,
and November 21, 1974, p. 9. See also Pravda, January 13, 1974,
p. 4; June 8, 1975, p. 2; October 17, 1975, p. 3; March 26, 1976,
p. 2; August 13, 1976, p. 1; and Izvestiia, February 27, 1975, p. 3,
and November 14, 1975, p. 3.

19. Mikhail Pervukhin, "Energy Resources of the USSR and
Their Rational Utilization," Planovoe Khoziaistvo, no. 7 (1974),
translated in Soviet and East European Foreign Trade 11, no. 1
(1975): 91-104.

20. V. A. Kirillin, "Power Engineering--Problems and Prospects," Kommunist, no. 1 (1975), pp. 43-51, translated in Current
Digest of the Soviet Press 27, no. 7 (1975): 10-11. See also his
comments reported in Pravda, November 28, 1974, p. 3.

21. Pravda, December 14, 1975, pp. 1-6.

22. Pravda, December 28, 1975, p. 3; and March 3, 1976;
p. 2. For comments on the further utilization of Urals coal, see
Pravda, November 16, 1975, p. 2.

23. Pravda, March 2, 1976, pp. 2-6.

24. Goldman, Spoils, op. cit., pp. 121-36. For poor abatement technology, see Kramer, Politics, op. cit., pp. 8-15, and
V. L. Mote, "The Geography of Air Pollution in the USSR" (Ph.D.
diss., Seattle: University of Washington, 1971), pp. 87-88.

25. Goldman, Spoils, op. cit., pp. 13-17; Norman Precoda,
"Left Behind--Soviet Mine Wastes," Environment 17, no. 8 (1975):
15-19; J. LaMothe, "Water Quality in the Soviet Union: A Review"
(U.S. Department of the Army, Medical Intelligence Office, 1971),
pp. 9-10; Pravda, August 26, 1975, p. 2, March 2, 1976, pp. 2-6,
and April 5, 1976, p. 4.

26. Pryde and Pryde, op. cit.; Goldman, Spoils, op. cit.,
pp. 142-44; LaMothe, op. cit., pp. 19, 48; New York Times,
June 14, 1974, p. 11, and May 26, 1975, p. 4.

27. Goldman, Spoils, op. cit., pp. 142-45; Pryde and Pryde,
op. cit.; New York Times, November 7, 1976, p. 18.

28. Elliot, op. cit., pp. 211-31; Chesshire and Huggett,
op. cit.; Pravda, March 30, 1973, p. 3; March 2, 1974, p. 2; and
August 3, 1974, p. 3; Izvestiia, February 4, 1975, p. 5; April 12,
1975, p. 5; July 5, 1975, p. 5; July 9, 1975, p. 3; July 11, 1975,
p. 5; November 21, 1975, p. 4; and December 2, 1975, p. 5;
Ekonomika i Organizatsiia Promyshlennogo Proizvodstva, no. 5
(1975), pp. 67-74; and Ekonomicheskaia Gazeta, no. 48 (1973),
p. 14.

29. Slocum, op. cit., pp. 22-23; Elliot, op. cit., p. 217.

30. Kelley, Stunkel, and Wescott, op. cit., pp. 84-85;
Kramer, "Prices," op. cit., pp. 364-73; Goldman, Spoils, op. cit.,

pp. 257-58; and Phillip R. Pryde, Conservation in the Soviet Union (New York: Cambridge University Press, 1972), p. 115.

31. Pravda, November 28, 1974, p. 3; Izvestiia, November 4, 1975, p. 5.

32. Pryde, Conservation, op. cit., pp. 107-12; Keith Bush, "Environmental Problems in the USSR," Problems of Communism 11, no. 4 (1972), pp. 21-31; Kramer, Politics, op. cit., pp. 38-75; and Kelley, Stunkel, and Wescott, op. cit., pp. 163-66.

33. Goldman, Spoils, pp. 185-205; Kelley, Stunkel, and Wescott, op. cit., pp. 166-72; Kramer, Politics, op. cit., pp. 24-26.

34. Goldman, Spoils, op. cit., pp. 177-210; Kelley, Stunkel, and Wescott, op. cit., pp. 173-80.

4

EASTERN EUROPE: CZECHOSLOVAKIA, ROMANIA, AND YUGOSLAVIA
George Klein

All the states of communist Eastern Europe copied the Soviet economic model when their respective governments came to power. This model had its virtues for states that were in the initial stages of industrialization; however, it was also applied uncritically to an advanced industrial state, Czechoslovakia. There it proved unsatisfactory because further Czechoslovak advances depended on the increased productivity of labor rather than on a massive transfer of labor from the agricultural to the industrial sector. Development throughout Eastern Europe was geared toward the attainment of a large volume of production at the expense of most other considerations. This was dictated both by Soviet influence and by the necessity for rapid reconstruction.

The East European leaderships were already accustomed to deferring to the Soviet lead and had frequently acted as the Soviet-dominated Comintern agents. In the aftermath of World War II, the Soviet leaders only deepened their ideological and political control because of Soviet domination of the economic and political institutions that facilitated it.

In all the East European states it was difficult to criticize the socialist sector because the industrial objectives set by the plan were proclaimed by the highest authorities in the states, parties, and governments. Any criticism of the production-centered objectives would have been viewed as a political attack on the system. While many legislative enactments designed to protect the environment graced the legal codes of the Eastern European states, many of them inherited from the precommunist era, the bureaucracy responsible for the execution of the national plans proceeded on its own order of priorities. This was partially dictated by the overwhelming need for increased production in all sectors of the economy and partially by an ideology that placed its faith in unbridled industrial expansion.

While in the West the academic community and other publics became alarmed about the deterioration of the environment in the 1960s, the communist states continued to voice optimism and faith in technology. The communist officials in many states viewed population and environmental questions as of little consequence. This was particularly notable in the Chinese positions on population in the 1950s. Marshall I. Goldman noted a similar lack of environmental sensitivity on the part of Soviet officials.[1] Moreover, most communist societies, with the exception of China, viewed the peasantry as a vanishing group that should be transformed into agroindustrial labor. It was only under the inexorable pressure of the problems generated by precipitous growth and urbanization that the authorities were forced to reconsider. The West, where the environmental movement was frequently linked with "progressive elements," served as a model. While all the communist states were amply supplied with legislation protecting the workers' health and well-being, it was only in the late 1960s that they began to examine the question of the environment comprehensively.

The three states under examination, Czechoslovakia, Romania, and Yugoslavia, have vastly differing traditions in environmental protection. In the areas that were formerly ruled by the Hapsburgs, protection of the environment dates back centuries. These areas, which include Czechoslovakia, Slovenia, and Croatia, bear testimony to the careful husbanding of cropland, forests, and water resources. Antierosion measures have been applied for centuries, and the conservation of fish and wildlife is a tradition. Those areas that were under Ottoman rule manifest a lack of investment and concern, which is visually apparent in Yugoslavia to the present day. Slovenia is an example of the careful husbanding of resources, while the former Ottoman territories of Yugoslavia bear the marks of raubwirtschaft. Czechoslovakia's rich tradition of conservation is particularly apparent in Bohemia and Moravia. It was the only area in prewar Eastern Europe that was truly industrialized and that had already experienced problems of large-scale industrial pollution in the nineteenth century, when Kladno, Plzen, and Ostrava suffered the fate of twentieth-century Gary, Indiana. Romania was so underdeveloped before the war that in most respects it represented the classic peasant culture, in which problems of modern pollution did not arise outside of a few major population centers and the Ploesti oil fields.

In the aftermath of World War II and after the communist takeover in 1948, Czechoslovakia faced much different problems from the other two states under examination. While Yugoslavia and Romania could effect a massive transfer of labor from the agricultural sector to industry, Czechoslovakia did not possess a reservoir of rural population. From the 1960s onward it became clear that

Czechoslovakia could achieve higher production only by increasing the productivity of the existing labor force. This meant increasing the horsepower at the disposal of Czechoslovak workers, which required an increasing energy output. Czechoslovakia embarked on a rapid buildup of its hydroelectric power system, although it was handicapped by a relatively low water volume in its rivers. Hydroelectric power, however, is scarcely the answer to the needs of a state that has one of the largest per capita steel production rates in the world.

While the ever-increasing demand for energy had an adverse effect on the environment of the cities, Czechoslovakia also experienced some significant environmental improvements. The expulsion of the Sudeten Germans in the aftermath of World War II depopulated many marginal farming areas, which have been reforested since. This increased the forest lands and habitat for wildlife. Due to its high level of technical development, Czechoslovakia faces many of the problems of the postindustrial societies, while Romania and Yugoslavia are still struggling to achieve full industrialization.

The marks of precipitous industrialization are visible in all East European states. Drab, low-quality construction saturated by a pall of lignite smoke is the hallmark of many development projects. The condition is seldom denied by responsible officials; but they point with justification to the need for rapid construction in areas of acute housing shortages and underemployment. In East Europe the principal source of pollution does not as yet derive from the automobile but from heating, which utilizes low-grade coals. The burgeoning automobilization is adding a new dimension to the pollution problems of East European cities. Such cities as Belgrade and Prague are quickly catching up to the West European rates of automobilization and complicating an already acute problem. In Belgrade, "good or bad air" residential areas are one of the favorite subjects of conversation. Until very recently the pollution-saturated urban environment was considered an acceptable price for rapid development, but since the mid-1960s, and particularly since the early 1970s, the situation has been a matter of major concern to both the populations and leaderships in all East European states.

In Yugoslavia the shift in focus was generated by controversy raised in such journals as Praxis. This journal raised the issue of whether the "vulgar economism" of the Soviet and Western models was worth uncritical emulation. The former editor of Praxis, Rudi Supek, in his book This One World, suggests the possibility of a stable society as a revolutionary contradiction to consumer society.[2] At present the environmental controversy has penetrated the communist states and commands attention from politicians, planners, and even national leaders.[3]

Energy policy is intimately linked with the entire range of environmental discussion in Eastern Europe; it was dramatized by the price rises in the wake of the October War in 1973. Nevertheless, energy policy will also determine the parameters of solutions to urban blight and pollution in the cities of Eastern Europe. Energy policy will determine the rate of conversion from polluting sources of heating to cleaner sources. The price of oil will determine investment in nuclear and hydroelectric projects, which are thought to have lower environmental costs than the burning of coal. Under the impact of rising oil prices, conversion to oil heating has been slowed both in home and industrial use. There has been a steady improvement in the atmosphere of some East European cities due to increased use of oil for heating. However, the price hikes in oil threw these developments into question and have forced a reexamination of energy priorities in all of Eastern Europe.

POLITICS OF ENVIRONMENTAL PROTECTION

The three states under examination have vastly differing political systems and equally differing energy resources. Their only claim to similarity is a shared geographic location, a common ideology, and proximity to the Union of Soviet Socialist Republics. Their commitment to Marxist socialism and practice has not prevented widely differing individual adaptations. Therefore it is necessary to examine each state separately.

Czechoslovakia

In Czechoslovakia, centralization has been a fact of political life for most of its history, especially since the communist accession to power in 1948. The state has always had a unitary government that exercised major control from Prague. During the communist era, centralization has been accentuated even further by the adoption of a planning system, in which all major economic divisions were subordinated to the wishes of a highly centralized government and party. The Prague Spring of 1968 only temporarily interrupted this practice. One of the few tangible results of the Prague Spring was a new federal constitution and new directives that would have placed Slovakia on an equal basis. The recentralization of the Czechoslovak Communist Party and the reimposition of tight domestic control in the wake of the Prague Spring may, however, have defeated the original purposes of the new constitution.

Energy policy in Czechoslovakia is now, as before, made by
state planning bodies that are responsible to the central planning
authorities and to the party. Since the mid-1960s, these planning
authorities have become sensitized to environmental matters by the
dismal statistics of the airborne and waterborne pollution that poison
the Czechoslovak environment.[4] The rate of pollution is among the
highest in Europe. The hazards of heating by coal have been augmented by a precipitously rapid automobilization. The pressure of
international concern, combined with increasing domestic concern,
has forced the authorities to put this issue in the forefront. This is
reinforced by the need of the communist regimes to appear to be the
avant garde of positive change. Laws have covered environmental
pollution for decades, but the enforcement was piecemeal and admittedly inadequate. Nevertheless, environmental initiatives were largely left to the governmental bodies, since the citizenry is not participating through spontaneously organized associations that could exercise viable criticism of the plan. Criticism of policy would be construed as criticism of the system itself. Therefore, when environmental policy and the productive goals of the state collided, it was
usually the environmental interests that had to yield. The absence
of a vigorous representation of consumers makes environmental concerns the prerogative of the bureaucratic apparatus, which is chiefly
concerned with day-to-day administrative control.

Central planning is not inherently antagonistic to environmental
protection if the controlling elites build high environmental standards
into the plans and back these by appropriate funding. The first step
that must be taken is to elevate environmental protection to one of
the goals of a centrally planned socialist society.[5] In Czechoslovakia,
environmental control has been receiving increasing attention from
the highest authorities and was an integral part of the party program
that was adopted at the Fourteenth Party Congress and the draft program of the Fifteenth Party Congress for the Sixth Five-Year Plan,
of 1976-80.[6]

In communist states, environmental costs are not calculated
into the economic plans, either in social or monetary terms. The
enterprise manager, who is principally concerned with fulfilling the
plan on which the structure of rewards for the enterprise is based,
is apt to view environmental concerns as a distraction from his major
responsibility. Most enterprise managers recognize that investment
in environmental measures reduces their profits with no immediately
visible return. The beneficiary of strict environmental control is a
far wider public, rather than the immediate constituency of the management.[7] Therefore, any major change in priorities will have to
come from party and government directives.

Environmental protection in Czechoslovakia falls within the jurisdiction of two ministries. The Ministry of Forestry and Water Economy of the Czech and Slovak Republics supervises the disposition of liquid wastes. The Ministry of Agriculture and Food is responsible for the supervision of dry waste and land conservation. The basic units of local government, the National Committees (Narodni Odbory), are responsible for the execution of the laws. The laws originate with the responsible ministries and party organs, which in effect control the enactment of implementing legislation by the national assembly.

The implementation of the laws is done at the behest of control and inspection bodies, such as the State Technical Inspection of Environmental Protection and the State Water Economy Inspection. In 1971 the Czech and Slovak governments set up councils for the environment as coordinating and consultative bodies. Their principal function is the drafting of environmental impact statements and the general supervision of all aspects of coordination between the central organs and the national committees. The success of their work essentially depends on the priorities of the national leadership and on the willingness of the control and inspection bodies to enforce environmental standards against enterprises that are under the control of the national leadership.

On the international level, Czechoslovakia is a member of the Council for the Environment, which was set up with Comecon. Prague also hosted the first UN conference on the environment in 1972.

Romania

Romania, like Czechoslovakia, is a highly centralized state. It is even more susceptible to central control because of the preeminent position of the Romanian nationality. As in Czechoslovakia, the leadership of both state and party is vested in one man, President Nikolae Ceausescu, who is also Party Secretary. While Ceausescu is highly accessible personally, he is not likely to brook interference with his highly personalistic style of decision making. The Romanians accept the highly centralistic style of leadership as the best guarantee of the maintenance of the nationally autonomous style that Romania has developed since the early 1960s. The political dynamics resemble those of Czechoslovakia, insofar as the protection of the environment does not depend on the pressure of associations but rather on the order of priorities set by the top authorities within the party and the government and planning bureaucracies. In recent years the Romanian leadership has manifested a high level of concern for the quality of the environment, and a particular determination not to pass on its effluents to its Danubian neighbors.[8]

The lower administrative levels in Romania are conditioned to subordinate their positions to the national leadership and would scarcely find strength to oppose national policy.[9] Thus opposition in matters on which the party and its leadership have gone on record would scarcely be conducive to fulfilling aspirations for upward mobility on the part of local officials. Romania is perhaps the most centralized system in Eastern Europe. Local officials are largely appointed and frequently transferred, to prevent the emergence of local power bases.

Romania is the only Comecon state that participated in the Stockholm Conference on the Environment. The leader of the Romanian delegation made the following declaration: "Romania views the protection of the environment as a precondition for progress. . . . In the struggle for environmental protection there is a community of interests between all states large or small, developed or engaged in development."[10]

While Romanian legislation in the area of environmental protection dates back to the 1950s, it received its greatest impetus only in the 1970s. The Tenth Party Congress of 1970 devoted its attention for the first time to a national policy toward the management of water resources. As of 1972 the results were not fully satisfactory: 7,000 of the 12,000 most important water users remained unlicensed, and apparently nobody dared to interfere with production plans on environmental grounds, lest this lead to the nonfulfillment of production quotas.[11] Despite the fact that the new legislation was hailed as a great step forward, no one has been quite willing to enforce it against the large enterprises. The funds devoted to purification facilities during 1971-75 doubled in comparison with the previous five-year period. This is not likely to prove adequate, however, because these facilities are not an integral part of the investment plans, but rather a separate item. The new dimension is the official attention that environmental problems are receiving in the highest policy-making bodies. In 1972 Ceausescu announced a strengthened environmental protection policy. This was achieved by invoking monetary penalties against responsible officials in polluting enterprises. The number of prosecutions for the violation of environmental laws has risen steadily in the past few years.

As in Czechoslovakia, the enforcement of environmental protection rests with a plethora of governmental agencies and commissions. The Ministry of Agriculture possesses a Directorate for the Protection and Purification of the Waters. The Ministry of Health is charged with the observation of the consequences of pollution. All ministries were put on notice to activate research groups. In

1969 the Romanian Academy of Sciences was commissioned to conduct a study that would classify air purity in all of Romania and identify all sources of pollution.[12]

Romania has a Commission for Environmental Protection, which publishes a journal, and Romanian universities have worked out curriculums dealing with environmental protection. Despite these efforts Romania, like other socialist states, will lag behind in the genuine improvement of its environmental qualities as long as the investments are not built directly into the initial construction plans. Romanian local officialdom exhibits the usual reluctance to interfere with projects that are significant sources of local employment and essential to the fulfillment of the national master plan. Thus the quality of Romanian environmental protection ultimately rests with the top leadership of the party and the bureaucracy.

Yugoslavia

Environmental concerns in Yugoslavia are expressed in the context of an entirely different political system than those of Romania and Czechoslovakia. Central planning in Yugoslavia has been limited ever since the 1950s, and at present there are several West European states that practice more rigorous central planning than Yugoslavia. Whatever remains of central planning is usually implemented by central banking and fiscal policy, which encourages investment in the less developed parts of Yugoslavia. The banking system is not centrally controlled. Most of the banks are based in republics and provide loans and customer services on a basis that is similar to that of their Western counterparts. Economic feasibility and profitability are the main criteria for granting loans. The federal government undertakes major investments in the infrastructure and in such major international projects as the construction of the Yugoslav-Romanian Djerdap hydroelectric complex on the Danube. The federal government aids underdeveloped regions through fiscal policies designed for that purpose. Most productive projects are left to individual enterprises, which must obtain support from republican and communal bodies* for their investment plans. In the republic of Slovenia, the banks participate in the protection of the environment by investigating the provisions for environmental protection in all proposed investment projects.

---

*The commune in Yugoslavia is the basic territorial subdivision of a republic or autonomous province, somewhat comparable to a county in the United States.

In contrast with other communist states, Yugoslavia tolerates
a plethora of essentially autonomous associations. Workers' self-
management organs and numerous local bodies are in a position not
only to act as pressure groups but also to implement policy. Thus
Yugoslavia is the only communist state that has interest groups that
are analogous to their Western counterparts, insofar as they may
dispose over sizable funds that are derived either from their earn-
ings or from their membership. Group expressions of concern over
national policy are not usually viewed as a challenge to an entrenched
bureaucracy and become merely disputes over policy in a decentralized system. The federal nature of the state, based on the hetero-
geneous character of its nationalities, endows the country with a
wide range of historic traditions. These traditions provide the
framework within which environmental concerns are expressed. The
efficacy of the various groups concerned with the protection of the environment differs vastly from republic to republic, depending on income levels and traditions in the realm of environmental protection.
The governments in those areas where conservation has been practiced for centuries, such as Slovenia and Croatia, are more likely
to act resolutely in support of protective measures than those in the
underdeveloped regions, which are desperately trying to attract investment and industrialize.

Sensitivity to environmental issues seems to vary with the
levels of income of the republics. It is perhaps more than accidental
that the largest generating plants relying on lignite fuel are located
in Kosovo, the most underdeveloped area. This area receives a
major share of investment money for the development of industries
that carry a high degree of environmental hazard, such as mining.
Any expansion of similar installations in Slovenia, such as the steel
mills of Jesenice, would cause a storm of criticism. The less developed republics would register little complaint about any investment.

Pressure groups in Yugoslavia consist of literally thousands
of self-managerial and working organizations, which govern the
economic life of the country. To these can be added hundreds of
voluntary associations, ranging from veterans' organizations to
hunting, sailing, and skiing clubs, which have a vested interest in
environmental protection. All these groups have relatively easy
access to the local media. Most environmental concerns are locally
generated and solved.

The classic case in Yugoslavia has been the ongoing struggle
between tourist and industrial interests on the Adriatic coast.[13]
This is a phenomenon that has been observable since the 1950s.
The discussion centered on the rapid expansion in the industrial
park north of Split, which contains the largest plastics industry in

Yugoslavia and competes for the Adriatic shoreline with a formerly prime resort area. The dispute between these two major local interests was vigorously fought in the local press, and the solutions had to be forthcoming from the Split communal council and from the republican government. Coalitions of interest groups emerged around both contending groups. While the environmental interests were not victorious, they were able to impose expensive environmental controls.

Such an interplay of groups does not signify that there are no limits on debate in Yugoslavia, especially when major investment projects are involved in which the state has a special interest. Individuals who question major policy items may be suspect in some quarters; yet their challenges in the daily press may force significant modifications of policy. Yugoslavia is the only state in East Europe that does not routinely practice precensorship of the press. What is permissible is decided by the editors, who are sensitive to the limits of the permissible in the system in which they operate. However, there are vast regional differences. What may be printed in Slovenia might be editorially proscribed elsewhere. Few would deny that the levels of political tolerance in Yugoslavia are directly proportional to the levels of regional development and modernization.

The efficacy of environmental policy, then, depends entirely on the dedication of republican and communal bodies as they directly respond to individual and group concerns. In Czechoslovakia and Romania, environmental protection is the function of locally implemented national legislation in a structured hierarchical situation. By contrast, the Yugoslav situation is anarchic and it is impossible to compare its efficacy with that of a system of total state control. In those areas of Yugoslavia where the level of environmental consciousness is high and income is high, environmental policy may achieve high standards. Local organs accurately reflect the concerns of an informed public and of the numerous self-managerial organizations and associations. In those areas of the country that do not have a tradition of environmental sensitivity, environmental protection depends on the dedication of the bureaucracy. It is impossible to speak of a nationally uniform Yugoslav policy toward the environment. There are as many policies as there are republics and provinces, and they each treat environmental issues in line with citizen and group expectations.

The years since 1973 have brought a growth in institutional substance to environmental policy because of the formation of the Yugoslav Council for the Protection and Enhancement of the Human Environment. The council consists of 80 members, delegated from each republic and autonomous province. It is headed by Ales Bebler, a former Partisan general and a distinguished diplomat. The council has a number of commissions concerned with the various areas of environmental protection, such as water and air. The principal duties of the council are to gather information, publicize it, and advise the policy-making bodies on matters concerning the environment. It does not have any direct policy-making powers, but it has access to the Federal Executive Council, which may act on its recommendations.

The Council of Ministers includes a federal coordinating body concerned with environmental questions, consisting of the deputy secretaries of relevant ministries and representatives of the trade unions, the League of Communists, and the Socialist Alliance. The Yugoslav Council for the Protection and Enhancement of the Human Environment is also represented on this body. Such institutions have their analogues on the republican and provincial levels.

The main effect of the new consciousness thus far has been new federal legislation and improvement of existing legislation for the protection of the quality of the environment. The federation has passed a law protecting the purity of rivers crossing republican boundaries. There has been an increase in the number of inter-republican and interdepartmental councils that attempt to address themselves to questions of enforcement. It would be premature to evaluate all the effects of the increased activity, but it is safe to predict that they will be far from uniform. For example, the Republic of Croatia has passed a law prohibiting the use of either alcohol or tobacco at workplaces, but it is doubtful that Macedonia, a major producer of tobacco, will follow suit. [14]

One of the greatest changes has been the organization of the scientific community for research in the area of the environment. [15] The Tenth Congress of the League of Communists of Yugoslavia set new tasks for the society and thus sanctioned the increasing environmental sensitivity at the highest levels. The increasing recognition that many of the problems defy purely national solutions leads Yugoslavia to participation in such international efforts as protection of the Mediterranean and the Danube.

ENERGY BALANCE

The structure of energy use in the countries under examination differs widely, insofar as the domestic resources of each of the states differ. The character and level of development in each state differ as well.

Czechoslovakia

Czechoslovakia is the only postindustrial nation in the Comecon bloc, with the possible exception of the German Democratic Republic. A diminishing and minor proportion of its population remains in the agricultural sector. Czechoslovakia, one of the largest steel producers in the world on a per capita basis, possesses a diversified and complex heavy industrial sector that is yet to be achieved by the other states under examination. Therefore the problems of Czechoslovakia are essentially different from those of Romania and Yugoslavia, which are both still striving to transfer population from agriculture to industry. Czechoslovakia has reached the limits of these possibilities if measured against the standards of the most industrialized states, and therefore it must make do with its existing labor force and render it more efficient. This requires expensive investment that carries over into the industrial sector.

Czechoslovakia is not striving to create new industry but to render existing plants more efficient. On environmental issues this has both advantages and disadvantages. One of the obvious advantages is that the Czechoslovak living standard has reached a level at which more resources can be devoted to the improvement of the quality of life rather than to the bare necessities of existence. Therefore Czechoslovakia, both out of necessity and because it is in a position to divert greater resources to it, will concentrate on effective environmental protection. It is a disadvantage because many of its plants are inherited from an earlier era, during which environmental concerns were not very high in the consciousness of either the engineers or the investors. Czechoslovakia must therefore devote much greater resources to making yesterday's plants meet the more exacting standards of today.

The rise in the price of oil has dealt a blow to plans for the use of cleaner fuels. In Czechoslovakia the availability of energy determines the level of industrial output. Apart from its fairly rich endowment in brown coal, Czechoslovakia is and will continue to be an energy-deficient state. Its rivers cannot be harnessed for significant output of hydroelectric power because their water flow is too low to contribute significantly to the solution of its energy shortage. The proportion of hydroelectric power has been steadily decreasing. In 1965 it totaled 18.8 percent, while in 1975 it contributed only 12.7 percent.[16]

Czechoslovakia is slated for considerable investment in the hydroelectric sector, due to the increased cost of the alternatives. Hard coal production has remained almost constant since 1969, while lignite mining increases have also not been significant.[17] Coal cannot meet the expanding energy needs of the Czechoslovak economy. The main burden of construction has been on oil-fired thermal plants. The price rises have led to the abandonment of construction of some projects, and the nation has been urged to exercise stringent energy conservation measures. The major hope for Czechoslovakia is the successful completion of its nuclear program and the introduction of Soviet natural gas from the Orenburg fields, slated for 1978. While it is not certain that these projects will be on target, eventually they will greatly ease the pressures on an economy that largely depends on imports for its energy needs. The oil price increases have already led to a greater use of existing coal-burning facilities as projects depending on oil and natural gas have fallen behind schedule. This does not promise much relief for the industrial centers blighted by air and water pollution.

Czechoslovakia imports 98 percent of its oil needs. Of this, 92 percent originates from Soviet sources.[18] It has been the claim of the Soviet bloc states that they are insulated from the price fluctuations common to the West. The Soviet price hikes, while not as dramatic as those of OPEC, materially worsened the Czechoslovak position and threw into flux all development plans based on the assumption of the availability of Soviet oil at fixed prices. This was bound to have adverse effects on the whole process of planning. The reevaluation of the proper energy mix for Czechoslovak needs continues.

Romania

Romania is in a unique position among the East European states, since it supplies about 80 percent of its oil needs from domestic sources. This enables Romania to avoid the constant drain of energy imports on its balance of payments. It has also contributed to the Romanian decision to chart its own economic development independently of Comecon planning. While Romania imports about 20 percent of its oil needs, none of this originates with Comecon countries. The principal problem the Romanians face is the depletion of their own domestic supplies. While Romanian production is still rising in small increments, any major expansion of production will have to come from the deep drilling of new fields or offshore oil, since the existing fields have reached their peak. *

---

*Oil production amounted to about 108 million barrels in 1974, compared to 106.1 million barrels in 1973. Estimated output for 1975 is 108.8 barrels. (World Oil 181, no. 3 [August 15, 1975]: 134.)

Due to an anticipated rise in consumption of oil products, Romania is making major investments in hydroelectric power. The next five-year plan calls for the construction of a chain of 29 power stations along the Olt River. Overall, hydroelectric power is projected to constitute 30 to 39 percent of total generating capacity by the end of the next five-year plan.[19]

The increased price of energy has also led to a rise in the output of coal. Coal and lignite have been substituted for the more expensive oil. Romanian planners have also approved the construction of a new thermal station at Onavita, to be fueled by bituminous shale. Increased emphasis is being placed on the recovery of gases in coking operations. Romania, with its relatively constant output of petrochemicals, will increasingly have to tap its coal resources, which have been largely underexploited.

The increased substitution of solid fossil fuels does not bode well for the Romanian environment, yet the emphasis on hydroelectric power, coupled with the abundance of oil, may yet provide Romania with the resources to maintain a fairly clean environment. The commitment of its planners in this direction is quite clear.

Yugoslavia

Yugoslavia has a rich and diversified resource base for domestic energy production. As yet, its potential resources for the development of hydroelectric projects have scarcely been tapped. The other resources, such as coal and uranium, suffer from underutilization. The Yugoslav problem is not resources, but the capitalization of the extractive industries, which could provide Yugoslavia with self-sufficiency. Domestic energy needs have expanded so dramatically that Yugoslavia, despite its rich resources endowment, is a net energy importer. Yugoslavia imports about 60 percent of the oil it uses, as well as direct electricity from Albania, Austria, and Italy.[20] The need becomes particularly acute during periods of drought, when the hydroelectric supply diminishes. The OPEC price hikes have placed a substantial burden on Yugoslavia's usually strained balance of payments. This has resulted in policy decisions that have focused Yugoslav development on coal-fired and nuclear plants, and a nuclear plant is presently under construction. It is to be augmented by three more nuclear projects over the next decade. Coal, however, with its questionable impact on the purity of the environment, is slated for the most rapid build-up, due to the initially lower investment and the domestic availability.[21] Coal and coal-fired thermal plants place the least burden on Yugoslavia's balance of payments and manifest a potential for rapid development.

Yugoslavia must consistently increase its production of both oil and coal in order to maintain a satisfactory energy supply. This is conditioned by both the rapid industrial expansion and by a growing automobilization. Despite significantly expanded domestic production, Yugoslavia will not be able to diminish its imports. It is estimated in a study projecting Yugoslavia's future needs that only 4.6 million tons of oil will be available domestically in 1980 and 5.3 million tons in 1985, despite new discoveries.[22] The Yugoslav need for oil imports will grow to 20 million tons by 1985, compared to the present level of 8 million tons. These are the forces motivating Yugoslavia's participation in the construction of the petrochemical complexes around Rijeka.

The Yugoslav socialized enterprise INA-Naftaplin is also active in operations abroad. It is drilling in conjunction with the Syrian national oil company. INA will also drill in the Bay of Bengal as the result of agreements concluded with Bangladesh.[23] In the next few years INA plans to seek oil off Yugoslavia's Adriatic coastline and has ordered an offshore rig. Most of the Yugoslav projects are behind schedule due to the economic measures exercised over investment. Only a slowdown in economic activity has kept Yugoslav energy shortfalls from being more severe.

THE CHANGING ENERGY OUTLOOK IN EASTERN EUROPE

In the 1960s the Comecon states based their planning on an assumption of stable oil prices. Most of the East European states, with the exception of Romania, must import energy supplies, largely from the Soviet Union. The communist press proclaimed that the Soviet oil price was not subject to the price fluctuations of the international market and that the Soviet bloc would therefore remain immune to Western inflation. The price of Soviet oil deliveries was fixed for five-year periods, but after the OPEC price hikes the Soviet Union decided logically that its energy exports to Eastern Europe were underpriced and that Soviet oil prices ultimately had to reflect world realities. The Soviet Union doubled its oil prices to East Europe and now insists on an annual price review.[24] During the 1960s Soviet planners believed that the USSR could maintain its position as a major oil exporter for an indefinite time, but by the late 1960s it was clear that domestic demand, both in the Soviet Union and in East Europe, was rising beyond Soviet projections.[25] Soviet industry and increased automobilization caused a rapid demand for both oil and natural gas energy;[26] however, the current Soviet five-year plan features a cutback in automobile production.

The new realities could not help but have profound effects on both Yugoslavia and Czechoslovakia. Yugoslavia imports most of its oil from OPEC states and thus was subject to the immediate effect of the OPEC-dictated price hikes.* Czechoslovakia, which imports practically all of its oil needs, was forced to adjust its plans to the Soviet price hikes. Romania, though faced by a growing discrepancy between domestic production and consumption, was the most immune, since it supplies 80 percent of its needs domestically and is a net exporter of oil products.[27]

All three of the states in question imposed conservation measures aimed at cutting back oil consumption. It is not clear whether these were in line with environmentalist maxims or largely aimed at preserving the balance of payments. In all three states the new realities produced changes of emphasis in energy planning.

Because of the centralized character of decision making in Czechoslovakia and Romania, the national authorities took a series of measures to conserve oil. The price hikes were passed on to the consumers in the hope that these would discourage consumption. All three countries passed their first effective speed limits for all types of vehicles, which are now posted not only on the highways but on commercial vehicles as well. Both Czechoslovakia and Romania imposed rationing during the emergency, which has since been rescinded. While the supplies of the states under examination were not threatened by the embargo, the price hikes led to serious attention to the effect of continued oil shortages on national planning. Such considerations have a direct impact on the quality of the environment.

The most serious impact is likely to be felt in the most import-dependent country, Czechoslovakia. The increased price of oil has led to substantial changes in the national plan. Until 1973 the plan called for a rapid substitution of oil and gas for coal. These plans have been curtailed significantly, and a number of conversion projects have been abandoned in the wake of the price hikes. Environmental quality has suffered, since the use of coal and lignite is far more polluting than the substitute fuels. The Czechoslovak planners also paid close attention to product modification, with the view of replacing materials that require high-energy expenditures.[28] The Romanian planners followed in the same path, and it is possible that the concern may have emerged out of Comecon directives. Both states pledged themselves to the rapid development of hydroelectric and nuclear sources of energy.

---

*Yugoslavia has benefited indirectly from the new-found Arab wealth, however, insofar as it has obtained substantial orders for Yugoslav products as well as investment funds for such major projects as the Adriatic pipeline.

NUCLEAR ENERGY

Since in all the states under study future oil deficits are predicted, their governments are pledged to the development of nuclear-
generated power. Czechoslovakia has made the largest investment
in nuclear power because it is the largest oil importer and also the
only state with a chronic and acute labor shortage. Czechoslovakia
has imported labor from other states within the Comecon bloc.
Nuclear power appears to offer an escape from both problems. The
country has domestic sources of uranium and the capacity to become
a major exporter of nuclear generating equipment, of which it is already a major producer. Czechoslovakia now has five nuclear energy
plants in operation or on order, and all of these should be in operation by 1980. By 1985 it is estimated that 30 percent of all generated
capacity will come from nuclear sources.[29]

Both Yugoslavia and Romania have nuclear power stations under
construction. In Romania present plans call for the construction of
nuclear power that would generate 20 percent of its electric power by
the end of the 1980s. Romania approved a national nuclear program
in 1969. At present there are 450 nuclear research units in enterprises and other institutions using nuclear technology. Personnel
are being trained, and a number of research institutes are working
on nuclear energy.

Yugoslavia also has a nuclear power station on order, from
U.S. sources. Interestingly enough, the Yugoslav nuclear station
has been the subject of the only publicly aired environmental controversy. Nenad Prelog, Secretary for the Commission for the Protection and Improvement of the Human Environment of the Youth League
of Croatia, engaged in a press controversy with the engineer responsible for the Yugoslav end of the technological arrangements in
the pages of the weekly Vjesnik u srijedu (Wednesday herald).[30]
Prelog expressed major reservations about the environmental safety
of the cooling arrangement for the projected plant. He pointed out
that during low water periods the entire flow of the River Sava would
have to pass through the plant's cooling system, and the flow might
still be inadequate, with unpredictable consequences for the biologic
life of the river and the ecology of the general area. The articles
caused considerable concern in Zagreb, Yugoslavia's second city,
which is close to the plant site at Krsko. This controversy generated so much pressure on the planners that eventually the plans were
altered to include the construction of an internal cooling system that
would not have such a major impact on the immediate environment.
The controversy entailed discussions about the disposal of nuclear
waste materials, and the dangers of nuclear development were publicized. To my knowledge, such issues have not been fully aired in
the other East European states.

The calculation is that nuclear energy will be competitive with other sources of power, particularly in the long run.[31] Even while admitting that initial construction costs are high, the Czechoslovak planners hold that the costs of nuclear-generated power will be advantageous whenever the transportation of fossil fuels exceeds 100 kilometers. The Comecon bloc, with the Soviet Union, East Germany, and Czechoslovakia in the lead, has made a commitment to achieve major nuclear generating capacity over the next 20 years.[32] In view of their rapid rise in demand for energy, which exceeds the world average, such a commitment appears logical to the planners.

THE INTERNATIONAL ASPECTS OF ENERGY SUPPLY

The area under study is covered by a series of energy transmission networks, which are under expansion. These include the Friendship Oil Pipeline, the Brotherhood Natural Gas Line, and the Peace Electric Grid. The Friendship Pipeline, with its terminal outlet in Bratislava, Czechoslovakia, augmented by the Adriatic pipeline originating in the port of Rijeka, Yugoslavia, promises to become a major factor in the oil resource picture of Yugoslavia, Hungary, Romania, and Czechoslovakia. Major projects underway will transmit large volumes of natural gas and electricity from the Soviet Union to Czechoslovakia and other states in Eastern Europe. The most ambitious of these is the 2,790-kilometer gas pipeline originating beyond the Urals in Orenburg and terminating in Uzhorod on the Czechoslovak border. The project is slated for completion in 1978 and will bring 25 to 30 billion cubic meters of natural gas per year to East European consumers.[33]

The other major project under construction is a 750 kilovolt power line linking the Ukraine with the rest of Comecon Europe. Due to high tension and high planned capacity, the environmental impact is not fully predictable. The plans call for bypassing areas with high population densities and constructing it in relatively uninhabited areas of the Ukraine and Hungary. It was determined that Czechoslovakia did not represent a "suitable environment" for the high voltage line because of its population densities. The technical experts also determined that the dust levels of Czechoslovak air are so high that the power would have to be stepped down to 400 kilovolts before it could be transmitted safely through the country.[34] This certainly bespeaks an awareness of environmental hazards.

The projects initiated are grandiose in scope. The Comecon meeting in Budapest in June 1975 led to the approval of $9 billion investment in joint Comecon projects. These also have profound political implications. It is assumed that the projects are designed to integrate the Comecon states and the Soviet Union into one comprehensive energy grid. The state that has resisted this policy of integration is Romania, which has steered an independent economic course since 1964. Romanian leaders warn that the new emphasis on an integrated energy policy might lead to Comecon autarchism, to the detriment of the entire bloc. Romania is not dependent on Soviet energy exports in any instance, and receives its substantial imports largely from OPEC sources.

Yugoslavia and Romania possess substantial port facilities that can receive tankers on the Adriatic and Black seas. This enables both states to contract for oil deliveries wherever they choose. While the Soviet Union offers the Comecon bloc attractive pricing by OPEC standards, Yugoslavia and Romania enjoy autonomy in their energy policies that cannot be matched by the other Comecon states.

The most important project that would link Yugoslavia with the Comecon bloc is the Adriatic pipeline centered in the largest Yugoslav port, Rijeka. The pipeline is largely financed by Arab capital and will have terminals in Romania, Hungary, and Czechoslovakia. This infusion of oil from non-Soviet sources will scarcely threaten the preeminent Soviet position as the principal supplier of oil and natural gas to Czechoslovakia, but it will enable Yugoslavia to be a direct source of supply to Romania and thereby strengthen the already strong ties between the two maverick communist states. It will also give Yugoslavia some voice in the affairs of the Comecon states because it will be within the physical capabilities of the Yugoslavs to turn off the flow. This will certainly bolster the political autonomy of Yugoslavia and Romania.

Despite these political hazards, the Soviet Union does not appear to oppose the Adriatic pipeline; the Czechoslovak and Hungarian tie-ins could scarcely take place without the Soviet blessing. The Soviet Union is preparing for the possibility that the East European states will augment their energy supplies from OPEC sources while the Soviet leaders are making increasing parallel agreements with Common Market states for greater oil and natural gas deliveries. Apparently the Soviet Union prefers to supply West European markets for hard currency rather than to maintain a monopoly with its East European clients such as Czechoslovakia and Hungary.

The pipelines and power lines raise serious environmental questions similar to those that surfaced when the Alaskan pipeline was proposed. Characteristically, the only state where these questions were aired publicly was Yugoslavia. It was feared that the terminal point of the Adriatic pipeline will damage the environment of the Kvarner Bay, a picturesque tourist area as well as the site of Yugoslavia's largest port, Rijeka. It was also feared that the pipeline would have an especially damaging effect on the dry areas it

must traverse. This issue of competition between tourist and industrial interests haunts all the urban areas along the Dalmatian coast.
In this instance, the environmental interests lost and construction is
going forward.

Recently Yugoslavia joined an international program for the
clean-up of the entire Mediterranean environment, which includes
all the Mediterranean states except Libya and Albania. Yugoslav
and East European energy policy will have a substantial bearing on
this issue, in case the Dalmatian coast becomes a major oil trans-
shipping center to Soviet bloc areas. At this point it is difficult to
predict how effective the environmental protection measures of the
Comecon states and Yugoslavia will be.

CONCLUSIONS

Czechoslovakia, Romania, and Yugoslavia differ in their degree of dependency on oil imports. This has a profound impact on
their respective domestic and foreign policies. Czechoslovakia is
almost entirely dependent upon imported Soviet oil and will therefore
continue to follow the Soviet lead in both domestic and foreign policy
because the Soviet leadership is in a position to paralyze the Czechoslovak economy. This ratio of dependency was a factor to be reck-
oned with during the Prague Spring of 1968.

Romania is largely self-sufficient in oil, and the relatively
minor proportion it imports is entirely from OPEC sources. Yugoslavia occupies an intermediate position by producing about one-
third of its needs from domestic sources and importing the remain-
der largely from the OPEC countries. If one takes a broad view of
what constitutes the environment, one may conclude that each country's politics, both in the domestic and international realms, accurately reflect the sources and degree of their oil dependency.

The policy-making processes of the three states reflect on the
quality of their domestic environmental protection. Czechoslovakia
and Romania maintain highly central planning systems, under which
the plans bear the imprimaturs of both party and state and cannot be
challenged from lower echelons. Therefore, any discussion of environmental impact takes place largely within the confines of the
party apparatus and state bureaucracy. It is only these groups that
have the power to translate concern into policy.

The Yugoslav political system rests on a different organization.
Central planning has been almost abolished, and most of the responsibility for environmental protection rests with republican or local
units of government. The six republics and two autonomous provinces
determine their priorities according to local custom and tradition.

Therefore the Yugoslav policy toward the environment reflects the historical concerns and wealth of the regions. The northern, more prosperous areas will continue to exercise greater control than the southern regions, where the main concern is to attract investment of any kind. The southern regions, however, have the advantage of being able to build environmental protection reflecting the new legislation as their investments come on stream. In Yugoslavia, workers' self-managerial bodies and numerous associations can force authorities to revise policy. In this, Yugoslavia differs uniquely from other socialist states, being the only state with an institutionalized system of grass-roots politics, and it is fair to assume that the Yugoslav authorities will be sensitive to this pressure.

Czechoslovakia has made the greatest commitment to the development of nuclear energy, and Yugoslavia and Romania share this commitment to a lesser degree. The reasons for this are self-explanatory if viewed in terms of the energy balance in each of these states.

The energy problem is merely one of many that will have an impact on the quality of the environment of the area under study. Rapid industrialization has diminished the environmental quality in all portions of Europe, East and West. Many of the problems, such as that of the preservation of the Danubian Basin or that of the construction of major hydroelectric power stations on the Danube, are not amenable to purely national solutions. Some of the consequences of the projected growth are imponderable at present. These may include the rapid expansion of oil and natural gas pipelines and electrical high voltage power grids. The potential effects of nuclear power have stirred such controversy that it is impossible for a layman to comment on their future impact in the face of divisions among technical experts. All the East European states are committed to more production and industrialization, and their environmental quality can be protected only if their national leaders show as much devotion to environmental protection as to growth itself. The national legislation that has been enacted and the direction of concern toward this problem by the highest party bodies is encouraging, yet the costs of environmental protection are not included in the plans for major industrial projects.

Certain effects of the energy crisis are already in evidence. At present the OPEC countries are producing below their rated capacity. It is doubtful that the present price structure will remain tenable as major new sources, such as the North Sea and Alaskan fields, come into production. The focus of concern has shifted from shortage to surplus.[35] The predicted rises in consumption of oil have not been realized. Under the circumstances it is difficult to predict whether recent measures taken by East European countries to convert from liquid to solid fossil fuels will be maintained.

NOTES

1. Marshall I. Goldman, The Spoils of Progress: Environmental Pollution in the Soviet Union (Cambridge: MIT Press, 1972), Chapter 1.

2. Rudi Supek, Ova Jedina Zemlja (Zagreb: Naprijed, 1973), p. 219.

3. Quarterly Economic Review: Rumania, no. 2 (1975), p. 10.

4. Quarterly Economic Review: Czechoslovakia, no. 1 (1975), p. 10.

5. Jana Klackova, "The Environment and the Structure of Social Goals," Eastern European Economics 14, no. 1 (Fall 1975): 96.

6. Hlavni smery hospodarske politiky strany v letech 1971-1975 (Prague: Svoboda, 1971), p. 149; "Smernice hospodarskeho a socialniho rozvoje CSSR v letech 1976-1980," Rude pravo (February 21, 1976), p. 6.

7. Klackova, op. cit., p. 91.

8. Adrian C. Caranfil, Umweltschutz in Rumanien (Koln: Der Bundesinstituts fur Ostwissenschaftliche und internationale Studien, 1973), p. 35.

9. Trond Gilberg, Modernization in Rumania Since World War II (New York: Praeger, 1975), pp. 82-91.

10. Caranfil, op. cit., p. 7.

11. Ibid., p. 34.

12. Ibid., p. 46.

13. Radio Free Europe Research: Yugoslavia, January 16, 1973, p. 5.

14. Tadija Popovic, Drustvena aktivnost na zastiti i unapredjenju covekove okoline (Belgrade: Jugoslovenskog saveta za saztitu i unapredjenje covekove okoline, n.d.).

15. Ibid., p. 18.

16. Quarterly Economic Review: Czechoslovakia, no. 1 (1975), p. 4.

17. Annual Economic Review: Czechoslovakia, 1975, p. 6.

18. John M. Kramer, "The Energy Gap in Eastern Europe," Survey 20, no. 3 (Spring 1974): 69.

19. Quarterly Economic Review: Rumania, no. 2 (1975), p. 8.

20. Quarterly Economic Review: Yugoslavia, no. 2 (February 1975), p. 14.

21. Ibid., p. 12.

22. Ibid., p. 14.

23. World Oil 181, no. 3 (August 15, 1975): 134.

24. "The State of Comecon," The Economist 258, no. 6908 (January 17, 1976): 68.

25. Kramer, op. cit., pp. 65-76.

26. The Economist 257, no. 6906 (December 20, 1975): 89.

27. "The Next Era for OPEC," The Economist 257, no. 6906 (December 20, 1975): 85.

28. Quarterly Economic Review: Czechoslovakia, no. 4 (1975), pp. 4-5.

29. Josef Wilczynski, "Atomic Energy for Peaceful Purposes in the Warsaw Pact Countries," Soviet Studies 26 (October 1974): 578.

30. Nenad Prelog, "How Much Is Zagreb Endangered," Vjesnik u srijedu, February 7, 1973, pp. 19-21; and "No, It Is Not at All Clear," Vjesnik u srijedu (Wednesday herald), February 28, 1973, p. 13.

31. Wilczynski, op. cit., p. 571.

32. Ibid.

33. "The State of Comecon," op. cit., p. 79.

34. Quarterly Economic Review: Czechoslovakia, no. 4 (1975), p. 8.

35. "Productive Capacity Grows as World Demand Falters," World Oil 181, no. 3 (August 15, 1975): 41-44.

5

DENMARK: THE
FRAGILE CONSENSUS
Joanne S. Wyman

The 1973-74 Arab oil embargo awakened the public in the industrialized nations to its fragile dependence on a continuous, abundant supply of energy. As a result of the embargo, shortages and
escalating prices combined to threaten the economic health and
social advancement of these societies. Consumerism and environmental protection, which had finally emerged as legitimate public
policy concerns, were threatened by the crisis.* As energy prices
continued to rise, the policies and programs designed to ameliorate
those problems became marginally important in many nations.

In the United States, for example, prominent political and
economic interests blamed the environmentalists for the nation's
dependence on foreign supplies, high prices, and periodic shortages.
Environmentalists ostensibly had contributed to the crisis by deterring atomic energy development, by advocating pollution-control
devices on cars and in factories, and by lobbying for unleaded fuel
and strip-mining controls. Although environmental protection programs have not disappeared entirely, public authorities have delayed
the adoption of new air quality standards and put off other programs.
Furthermore, the United States only began to formulate a unified policy for both energy and the environment during the 1976-77 period.
Policy making on all issues appears to occur within the context of

----

*The embargo was not the first indication of an energy prob-
lem. In the summers of 1972 and 1973, the United States had experienced periodic gasoline shortages and price increases in some
sections of the country, particularly the Northeast. In Denmark
the possibility of a shortage for the winter existed even before the
Arab imposition of an embargo.

issue competition for finite political, economic, and manpower resources.

In Denmark, on the other hand, the environment and energy issues have not placed conflicting demands upon the political system until 1976 despite the serious economic impact of the oil embargo and Denmark's commitment to environmental protection. This absence of substantial conflict reflects both the nature of Denmark's energy problems and the traditional political characteristics of its policy process. First, the environmental policy of Denmark is relatively new; in fact, the oil embargo preceded the implementation of many environmental protection measures.[1] Therefore the energy crisis and the subsequent economic problems have not been attributable to the environmentalist movement.

Second, the emergence of the environmental issue and the formulation and adoption of legal, administrative, and economic programs generated little controversy. Danish industry, unlike its U.S. counterpart, played a cooperative role in environmental policy making, thereby denying antienvironmentalists a focal point for their activities.[2]

Third, Denmark has no energy industry comparable to that of the United States, Britain, or even Norway. This also has prevented the coordination of any substantial energy challenges to environmental policies.

Fourth, the fusion of power, or quasi-corporatism,[3] that has traditionally characterized decision making in Denmark has precluded the development of intense issue conflict.[4]

The nuclear power plant development and siting issue, however, has raised safety and environmental questions that have threatened the formulation and implementation of comprehensive energy policies. The Danish government, with limited success, has attempted to guide a carefully orchestrated public debate on nuclear energy to forestall the potential divisiveness of a public referendum. At times the government's inclusion of a wide variety of interests in the decision-making process and its attempted manipulation of political relationships appeared to have provided the foundation for the formulation of an integrated energy and environment policy. Disagreement within the ruling party and public clamor for a referendum, however, threaten an already unstable government.* A special

*In the December 1973 election the five major parties (Socialist People's Party, Social Democrats, Radicals, Liberals, and Conservatives), suffered a severe blow, leaving open to question the amount of support for traditional values and alignments. In the January 1975 election two of those parties, the Social Democrats and

parliamentary session was scheduled in September 1976 to deal with
the nuclear issue, but continued political instability and emerging
differences between industrial and environmental interests led to its
cancellation. Until this question is settled, Denmark will be unable
to effectively pursue a comprehensive energy policy.

ENERGY

Of significance in assessing Denmark's new energy policies is
the fact that its energy problems reflect global conditions rather
than short-sighted domestic energy programs. Despite its rapid
increase in energy consumption during the 1960s, Denmark, compared to the United States, traditionally has not used a dispropor-
tionate share of the world's energy.[5] However, Denmark is completely dependent on foreign supplies. Unlike Britain and the United
States, it possesses no coal deposits. It does not have the hydroelectric capacity of neighboring Sweden and Norway. In addition,
its North Sea oil and gas exploration has been relatively unsuccessful, and unlike Sweden it has no commercial nuclear plants.

Consequently, Denmark imports 99.5 percent of its energy.
In 1973 its principal crude oil suppliers were the Middle East (86
percent) and Nigeria (11 percent). Of other petroleum products,
75 percent came from European Community members and were
based on Middle East oil and 10 percent came from Eastern Europe
and the Soviet Union.[6] Therefore Denmark's supplies were vulnerable to the whims of international politics. Its African supplies
could be and were reduced through nationalization, and its Middle
Eastern supplies proved to be vulnerable to embargo. In addition,
the East European suppliers took advantage of Denmark's vulnerability: not only did Denmark contend with price increases from the
Organization of Petroleum Exporting Countries (OPEC) but also
with increases from non-OPEC countries. The Polish coal organization, for example, demanded 1973 price increases of up to 100 percent on long-term contracts. In 1974 it demanded and received
additional price increases.[7]

Escalated world energy prices resulting from the oil embargo
had a serious impact on Denmark's economy, causing an inflationary
price spiral on a wide range of goods and services and also rapidly
rising unemployment. Oil price increases were directly and

---

the Liberals, made substantial gains. However, the Social Democratic government has not had much more success in solving economic problems than the Liberal government had.

indirectly responsible for a severe 1974 trade deficit of nearly $2 billion and a balance of payments deficit of $1.1 billion. During that same period, prices rose at an annual rate of 15 percent, mostly as a result of the increased costs of petroleum and petroleum-derived products. In one year, unemployment rose from 2.4 percent of the work force to 5.8 percent.[8] The economic deterioration has intensified political instability, and full economic recovery is elusive.[9]

Two factors in particular contributed to the seriousness of Denmark's energy problems. First, following a trend that began early in the twentieth century, Denmark has evolved since World War II from an agricultural, rural nation to an urban, industrialized one.[10] Urbanization and industrialization included a national commitment to motorized transport of people and goods. Much of the surge toward urbanization, industrialization, and increased motor transport occurred in the 1960s, a fact reflected in significant energy consumption increases during that period. Throughout the 1950s energy consumption rose only 3 percent per annum. In 1960-65, however, it increased 8 percent per year, dropping back to 4 to 5 percent between 1965 and 1973. Government-imposed restrictions in 1974 produced a decline in consumption.[11]

Second, the shift in energy sources from coal to oil made Denmark virtually dependent on politically vulnerable African and Middle Eastern supplies. A Pollution Control Board report documented the nation's transition from coal to oil. In 1969, for example, Denmark consumed 6.4 million tons of fuel oil, 41 percent of which went to power plants. Between 1968 and 1969, Denmark's total use of oil rose by 35 percent, and for power plants by 68 percent. During the same year, total national coal usage was 3.7 million tons, a 7 percent decrease. The power plants decreased their coal consumption by 78 percent.[12] Despite its dependence on Middle Eastern supplies, Denmark did not seriously consider the prospect of an oil embargo.[13] Even at the outset of the embargo, the government's position was one of cautious optimism, despite press reports prior to the embargo indicating a potentially significant winter shortage.

POLITICS OF ENERGY AND THE ENVIRONMENT

The Danish government has attempted to formulate both energy and environmental policies within the context of traditional political relationships and decision rules. The energy issue, however, had and continues to have a greater potential for disrupting traditional relationships and opening up the political process to new groups because of the prominence of its discussion of nuclear energy development and power plant siting. Whereas the incremental transition from conservation to an ecological orientation deterred the development of substantial opposition to the environmental policies, the unexpectedness with which the energy issue assumed crisis proportions requiring immediate, drastic action was conducive to the eventual emergence of a widespread public debate. Until recently the Danish government appeared to have succeeded in manipulating the degree of change resulting from the energy policy-making process. The government's continued ability to lead the debate will significantly influence the ultimate impact of the issue on traditional political relationships.

A potential source of energy-environment issue competition was the government's regulation of pollution from fuel. Until the early 1970s, fuel oil used in Denmark usually had a 4 percent sulphur content. A Pollution Control Board report, however, had alerted the public and political officials to the pollution generated by energy consumption in heating, transportation, industrial production, and electricity generation. During 1969, for instance, Denmark's electricity generation facilities emitted 91,500 tons of sulphur in gaseous and particulate form.[14] Additional pollution resulted from the population's dependence on motorized transport. Between 1954 and 1972 the number of cars per capita rose from 1 in 23 to 1 in 4.[15] During this same period, public transportation usage declined.[16] In addition, although in 1967 fewer than 30 percent of the Copenhagen households owned cars, 42 percent possessed them in 1973. In the remaining capital-region communities, car ownership was even higher. Although the three principal capital-region municipalities, Copenhagen, Frederiksberg, and Gentofte, are linked by an extensive bus and train system, 20 percent of the work force commutes by car. From neighboring communities 41 percent commutes by car, a large percentage of which goes to downtown Copenhagen, contributing to a significant air pollution problem.[17]

Responding to the nation's growing concern about environmental protection, the 1971-72 session of Parliament enacted legislation requiring a gradual reduction in sulphur content to 1 percent in the capital region and 2.5 percent in other areas.[18] Subsequently, however, the Mideast crisis, the African nations' nationalization of oil companies, and the increased oil imports by the United States and Japan threatened Denmark's short-run access to low-sulphur fuel. Therefore the government suspended the regulations for one year, a decision that reflected information from industry that the Ministry of Commerce had double-checked.[19] Suspension of the regulation both illustrated the corporatist ties between the public and private sectors and eliminated a measure that could have provided anti-environmentalists with ammunition against the environmentalist movement.

The nuclear energy issue, which gained public prominence as a result of the oil embargo, provided a second potential arena of conflict. Without the appearance of the embargo, the nuclear energy issue would have emerged more gradually. It began to attract limited public attention when in 1971 the Elsam Power Company, an association of Danish utilities in west Denmark, began to consider the introduction of atomic power stations into the power supply grid. In December the consortium applied to the Atomic Energy Commission, the National Health Service, and the Ministry of Public Works for permission to develop atomic energy plants. The government, following traditional policy-making procedures,[20] established a committee under the leadership of the Housing Ministry to study siting. Recognizing the potential for serious public and political opposition to nuclear power, the government appointed representatives from all ministries to participate in the committee. The group was asked to prepare proposals for one or more sites. In 1973 the government established the Inspectorate of Nuclear Installations under the Ministry of Education. Both the establishment of the Inspectorate and its administrative placement reflected a perceived need to separate atomic research functions from regulatory ones.* In its January 1974 report on potential sites west of the Great Belt, the group recommended 9 out of 45 sites for further consideration. It then proceeded to an investigation of several sites east of the belt.

The oil embargo interrupted the normal pace and processes of Danish policy making. The government instituted several emergency measures. On November 16, 1973, it notified industry of an expected 5 percent oil supply reduction and advised the public to prepare for carless Sundays. In addition, thermostats in Copenhagen municipal buildings were lowered to five degrees centigrade.[21] Throughout the fall, a government-appointed energy savings committee conducted a media campaign urging consumers to use less energy, particularly oil products. Speed limits were reduced throughout the

---

*According to recently enacted legislation establishing environmental and safety conditions for nuclear facility development, a utility must apply to the Environment Ministry for a permit for each proposed nuclear site. The Environment Ministry is required to hold a hearing, in which local authorities and the public may participate. Although the passage of this law was intended to represent a national commitment to the development of nuclear energy, the political sensitivity of the issue dictated the calling of a special session of Parliament to discuss the actual procedures for implementing nuclear power development.

country. Despite these conservation measures, however, the oil embargo had serious economic consequences and aggravated an already relatively unstable situation. The nuclear energy issue remains unresolved and was to have been the highlight of the agenda of a special parliamentary session, originally scheduled for September 1976 but postponed until 1980 or 1981. This issue, together with Denmark's continuing poor economic performance, threatens to bring down the Social Democratic government of Anker Jorgensen. [22]

ENERGY POLICY, 1973-76

On the surface the initial responses of the Danish political system to the energy issue in general and the nuclear question in particular appeared to follow traditional patterns. Specifically, the government attempted to supervise the input of viewpoints, orchestrating a consensus that would have nationwide application; yet the emergence of an anti-nuclear-energy citizens group and increasing debate in the press demonstrated an underlying current of public opposition. As in the United States, this position focused on (1) the possibility of a meltdown and/or accidental explosion, (2) the potential for radioactive leakage, (3) the dangers of nuclear material transportation, (4) the possibility of sabotage, and (5) problems associated with nuclear waste storage. [23]

In response to Elsam's nuclear power plant petition, the government established a special study committee similar to the Hygiene Commission and Pollution Control Board, which had been set up to study previous issues. In response to the oil embargo, the government also established committees for public information and the study of heating and energy. It also took additional administrative and legal steps analogous to its actions on other issues. For example, in the same way as initially environmentally responsibilities had been fragmented, the housing, commerce, and education ministries all had responsibility for energy policy until the government eventually concentrated all tasks in one organization, the Trade Ministry, just as in 1973 it had transferred the traditionally fragmented environmental responsibilities to the Ministry of Environment.

Following the traditional pattern of discussing major issues in Parliament, the 1974 session held an energy debate centering around a Commerce Ministry energy policy recommendation and a statement on coordinated power development in the 1980s that the Electricity Works Energy Committee had prepared.

Not until April 23, 1976, however, did the Parliament enact major energy legislation, when it adopted the Act on Energy Policy Measures. This act, which entered into force on April 29, 1976, abolished the Danish Atomic Energy Commission at Riso, which was established in 1955. The new Danish Energy Agency, which replaced it, was placed under the Ministry of Commerce. Its responsibilities included review and assessment of both Danish and international developments in energy research, supply, production, and consumption. The Research Establishment Riso, formerly part of the Atomic Energy Commission, remained as a research center devoted to the development of atomic energy for peaceful purposes. In addition, the research laboratory, also under the Ministry of Trade, would conduct other types of energy studies as needed.

Beneath a veneer of traditional responsiveness, however, the government exhibited vulnerability to the potentially disruptive nature of the energy issue. The potential for disruption stemmed from the nuclear power plant siting question and was manifested during the Ministry Committee siting study. In January 1974 the committee published its report on potential sites in western Denmark. Researchers and officials from the Danish Atomic Energy Commission asserted that fears about meltdowns, explosions, and radiation hazards were unfounded and based not on scientific fact but rather on psychological fears and cultural taboos associated with atomic weapons.

Nevertheless, doubts regarding the wisdom of a commitment to nuclear energy continued to develop within the government. In cooperation with the various ministries, the Atomic Energy Commission had developed safety plans for almost all of the original 45 proposed sites. In one of the final selection meetings, however, the Ministry of Environment expressed reservations about the recommendations. After the many months of discussion, it had just begun to recognize the complexity of the issue and wanted additional time to study the sites. [24]

This type of hesitancy, coupled with antinuclear campaigns by civic groups, contributed to a long delay in the nuclear decision. The April 1974 parliamentary energy debate showed that although the political parties generally supported the power plants' interest in introducing atomic energy, the politicians wanted additional public participation in the planning and siting of atomic energy plants. In fact, prior to what was to have been the special September session of Parliament the press reported continuing disagreement over the nuclear energy issue within the ruling Social Democratic party. Members of the party, as well as those of other parties, expressed a desire to hold a national referendum on the atomic issue. To prevent continued internal rifts, one compromise discussed by the government leadership was to have the Parliament vote not only on the principle of introducing nuclear power but also on each request for an atomic plant permit thereafter.

ENERGY AND THE ENVIRONMENT: A PROGNOSIS

In Denmark the energy issue, in particular the nuclear energy debate, must be interpreted within the context of a society that is highly committed in principle to environmental protection.[25] This philosophical commitment, even more than the cultural taboo against atomic energy, has contributed to the underlying tension and potential for disruption of traditional decision-making networks. Initial responses to the energy issue, as illustrated above, appeared to follow traditional decision-making patterns. Only with the increasing importance of the nuclear question and the intrusion of serious economic and political problems did energy and environmental policies conflict with each other. In contrast to the U.S. experience, the energy issue did not challenge environmental programs at that point, but rather, environmental goals deterred the decision on nuclear energy development.

From the U.S. perspective the environment policies of Denmark are innovative. Although they do not depart radically from the various legal, economic, and administrative strategies discussed globally, they are a nationwide application of a synthesis of several of those strategies.[26] For example, the 1969 establishment of a Pollution Control Board was a deliberate political decision to commit Denmark to the development of an environment protection policy. The goal of the board was to survey domestic pollution problems and existing remedies as well as to survey the international literature. On the basis of these surveys the board recommended various technical, political, and economic remedies. The final reports resulted in centralization of the environment protection functions in a Ministry of Environment (1971) and the enactment of a comprehensive Environment Protection Act (1973). Subsequently the Parliament enacted legislation to provide government subsidies to established industries installing new pollution control equipment.

The relatively swift formulation, adoption, and implementation of significant environment protection programs was due in large part to the fusion of power, or corporatism, characteristic of the Danish political system.* Political parties are organized on a

---

*In the United States, formulation and implementation of environmental policy is fragmented. First, the National Environment Policy Act of 1969 and the Council on Environmental Quality guidelines have only established a framework. Individual federal government agencies issue their own directives on environmental policies and procedures. Second, the Environment Protection Agency does not have the comprehensive functions and authority exercised by

national basis, unlike the autonomous U.S. local party machines,
which are loosely linked by national committees. Members of the
Danish Parliament often hold local elective office as well, and sometimes they retain their civil service positions on a part-time basis. [27]
Most interest groups in Denmark have strong, active, national organizations. Through their trade organizations, the major economic
interests have extensive formal and informal ties to the political
parties. [28] In addition, the central authorities traditionally have
had extensive control over both the formulation and implementation
of policy. Local authorities have had little autonomy, although this
is changing. [29] Within this framework, coalition or minority governments have ruled Denmark increasingly in recent years. Many
policy decisions, therefore, require consensus, with several parties
individually possessing a veto power. [30] Consequently, on any given
issue the government will attempt to orchestrate a political discussion that will produce widespread agreement among the parties.

This fusion of power deterred the development of substantial
resistance by industry and the Conservative People's Party toward
environmental protection measures. In fact, the 1969 decision to
establish a Pollution Control Board, the 1969 party platforms, and
the 1971 party replies to press inquiries identified support among
most political parties for the principle of environment protection,
although strategy details differed. [31] Only the Communists and Left
Socialists actively criticized environment protection policies, as-
serting that capitalist societies could not cope with the issue effectively.

Although Denmark's industries are relatively small, they
nevertheless pollute considerably and are a visible target for environmentalists. [32] However, despite its objection to being singled
out for its contribution to Denmark's pollution problems, [33] the
industrial sector has been supportive of environmental policies. It
neither supported nor thwarted the emergence of the environmental
issue and its placement on the political agenda. Like other non-
conservation-oriented interest groups, it followed a policy of
silence. [34] As later events exhibited, industry was able to avoid an
adversary position largely because most environmentalists accepted
the interests of industry as legitimate and necessary. Thus industry

---

Denmark's Ministry of Environment. The principle of federalism
limits the authority of the EPA over the actions or nonactions of
state and local governments. In addition, in some cases, the Federal Aviation Administration or Department of Housing and Urban
Development may issue guidelines conflicting with those of the EPA.

through the Conservative People's Party, joined with the Social Democratic government in enacting the 1973 Environment Act.

The representatives of industry acknowledged that the environmental issue presented them with an excellent opportunity to improve their political position. Given strong public pressure for environmental protection programs, failure to support such programs could have had costly political consequences. By appearing responsive, however, industry obviated the need for new articulation channels and rules of decision. Its representatives were able to influence considerably the content of the statutes and guidelines that would control industrial pollution.[35]

Initial government responses to the energy crisis appeared neither to pose a threat to environmental protection programs nor to generate substantial controversy. All political and economic factors acknowledged the seriousness of the crisis and the need for both emergency and long-range conservation measures. As with past issues, these factions participated in government-established committees to develop long-term policies. The immediate savings were concentrated in the housing and transportation sectors rather than in the industrial sector, thus deterring the development of resistance from industry. In addition, the government suspended the restrictions on sulphur content in fuel. The crisis situation, in fact, produced an intense concern about community welfare and recognition of the need for collective action and cooperation.

The absence of a public perception of environmental programs as a cause of the energy crisis or a deterrent to the development of an energy policy also minimized the potential for controversy. However, the economic issues arising as a result of the oil embargo did generate discontent and controversy. The minority Liberal Party government of Poul Hartling attempted to devise an emergency economic plan, the provisions of which included a freeze on wages. This plan constituted an unusual governmental interference in the self-regulated management-labor negotiations and was particularly unpopular with the Social Democratic Party.

The government's failure to obtain enactment of a legislative package and Parliament's subsequent failure to give the government a vote of confidence produced the second national election in 13 months.[36] Recent reports indicate that the minority Social Democratic government, which took office after a controversial and inconclusive election, has not had much better success in putting Denmark on the path to economic recovery. In addition, the controversy over nuclear power plant siting has exacerbated the tension surrounding the state of the economy and the weakness of the government.

To ease tensions, or at least the rift in the Social Democratic party, the government leadership announced new tactics for the

afterwards postponed special session of Parliament. It would not
offer for consideration the question of a national referendum on
nuclear power, but rather it would recommend a parliamentary
commitment to the principle of nuclear development and parliamentary consideration of each individual permit application.[37]

Legislation in 1973-75 provided the foundation for a commitment to nuclear energy. The Danish Energy Agency replaced the
Atomic Energy Commission; the Riso establishment continues its
peaceful nuclear research; the Inspectorate of Nuclear Facilities
was transferred from the Ministry of Education to the Ministry of
Environment; and the latter ministry was given an expanded role in
the nuclear area.[38]

Nevertheless, the Social Democratic government will have a
difficult, if not impossible, time in achieving a parliamentary commitment to nuclear development and consensus on the methods of
its implementation. In fact, the combined impact of the economic
and nuclear issues could be a deadlock resulting in the calling of a
new election barely two years after the previous one. The uncertainties about the postponed special parliamentary session have
certainly suggested that the strains linked to nuclear policy decisions
are indeed growing. Eventually the government must resolve the
nuclear energy issue. Nuclear energy is Denmark's one feasible
avenue to a reduction of its dependence on foreign fuel supplies in
the near future. Without such a reduction, Denmark's industrial
growth and therefore its economic health and domestic political
stability remain vulnerable to the conflicts and vacillations of international politics.

NOTES

1. Letter from Jean Grandjean, former press secretary,
Danish Environment Protection Agency, March 3, 1975.

2. Interview with Elo Hartig, Federation of Danish Industries,
Copenhagen, June 28, 1974.

3. Samuel Beer, "Pressure Groups and Parties in Britain,"
The American Political Science Review 50 (March 1956).

4. Joanne S. Wyman, "The Impact of Issues on Political Relationships: A Case Study of Denmark's Environmental Policy 1969-
1976" (Ph.D. diss., Brandeis University, forthcoming).

5. Hvem, Hvad, Hvor 1975 (Copenhagen: Politikens Forlag
A/S, 1974), pp. 269-71.

6. Danish Information Service, "Energy in Denmark," (fact
sheet, New York: the Service, 1974).

7. Nordel, <u>Nordel Annual Report 1974</u> (Helsinki: Nordel, 1974), p. 57.

8. Ibid.

9. "Denmark: Recession Cuts Buying; Caution Current Mood," <u>Commerce Today</u>, January 20, 1975, p. 19; Claus Kallerup, "113,000 Ledige," <u>Politiken</u>, December 6, 1975, p. 1; "Hartling: Et Mindretal Har Baaret Byrdene," <u>Politiken</u>, December 4, 1974, p. 4; Hilary Barnes, "Danmark Staar Staerkt-Tog Afgorende Konsekvens af Prisforhojelser paa Olie," <u>Weekendavisen Berlingske Aften</u>, February 28, 1975, p. 14.

10. Denmark, Royal Ministries of Foreign Affairs, Housing, Cultural Affairs, and Environment Protection, <u>Environment Denmark: Denmark's National Report to the United Nations on the Human Environment</u> (Copenhagen: Statens Trykningskontor, 1974); Danmarks Naturfredningsforening, <u>Saadan Ligger Landet</u> (Copenhagen: Det Berlingske Bogtrykkeri, 1970); Danmarks Naturfrednings-forening, <u>Miljoets Forurening</u> (Copenhagen: Danmarks Naturfrednings-forening Forlag, 1970).

11. Nordel, op. cit.

12. Denmark, Forureningsraadet Sekretariatet, <u>Luftforurening: Industriproduktion og Elektricitets Fremstilling</u> (Copenhagen: Statens Trykningskontor, 1971), p. 67.

13. "Den Arabiske Olie Vil Altid Flyde," <u>Politiken</u>, September 19, 1973, p. 2; Stig Andersen, "Nyt Smaek paa Oliepriserne," <u>Politiken</u>, September 19, 1973, pp. 1, 17.

14. Denmark, Forureningsraadet, op. cit., p. 68.

15. Denmark, Ministry of Foreign Affairs, <u>Denmark: An Official Handbook</u> (Copenhagen: J. H. Schultz A/S, 1974), p. 413.

16. Interview with Helge P. Olsen, press secretary, Danish State Railways, Copenhagen, October 10, 1973.

17. Forenede Danske Motorejere, <u>Bilen i Danmark og Alternativer</u> (Copenhagen: Gallup Markedanalyse A/S, 1973), p. 10; City of Copenhagen, <u>Luftforurening i Storkoebenhavn 1967-1972</u>, Rapport fra Storkoebenhavns Luftforureningsudvalg [A report from greater Copenhagen's Air Pollution Committee], 1973; Akademiet for de Tekniske Videnskaber, Rogudvalget 62 [Academy of Technical Sciences, Smoke Committee 62], <u>Rapport over Luftforurenings-maalinger 1965-1967 i Koebenhavn, Aalborg, Norresundby, Odense, Vejle, og Maribo</u> (Lyngby: Academy of Technical Sciences, Smoke Committee 62, 1968); Akademiet for Tekniske Videnskaber, Rogudvalget 62, <u>Rapport over Supplerende Forureningsmaalinger 1970 i Koebenhavn og Aalborg</u> (Lyngby: Academy of Technical Sciences, Smoke Committee 62, 1971).

18. "Ministeren Dispenserer Fra Lov om Svovl i Olie," <u>Politiken</u>, October 30, 1973; "Krav om Svovlfattig Olie Udsaettes," <u>Berlingske Tidende</u>, October 30, 1973.

19. Ibid.

20. Wyman, op. cit.; Joanne S. Wyman, "Conflict and Co-operation: Environment Decisionmaking in Denmark" (Paper presented at the Northeastern Political Science Association annual meeting, Saratoga Springs, N.Y., November 7-9, 1974).

21. "Energikrisen: Koebenhavn Vil Blive Koldere- Og Moerkere," Politiken, November 15, 1973, p. 1; Finn Sivebaek, "Vi Maa Fryse for At Hjulene Kan Snurre," Politiken, November 16, 1973, p. 1; "Forsoeg paa Oliepression," Politiken, October 19, 1973, in Presseklippe, ed. Denmark, Ministry of Environment, Copenhagen, October 19, 1973; "Ingen Koersel i Weekenden Hvis Olie Udebliver," Politiken, October 11, 1973, p. 3.

22. Geoffrey Dodd, "News of Norden," Scandinavian Review, September 1976, pp. 49-51.

23. A. R. Mackintosh, "Dansk Energipolitik og Atomkraften," Berlingske Tidende, February 24, 1974.

24. Danish Atomic Energy Commission, Eighteenth Annual Report 1973-74 (Copenhagen: Nordlunds Bogtrykkeri, 1974), p. 6.

25. Gallupundersoegelse af den Danske Befolknings Holding til Ressource og Forureningsproblemerne, Copenhagen, December 1973; Jean Grandjean, "Forureningen, Pressen--og Hvad Folk Mener," commentary on the Gallup poll.

26. Lynton Caldwell, In Defense of Earth: International Protection of the Biosphere (Bloomington: Indiana University Press, 1972); Organisation for Economic Co-operation and Development, The Polluter Pays Principle: Definition, Analysis, Implementation (Paris: OECD, 1975); Joanne S. Wyman, J. M. McLoughlin, Law and Practice Relating to Pollution Control in Member States of the European Communities (London: Environmental Resources Ltd., 1975).

27. Interview with Mogens Camre, Member of Parliament, Copenhagen, October 30, 1973; interview with Ejler Koch, alternate Member of Parliament, October 24, 1973.

28. Danish Federation of Trade Unions, The Danish Trade Union Movement; Erik Vagn Jensen, De Politiske Partier (Copenhagen: Det Danske Forlag, 1964); Joanne S. Wyman, Bent Stuckert, "Hvor Ophoerer LO og Hvor Begynder Socialdemokratiet?" Weekendavisen Berlingske Aften, February 28, 1975, pp. 1-2.

29. Olaf Ingvartsen, Democracy and the Environment (Copenhagen: National Association of Local Authorities in Denmark, 1973); Walter Gellhorn, Ombudsmen and Others: Citizen's Protectors in Nine Countries (Cambridge: Harvard University Press, 1966); Ole Norgaard Madsen, "Dansk Kommunalreform: Vaerdigrundlag, Finansielle Konsekvenser, Konsekvenser for Kommunalt Samarbejde og Konsekvenser for Participation," Den Nordiske Statskundskabskonference i Aarhus, August 21-23, 1975.

30. Beer, op. cit., p. 15.

31. "Informations Sporgsmaal til Partierne: Hvem Skal Betale for Forureningsbekaempelsen? Alle, over Skattebilleten, eller den der Forurener?" Information, September 13, 1971, pp. 2-3.

32. Denmark, Folketinget, Sporgsmaal til Skriftlig Besvarelse af Camre til Ministeren for Forureningsbekaempelse, "Vil Ministeren Fremme en Undersoegelse af Udledningen af Industrispildevand i Koge Bugt?" Sporgsmaal nr. 345, September 5, 1973; Peter Kramer, "Fiskere Vil Have Erstatning for Svineriet i Koge Bugt, " Aktuelt, October 1, 1973.

33. Elo Hartig, op. cit.

34. Sven Th. Jensen, Miljobeskyttelse og Erhvervslivets Inflydelse (Aarhus: Institut for Statskundskab, Aarhus Universitet, 1973), p. 86.

35. Denmark, Miljostyrelsen, "Ekstern Stoj fra Virksomhder, " May 1974; Miljostyrelsen, "Begraensning af Luftforurening fra Virksomheder, " August 1974.

36. "De 20 Punkter i Kriseplanen, " Politiken, December 4, 1974, p. 4; "Partierne Afviser Kriseplanen- Det Tyder Paa et Valg, " ibid., p. 4; "L.O. om Kriseplanen: Hold Krudtet Tort, " ibid., p. 15.

37. Stig Andersen, "Regeringen Aendrer Taktik for at Faa Ja til A-Kraft, " Politiken, June 21, 1976.

38. Denmark, Lov om Sikkerhedsmaessige og Miljomaessige Forhold Ved Atomanlaeg m.v., May 12, 1976. Helge P. Nielsen, "Energi-Politik, Miljo og Sikkerhed, " Politiken, April 30, 1976, Section 2, p. 5.

6

WESTERN EUROPE: ENERGY AND THE ENVIRONMENT IN THE NINE

Robert A. Black, Jr.

Energy crises in Western Europe are not new. In 1255 A.D. the wood consumed in Henry III's English forges had greater value than the iron they produced. The woodlands were being devastated not only for fuel but also to create arable land to support a threefold jump in the English population. The pressure on this primary energy resource was relieved only by famine and the Black Death in the fourteenth century.

Historically, European governments have made considerable efforts to secure and manage energy supplies, such as the Prussian intervention in coal to guarantee fuel for railroads and certain industries, the French reaction to international oil efforts in the 1920s, the Nazi efforts to secure enough fuel to carry out their war policies, and the contemporary European efforts to manage all energy sectors. The 1958 European coal crisis was handled largely by an upsurge in oil supplies from the multinational oil majors operating in North Africa and the Middle East. This led to a Western European dependency on these areas, contributed to the effectiveness of OPEC, and was a necessary precondition for the 1973 oil crisis in Europe.

The author wishes to thank Harald H. Bungarten, an engineer, economist, and research fellow at the Forschungsinstitut der Deutschen Gesellschaft für Auswärtige Politik, for his considerable assistance in giving crucial knowledge on European environmental issues and policies. Without full, wholehearted dialogues with him, it would have been exceedingly difficult to locate the information necessary to complete critical parts of this chapter dealing with the environment.

It is manifestly clear that one prerequisite for an advanced industrial market economy is an adequately developed energy resource base, whether indigenous or from relatively stable imports. The quality of life in Western Europe is directly dependent on this. In the Nine of the European Communities (EC), where the quality of life is considered equal to (or even better than) that of the United States, per capita energy consumption is about half that in the United States. * Historically and culturally, this stems from a somewhat innate European perception of the value of those resources required to maintain a better quality of life.[1] That perception, learned over centuries, has become a realization that resources for a relatively higher density of population in an industrial era require thorough consideration of those aspects now called environmental.

The 1973 oil crisis precipitated the intense U.S. energy-environment debate discussed in Chapter 1, with its resultant industrial interest-group pressure to retard or roll back environmental protection gains. A different response, however, emerged in the EC and the Nine. This was directed more at managing energy resources and stabilizing supplies so that national economies would not be totally disrupted. The absence of serious industrial interest-group efforts to stymie or roll back Western European environmental protection following the 1973 crisis is attributable to a number of factors that are peculiarly European.

First, the structure and civic development of politics in the past in the Nine generally precluded the establishment of the effective class-action interest groups found in the U.S. environmental movement. The political bargaining games in the Nine had developed means by which environmental issues were routinely taken into account with other issues to varying degrees, depending upon the nature of the issue and its impact on a particular local group. Some of these larger rubrics have been public health; water quality; conservation of nature; and, in some areas, air quality. More recently, solid waste management, noise abatement, and pollution from energy

---

*The European Communities (colloquially the Common Market) are composed of nine member states, Belgium, Denmark, the Federal Republic of Germany, France, Ireland, Italy, Luxembourg, the Netherlands, and the United Kingdom, drawn together in a single set of common intergovernmental and transnational institutions specified by multilateral treaty law--the Treaty of Paris (1951) for the European Coal and Steel Community (ECSC), the Treaties of Rome (1957) for the European Economic Community (EEC) and the European Atomic Energy Community (Euratom), plus the Treaties of Accession (1972) for the newest members, Denmark, Ireland, and the United Kingdom.

use have become major issues, along with the emergence of the overall environmental issue. This can be traced in the EC with the shift from separate sectoral policy concerns to the treatment of the environment as an overall policy affecting basic policies in all other functional sectors.

A second major factor has been the general absence of severe interest group pressure (except for labor disputes in the coal sector) against energy industries in the Nine. In the United States, environmentalist pressures against various sectors of the energy industry considerably predated the 1973 crisis; in Europe the crisis marked the emergence of more effective environmentalist pressures. In the United States, energy industry interests saw the 1973 crisis and public concern for adequate supplies as an effective means of discrediting and fighting the environmentalists; the EC energy industry responses were more rational initially and directed not so much against environmentalists but toward more stable supplies at an economically viable cost. European energy interests and government officials did not perceive a threat from environmentalists at that time and so did not direct any counterenvironmental campaign as a result of the 1973 crisis. Where there was industrial-interest, public, or governmental reaction against proenvironmental policies relating to energy, it stemmed more from the desire to strike down an individual policy that had been used by one or another politician for that person's political gain than a desire to strike against environmental policies in general. Notable among such reactions was the effort to counter the FRG lead-free gasoline policy.

Also contributing to the lack of severe interest-group pressure in this area is the different manner in which continental courts can and cannot be used for class action suits. Where U.S. environmentalists drew on the precedents set by the civil rights activities of the 1960s, Western Europeans have had no such class use of their courts to set precedents, and in some countries, such as Belgium, are precluded by law from class action even when strong pro-nature laws exist. Often, only the individual who can show true damage and suffering to self-owned property has access and standing to sue.

A third major aspect is found in the structure of energy in the Nine and the EC. This is complex and not readily conducive to brief analysis. The major problems here center around disparate energy situations among the Nine; individual national approaches to energy issues, with their respective national energy industry structures; the intractability of energy as a domestic issue in each of the Nine because it is perceived by national elites as a necessary basic to each national economy; the significant governmental intervention in this area in the Nine; the intersectoral dynamics of energy; a globally integrated rather than truly regional energy market; the role of

multinational firms in these markets; and the existence of multiple
international forums in which solutions to various energy problems
can be sought. The results have been generally haphazard energy
policy choices, based predominantly on perceived short-term individual national interests.

Over time this has led to a "cheap-and-stable" supply policy,[2]
since the higher value in the Nine has been economic growth. Supply
security had been subordinated to this. Environmental concerns had
been subsidiary, especially since per capita energy consumption had
not reached U.S. levels.

The real impact on the environment from the 1973 crisis was
in governmental decisions in the largest four members of the EC
and the efforts of the EC Commission at the center of the EC system
to push nuclear power for electricity generation. The smaller member states have little means of opposing such decisions and would be
affected by their neighbors' policies. The original proposals were
for an installed capacity of 200 Gwe by 1985, to handle 50 percent of
all electricity generation. * By 1976 these proposals led to a major
backlash and the evolving of somewhat effective antinuclear lobbying
by environmentalists. Thus the impact of the 1973 crisis was to generate throughout the informed public a greater environmental concern over energy production and use than had existed before.

In most cases this impact cannot be disaggregated for analysis
from other political changes occurring in Western Europe. In many
cases it has been linked to greater public demand for increased
political participation at the local level and less technical bureaucratization. It has been part of the general trend against "bigness"
occurring globally. It has occurred particularly in Denmark, in the
United Kingdom (with its dual problem of devolution and increasing
local government), in Italy, and to a lesser extent in France. In the
Federal Republic of Germany it has emerged as a struggle to retain
local Land control against a growing tendency to increase central
federal control over environmental issues.[3]

Because the impact of the energy crisis on the environment in
the Nine cannot be reduced to any single factor for analysis, it is
best to examine the energy situation first, and then the environmental situation. Clearly, in all the Nine (and reflected in the EC),
there is a commitment to economic growth and a rising standard of
living, hopefully while keeping a higher quality of life. These are
paradoxical goals with conflicting objectives, and the conflicts cannot be eliminated. The Nine, however, have at least chosen to cope

---

*One gigawatt electric (Gwe) is equivalent to 10 million 100-
watt light bulbs: 1 Gwe = 10^9 watts.

with these goals in somewhat flexible ways suiting their national styles. They have generally rejected the extreme view of the first report to the Club of Rome (The Limits to Growth).[4] They have attempted to bring more medium- to long-range planning into national policy making and have sought to maintain local participation in their various environmental policy processes.

A notable exception to the last has been France, where all societal demands continue to be handled by bureaucratizing them at the center. With regard to energy and environment as linked issues, reaction to this has proven violent on occasion, as in the bombing of French nuclear power station sites at Fessenheim. People clearly want a say in determining their quality of life and not arbitrary bureaucratization of their environmental needs.

The conflicts between desired energy consumption and environmental degradation is more acute for energy than for any other natural resource use. The production and use of energy is central to pollution in the industrial era. What is at stake is the power for machinery, for all forms of transportation, for space heating and cooling, and for those things people in industrialized societies believe they need in order to live.

THE ENERGY SCENE

Public policy making for energy is by nature arcane and complex. This has discouraged direct mass public participation in the debate over energy issues and its policy-making process. Thus the energy policy-making arena remains dominated by professional and technocratic interests, though the trend is for medium-term changes caused by ongoing environmental group activities. Immediate energy needs in the Nine are usually handled through bilateral relations between producers and consumers. More and more long-term needs are being managed through various multilateral frameworks, including the International Energy Agency (IEA), an ancillary to the Organization for Economic Cooperation and Development; the OECD itself; FORATOM, a transnational industrial grouping; and the tripartite producer-consumer-developing nations' Conference on International Economic Cooperation (CIEC), as well as through the EC itself.

An adversarial style marks the EC process, with each of the ten principal actors, the Nine plus the Commission, "pulling and hauling" in a political manner. For energy this process is nonintegrative, and consensus results only when long-term aspects or general principles are being debated. This means that effective EC energy policies have surfaced only when the Nine have agreed to

some extent on the issues in other forums in which there was no
requirement to emerge with concrete results for public consumption.

Physical and Technical Aspects

The concern here is with "primary energy" as well as with
electricity generated from primary sources. Primary energy is
usable in its basic form and encompasses the traditional solid fuels
(various coals and peat or turf), hydrocarbons (oil and gas), nuclear
fuels (uranium, enriched uranium 235, plutonium, and thorium), and
"other sources" (hydroelectric, wind, solar, tidal, wave, and geothermal energy). Secondary energy is that made from the basic
sources and used to do productive work for society. Electricity
from thermal and nuclear plants is the most important form of
secondary energy.

In the early 1970s primary energy in the Nine was consumed
at an average rate of 4.95 metric ton equivalent of coal (tec), or
3.96 metric ton equivalent of petroleum (tep) per capita per year,
representing some 35 million kilocalories per capita per year. The
range in the Nine is from 3.19 tec in Italy to 19.6 tec in Luxembourg
(due to presence of iron and steel industry, some 60 percent of the
Grand Duchy's consumption). The United States expects a per capita
consumption rate of 14.7 tec by 1980. A tec, at 7,000 kilocalories
per kilogram, equals 1.43 tep, at 10,000 kilocalories per kilogram.
This factor is the continental conversion figure based on the higher
commercial grades of coal used there, whereas the U.K. conversion
factor is 1:1.7. The 7,000 kilocalories per kilogram heat value is
assigned as the EC's standard measure of equivalency. Differences
do exist among econometricians about the validity of caloric comparison, with some maintaining that only cost data are valid. The
difficulty of finding standard concepts on which to base measures so
that economic data can be commonly analyzed is an ongoing problem for the EC.

The use of primary energy in the Nine is predicted to increase
to 7.1 tec per capita per year in the 1980s, or about 50 million kilocalories per capita per year, a yearly total of 1.6 billion tec. So
far in the Nine the proportion of national investment expended on
energy has averaged 7 percent, requiring a total annual investment
of around $18 billion to $20.4 billion in the 1980s.[5] These forecasts
have been debated and revised downward in the wake of the oil crisis,
but knowledgeable national experts consider the financial values to be
valid--that is, energy will cost more, not less--and they also consider that any resurgent economic growth will reestablish the validity
of these forecasts. The OECD post-1973 forecast placed the rate of

growth in energy consumption for the 1970s at 5.1 percent, down
from the 5.5 percent rate in the 1960s.

Generally there is an external energy dependence of about 60
percent in the EC. Commission officials forecast that dependence
dropped to 55 percent in 1975, with a considerable assist from the
global economic slowdown. This dependence is not limited to oil but
cuts across all energy sectors. Tables 5 and 6 show the disparities
and relative dependence in the Nine.

TABLE 5

External Energy Dependence, 1973

Member State	Percent of External Supplies
Luxembourg	99.6
Denmark	99.3
Belgium	86.7
Italy	83.4
Ireland	81.7
France	78.0
Federal Republic of Germany	54.9
United Kingdom	48.2
The Netherlands	5.7
Average for the Nine	61.4

Source: "The European Community and the energy problem,"
European Documentation (Commission of the EC) 75, no. 2.

Additionally, there have been major shifts in the pattern of
energy consumption in the EC since the coal crisis of 1958, as shown
in Table 7. Although a sectoral decrease for electricity is shown,
the actual amount produced has increased, whereas for coal, production has decreased. In order for EC policy makers and consumers
to choose among alternative sectors, the physical and technical
aspects of those sectors must be known.

Nuclear Energy

There are two types of nuclear energy--fission and fusion.
These are used to produce heat, which in turn can be used in direct

TABLE 6

External Dependence of Member States, 1972:
Primary Energy by Sector
(in percent)

Member State	Solids	Oil	Gas	Primary Electricity
Luxembourg	100.0	100.0	100.0	99.5
Denmark	100.0	99.3	n.a.	0[a]
Belgium	42.7	100.0	99.5	0[a]
Italy	97.3	98.6	70.4	9.4
Ireland	25.0	100.0	n.a.	0
France	31.7	98.6	49.7	0[b]
Federal Republic of Germany	0[b]	95.0	36.8	35.7
United Kingdom	0[b]	99.5[c]	33.8	1.2
The Netherlands	36.7	94.6	0[b]	0[a]

[a]No significant exports.

[b]Significant exports.

[c]North Sea oil not in production.

Notes: External dependence is defined as the ratio of consumption minus production over consumption.

n.a.: not applicable.

Sources: Computed by the author from "The European Community and the energy problem," European Documentation (Commission of the EC) 75, no. 2; "Les problèmes de l'énergie, perspectives d'avenir," Documentation européene (Commission of the EC) 74, no. 1 ; Prospects of primary energy demand in the Community (1975-1980-1985) (Luxembourg: Commission of the EC--Office of Official Publications of the EC, 1972); Selected Figures: Energy in the Community (Brussels: Commission of the EC-- Eurostat, 1974, 1975).

TABLE 7

Primary Energy Consumption in the European Communities
(in percent)

Type	1960	1973	1985[a]	1985[b]
Solid fuels	63.9	22.6	10	16
Petroleum	28.6	59.5	64	41-49
Natural gas	1.7	12.6	15	23-19
Electricity	5.8	4.3	2	3
Nuclear and other	--	0.2	9	17-13

[a]Forecast prior to 1973 oil crisis.

[b]Revised 1974 forecast, with low and high oil import and high and low nuclear production hypotheses respectively.

Sources: Compiled by the author from "The European Community and the energy problem," European Documentation (Commission of the EC) 75, no. 2; "Les problèmes de l'énergie, perspectives d'avenir," Documentation européene (Commission of the EC) 74, no. 1; John Bradbeer, "Energy in the EEC," European Studies (London) 18 (1974); "L'Energie en Europe," L'Europe des Communautés (Paris: Documentation Francaise, 1974).

heating applications such as industrial process heat, urban district heating, or shale oil production, or they may be used to heat steam for electricity generation. The current usable technology is fission, which in reality is a medium-term solution. The development of fusion technology (magnetic torus, laser ablative method, or otherwise) has not yet reached any commercially feasible "breakthrough" point, and in spite of prior forecasts, this point cannot be adequately predicted. It could in fact come in the late 1970s, or it might not become feasible until the turn of the century, yet to emphasize nuclear fission energy in face of this uncertainty could be as disastrous as being overly optimistic about a fusion breakthrough. This also relates to uncertainties in the alternative energy sectors. As long as uncertainty exists with regard to specific long-range alternative sources, any overemphasis on current nuclear fission plans and objectives to 1985 means that there is a high probability of burdening the densely populated areas of the EC with major fission products and radioactive wastes while simultaneously squandering billions of dollars on an interim technology that may not be needed at all in such concentration as is now being planned in some of the Nine.

Nuclear energy itself may be best used in direct heat applications rather than for electricity generation. Heat loss and electrical transmission loss make a nuclear-powered electrical system only about 30 percent efficient overall. No real heat transport engineering and technology is on line or far enough developed to come into full operation in the short or medium term. High-temperature gas-cooled reactor (HTGR) technology would be required, and only the Federal Republic of Germany is now allocating significant resources for this.[6]

Light water reactor (LWR) technology is well developed and sufficient for district heating schemes, but the lack of fully tested engineering technology adequate for such applications adds to the uncertainty involved with nuclear energy, in spite of the considerable experience with LWR systems. The emphasis has been on reactors and not on the peripheral equipment needed to make LWR systems work reliably and properly.

There is also the entire question of reactor reliability, system reliability, and general public safety from nuclear energy systems. There have already been core meltdowns without serious failures of emergency systems, failures of emergency systems without other complications, and a host of engineering problems in the current technology, including hairline cracks in cooling pipes, foundry problems in valving, fuel rod splitting, fuel densification, and problems of quality control at all stages. The problems encountered point to the probability of reactor vessel blowouts and blowdowns. Debate on this probability leaves this an unsettled issue at best.

Out of this debate has emerged the frightening Colgate Hypothesis (or Krakatoa effect) on dynamic self-mixing, which states basically that the physical process of any blowout or blowdown would be a violent explosion greater in magnitude than perceivable due to the shock effect of cooler water being dumped into the superheated reactor vessel, through which a small initial explosion from initial dynamic self-mixing would self-propagate mechanically and thermodynamically to a worst-case detonation of the equivalent of 19 tons of TNT. Such "steam explosions" are not new and are considered in the 13-volume Rasmussen Report.[7] Granted, this is a dimension of uncertainty encountered only in water-cooled or water-moderated reactors with pressurized reactor vessels.

The power reactor systems on line in the Nine and projected through medium-term use include two types, the British second-generation gas-graphite Magnox system (GGR) and the U.S.-licensed pressurized water (PWR) and boiling water reactors (BWR). The Magnox GGR has been reliable though expensive. Its major problem has been excessive oxidation of "mild" steel components in the core as well as the heat exchanger, which is overcome by reducing loading, which in turn reduces CO_2-coolant temperatures. Thus it cannot operate at maximum generative capacity. Another problem has been inadequate design engineering of peripheral equipment unrelated to reactor operation or design. The relative success and reliability of this system is leading some in the United Kingdom to seek an advanced Magnox design, the advanced gas-cooled reactor (AGR). However, the U.K. government has been placing orders for the steam-generating heavy-water reactor (SGHWR). LWR technology developed in the United States was used elsewhere in the Nine with a BWR to PWR ratio of 1:1 until 1973, when orders for PWR exceeded BWR almost 5:1, costing (prior to the oil crisis) about $600 per kilowatt electric (Kwe) installed capacity or more.[8]

The Commission of the EC projects a nuclear power objective of 160 Gwe (minimum) to 200 Gwe installed capacity in 156 new plants by 1985. The most optimistic forecasts from other sources show only an overall installed capacity of about 134 Gwe maximum. Table 8 shows the capacity forecast in each of the Nine.

The Bonn government's post-crisis policy projection was expected to cost a total of $150 billion by 1985, excluding fuel costs. The French plan for fifty 1,000-Mwe stations by 1985 will require an investment from Electricité de France (EdF) of $20 billion between now and 1980 for the first phase of stepped-up production of six to eight stations per year. The Irish have sensibly refrained from jumping into the nuclear muddle with their national energy plans; however, they have made EC treaty commitments to cooperate in the nuclear efforts of the Nine, which is a somewhat ambiguous position for their national policy.

TABLE 8

Installed Nuclear Capacity Forecasts for 1985

Member State	Forecast* (in gigawatts electric)	Government Policy Projection
Belgium and Luxembourg	5.5	
Denmark	1.5	not yet determined
Federal Republic of Germany	38.0	45-50
France	32.5	35-50
Ireland	--	0
Italy	18.0	
The Netherlands	3.7	
United Kingdom	35.0	
Total	134.2	160-200

*Range could vary by +11 percent or -16 percent, depending on many uncertain factors according to the source material.

Sources: Commission of the EC projections found in: "The European Community and the energy problem," European Documentation (Commission of the EC) 75, no. 2; Situation and prospects of the industries producing heavy electrical engineering and nuclear equipment for electricity generating in the Community, SEC (75) 2770 (Commission of the EC, July 23, 1975); forecast data from "Croissance énergétique nucléaire mondiale," table in "Uranium-- Resources, production, et demands," AENE/AIEA, Rapport du Groupe de travail, August 1973.

The Danes have yet to decide whether to take on a nuclear power program or not, although the Social Democrat government is inclined to push for some minimal program even though this will cause a cleavage in its party. The British are in the process of deciding among three systems for their future capacity, AGR, SGHWR, or HTGR, but the last has been dropped de facto and some orders have been placed for the second. They are not yet able to forecast projected costs for this capacity with adequate certainty. Italy is negotiating with Canada to construct CANDU heavy water reactors (HWR)* and has entered into agreements with France and the Federal

---

*The CANDU is considered the safest reactor at this time because it does not use a pressurized reactor vessel. However, its

Republic of Germany for fast-breeder (FBR) generation of electricity. The plants will be in France and the Federal Republic of Germany, and the electricity will be transmitted to Italy. [9]

A major uncertainty about fission reactors is being created through the increasing size of such systems as economies of scale are sought for cost and energy efficiency. In the Federal Republic of Germany, reactor size increased from 50 Mwe in 1965 to 1,300 Mwe in 1976. Bilbis I, near Worms on the Rhine, is operating at a capacity of 1,204 Mwe, and Bilbis II (under construction) is to operate at 1,300 Mwe. Four reactors are planned for this site, to cost $3 billion each for the complete system (excluding fuel)--reactor, peripherals, security, and environmental protection systems. [10] The French are planning 1,000 Mwe stations at the rate of six to eight per year.

Medical critics maintain that a single 1,000 Mwe reactor operating under current standards would release levels of radioactivity sufficient to kill 1,000 to 10,000 people annually; experience with plants of this size is minimal, and to enter into such a rapid construction program is to rush in where the proverbial angels fear to tread. [11]

Another problem involves the personnel and means of funding needed to reach national and EC nuclear energy objectives. Currently the significant work force in the Nine for electricity generation equipment construction (nuclear and conventional) is 0.7 million and handles a pretax annual turnover of $12 billion. Of necessity this force would expand to keep up with projected construction, and qualified operating personnel would have to be increased tenfold. With a seven- to ten-year lead time to finish nuclear plants, this means completion of one reactor per week in the last two years to meet 1985 objectives. Additionally, the total needed to build 156 new plants properly is estimated between $300 billion and $450 billion, about one-half to two-thirds of the estimated surpluses of the Organization of Arab Petroleum Exporting Countries (OAPEC) at that time. Even if all EC investment were concentrated in the projected nuclear program, it still would not cover the needs.

The final problem in the nuclear sector is nuclear fuel for the EC program. First, the Nine have neither adequate indigenous uranium resources to meet their needs nor on-line enrichment process plants for their LWR systems, which require slightly enriched uranium 235. Uranium ores are sufficiently dispersed globally

---

use creates weapons-grade fissile materials suitable for use in bombs, thus contributing to the risk of major nuclear incidents, since its sales are global.

that obtaining yellowcake (U_3O_8) is not a major problem for the EC. The oil crisis drove up its cost threefold, from $8 per pound to $24 per pound; however, this has had a positive effect by providing an economic incentive to develop new reserves, such as those believed to be in the Black Forest of the Federal Republic of Germany. The U.S. Energy Research and Development Administration (ERDA) survey shows yellowcake averaging $12 per pound in 1976 and projects average costs of $13 per pound in 1977, $14 in 1978, and $20 by 1985. These shifting costs will exacerbate the uncertainties over fuel as they affect prospecting, although they do reflect a reduced demand for nuclear fuels. The Commission of the EC has scheduled negotiations with Australia, which is reviewing its uranium exporting policy, in order to obtain some commitment for the uncommitted Australian reserves. The EC consumes about one-fourth to one-third of the global demand, and by 1985 it will need 40,000 metric tons annually. [12]

Until 1974 the United States was the sole supplier to the EC of enriched uranium 235. The first delivery of slightly enriched Soviet uranium 235 to West German reactors took place in that year, and the Soviet Union now supplies 21 percent of EC needs, while the United States supplies the rest. The 1974 total of slightly enriched uranium 235 was 11,836 kilograms, corresponding to about 454 metric tons of yellowcake. The United States is still the sole supplier to the EC of slightly enriched uranium 235. [13] This de facto U.S. monopoly stems from the commercial success of its LWR technology, which requires slightly enriched uranium 235. The Nine are ending this dependency with the establishment of their own facilities-- EURODIF at Tricastin, France (gaseous diffusion consortium from France, Belgium, Spain, Sweden, and Iran) and URENCO+CENTEC at Almelmo, the Netherlands (gas ultracentrifugation consortium from the United Kingdom, the Federal Republic of Germany, and the Netherlands). These come on line fully by 1985.

In spite of this, the dependency on the United States for enriched uranium 235 may arise anew. The U.S. decision to seek commercial enrichment services to meet its own energy needs will have great effect on how far the EC must push its enrichment process programs. Two prospective U.S. consortia are already preparing to construct another diffusion plant (Bechtel/Union Carbide/Westinghouse) and an ultracentrifuge (Exxon/General Electric). Additionally, a nozzle process (from STEAG, of Karlsruhe, in the Federal Republic of Germany) which involves low capital cost and high energy use; a laser separation process (AVCO/Exxon and LASL), which uses low cost, lower energy use, low-grade yellowcake; and a second laser process (in South Africa) are being developed, all of which promise low-cost enriched units of separative work (usw). The estimated costs of the first two proposed U.S. commercial plants are less than or on par with the EURODIF price and about 75 percent of the URENCO price, respectively.[14]

As these plants come on line, they could drive the actual cost down, creating an incentive for EC power producers to seek U.S. enriched uranium 235 again. The investment cost for a new diffusion plant is about $150 per usw, and it requires 2,400 kilowatt hours of energy per usw. Ultracentrifuges may average $165 per usw, but the energy use is only 200-300 kilowatt hours per usw. The diffusion cost structure is about 50 percent for energy and 40 percent for capital, whereas ulticentrifugation needs about 15 percent for energy, 65 percent for capital, and 10 percent for centrifuge replacement. The usw capacity of EURODIF has been planned to reach a total level of 12 million usw by 1985, costing some $1.8 billion in investments. URENCO has planned a capacity of 10 million usw by 1985, with an investment cost around $1.6 billion. Where EURODIF capacity would remain about 12 million usw, however, URENCO plans to increase capacity to 20 million usw by 1990, increasing investment costs to a $3.2 billion total at current projections. Moreover, centrifuge capital replacement costs over this period would run to $500 million.[15] Normally the fuel cycle is nine to thirteen years, with eight to ten for ore exploration and one to three for processing. Eight years are required currently between contracting and shipment of U.S. enriched uranium 235.

For the long term, active consideration of projects as well as projects themselves have been underway for various advanced systems: HTGR (an AVR pebble bed by the Federal Republic of Germany and the British-led DRAGON); SGHWR and AGR (United Kingdom); liquid-metal fast-breeder reactors (LMFBR) (France's Rapsodie and Phénix; Britain's DFR and PFR; Italy's PEC; and the Federal Republic of Germany's SNR-300 and SNR-2000); the gas-cooled breeder (GCBR) (Shell/Gulf/General Atomic); and the heavy-water homogenous-breeder reactor (HWHR) (KEMA corporation). Also, a promising U.S. experimental-design molten-salt breeder reactor (MSBR), which has on-site reprocessing and obviates fuel refabrication and transportation, is undergoing R&D. R&D costs are expensive, however; the MSBR had a project restart cost of $4 million, and the Commission of the EC wants to allocate $3.6 million to exploit the results of the now-defunct DRAGON project. Additionally, the EC and the Nine have budgeted for 1976-80 some $0.7 billion for nuclear fusion R&D on the Joint European Torus/Tokomak (JET). The major fission R&D item is the LMFBR.[16] The probable outcomes of these projects are not accurately foreseeable.

In sum, nuclear energy in the EC is marked by great uncertainty because of: system reliability problems (even with experienced designs); inability to adequately forecast needed capacity or make sound policy projections; exceptionally large capital as well as R&D costs; long lead times; unknowns regarding radioactivity; uncertainties about uranium dependency, enrichment capacity, and fuel reprocessing; and an excessive number of inadequately proven (or even unproven) designs competing for too small a share of the global nuclear energy market.[17] This sector is fraught with major problems without even taking into account rising environmental and land-use siting concerns. Also, the social reaction to nuclear power varies in different members of the Nine, and although it has been studied, it has yet to be thoroughly assessed.

Coal

Physically, the economically recoverable coal and lignite reserves of Western Europe are set at 48 billion metric tons. In the mid-1950s almost 75 percent of EC energy needs in the Six were met by coal, 95 percent of this from indigenous production. EC coal reserves can replace all the oil consumed in the Nine and continue doing so well into the twenty-first century. World coal reserves comprise 93 percent of all fossil fuel reserves known at this time.

Technical and economic factors greatly limit its substitutive elasticity, however. The 0.7 million-person work force of the 1950s has been cut by 80 percent to around 0.2 million. The cutback in production in the Nine in the 1960s and 1970s fell from 475 to 250 million tec.[18] Many coalfields are now closed and their pits sealed; reopening now, in view of other alternatives, would be prohibitively expensive to the governments of the Nine. Assuming immediate full availability, which is not the actual case, EC mines are not conducive to greater mechanization, based on experience elsewhere. Some of this limitation is due to geologic structures, but much of it is because it is impossible to make simplistic introduction of modern extractive equipment in old mines without adequate design-matching of coal-handling and peripheral equipment to the coal-cutting machinery.[19] Strip mining would be suitable in many EC areas, and, if done as it is in the Federal Republic of Germany, which has similar requirements to those of Pennsylvania, but with much better social cooperation and consensus, it can be environmentally acceptable at minimal cost.

In the EC the major impact on coal now comes from the steel industry and electric utilities, which consume 80 percent of output and imports. The ECSC's Steel Club is trying to get out from under the burden of providing de facto support for EC coal industries. Without adequate investment, coal production will continue to decline; but investment climates are created by public policies.

The EC steel interests are generally dissatisfied about having to shoulder the bulk of the financial burden of coal and are seeking a policy that places the cost of current and future coal aids on the EC economy as a whole. West German laws give mine owners priority in allocating coal supplies, and so seven major steel firms control one-third of the FRG output. These firms threatened to move from the Federal Republic abroad unless they could get adequate supplies of coking coal at prices permitting their products to compete globally. The impact of steel on coking coal is severe, with its demand exceeding EC abilities but not EC reserve capacity. This led the United Kingdom to import hard coal from North Vietnam in 1975; its own Welsh fields had been plagued by strikes and could not meet steel mill demands. The mines of the Netherlands are now closed completely, and contraction or rationalization continues in other EC countries.[20]

These economic dynamics have led to import policies for coal. Based on the best estimates of import availabilities from various sources, the EC can count only on 125 million metric tons through 1980, as shown in Table 9. This pressure to import rather than maintain EC production continues, especially in the case of coking coals.

TABLE 9

Coal Imports by the European Communities, 1974-80

Source	Amount (in millions of metric tons)
United States	50
Australia	25
German Democratic Republic	10
Poland	10
USSR	10
Canada	10
South Africa	10
Total availability	125

Sources: Derived from S. Schmitt, "Coal as a Substitute," in Energy in the European Communities, ed. F. A. M. Alting von Geusau (Leyden: Sijthoff, 1975), Chapter 5, plus Eurostat data (unpublished, Commission of the EC, 1974).

The prospects for short-term substitution of coal are problematic if not poor. Only the Federal Republic of Germany has enough flexibility to meet 10 percent of its current oil needs by an immediate increase in coal production. This is linked to the federal and Länder systems of governmental aid to the coal industry. Only 17 percent of current thermal power-plant oil use could be switched easily from oil to coal, and this dual-firing capability has come from pressures generated out of the 1973 oil crisis. Twelve new coal-fired plants and ten new dual coal-oil plants are due in service by 1980, somewhat enhancing this capability.

Medium- and long-term coal prospects are not so bright in the face of EC nuclearization policies. Only in combining rationalization of EC production with coal liquification and gasification will an EC production of 250 million metric tons in 1985 be maintained and economically feasible. Only Ireland, the United Kingdom, and the Federal Republic of Germany are planning to maintain significant coal capacity. The hope here lies in advanced technological uses of coal for synthetic fuel, which under current economic conditions requires higher stable oil and gas prices. Ten members of the IEA have signed five agreements, with a budget of $24 million, on triannual coal R&D projects to develop this alternate source. Four are studies and technical data projects, totaling $8 million. The rest is for a joint program of the United States, the United Kingdom, and the Federal Republic of Germany on a fluidized-bed combustion rig. This full design, construction, and operation program will be set up in the United Kingdom under the aegis of the National Coal Board (NCB), in NCB (IEA Services) Limited.[21] Although this is a highly desirable R&D project, it took two full years following the 1973 oil crisis to get any concrete action on alternate sources of energy, in spite of the fact that other international machinery existed in which this and other IEA cooperation could have been pursued immediately.

A number of factors contributed to the decline of the EC coal industry, including price competition with oil (over a ten-year period), different market structures for coal and oil, a preoccupation with enhancing the technical changeover from coal to oil, the lack of comparable convenience for coal, a belief that energy costs were the most significant part of industrial costs, "dumping" of low-cost fuel oil to compete with high-priced coal for the benefit of the oil companies, the lack of rules for the operation of multinational oil firms in the EC, and strict EC rules for coal.[22] Coal can still be more economically extracted and shipped to the Nine from Poland, the German Democratic Republic, and the United States. Also, in the EC nuclear power is expected to cost 10 to 40 percent less for the foreseeable future according to some forecasts. In short, there is little relative flexibility for coal in the EC market structure, and its medium- to long-term prospects are not the brightest.

Gas

Natural gas is the most environmentally sound energy source. Unfortunately, it is linked to oil production and falls into the international and multinational oil struggle. Today it could meet over a third of total EC energy supplies if it were equitably distributed. The Groningen reserves of the Netherlands, the southern British sector of the North Sea, France's Lacq fields in Aquitaine, and the Italian Cortemaggiore fields are the major developed EC natural gas sources. Recoverable reserves are estimated at 7.5 trillion cubic meters (m^3) currently. As developed by 1980, these should increase to 10.4 trillion m^3.* Today's production of 105 million tep of natural gas will increase by 1985 to an estimated 210-450 million tep, some 500 billion m^3 annually, or about 22 to 25 percent of total energy demand then. The EC reserves, if used exclusively, could be exhausted by the turn of the century.[23]

In 1976, imported Norwegian North Sea gas started flowing to Emsland in the Federal Republic of Germany. An extensive pipeline network to import Soviet gas is being developed at significant cost by FRG producers and distributors. The Federal Republic of Germany also concluded negotiations for Iranian gas, which will be sold to the Soviet Union in order that additional Soviet gas can be piped to West Germany for EC use. The West Germans were driven to this diversification when the Dutch became the "Arabs of the North" with respect to their gas reserves by limiting production. The deal involves Soviet gas in exchange for large-diameter pipe, with huge costs requiring FRG government financial and negotiating support.[24] A minor dependency over the short and medium term might be built for liquified natural gas (LNG) by France, which does not want to participate directly in the Soviet-Iranian-FRG plans. This diversification of sources suitably complements the very large-scale medium-term production of gas by the EC itself.

---

*P. R. Odell's restatement of oil and gas data suggests that developed total reserves of 10.4 trillion m^3 will be depleted at an annual rate of 0.48 trillion m^3, exhausting the indigenous gas potential of Western Europe by 2005 A.D. This depends, however, on such factors as actual investment patterns, use patterns, and governmental intervention over the long term.

The controlling factor is a system of pipeline networks. These are best developed in the United Kingdom, the Federal Republic of Germany, Benelux, northern Italy, and northeastern France (plus the French supply line from Aquitaine). The FRG-Soviet deal will extend the system through the north German and Polish plains, and through Austria (a later pipeline to the USSR). This will undoubtedly generate additional demands on Soviet (and Iranian) gas along the pipeline route. The Germans want to extend the lines to France, but the French are not keen on any hookup because they want to develop their own relationships for LNG, an environmentally questionable source because of the lack of experience with and unproven designs of LNG carriers. Forecasts show a global shipping requirement of 70 to 80 ships of 12,000 m^3 capacity in order to transport 0.2 billion tep, with about one-fourth of this going to Western Europe.[25] The outlook for natural gas remains fair to good, and the Federal Republic of Germany may push this sector in lieu of its nuclear power program if it is willing to sacrifice a degree of security or energy autonomy.

Oil

The oil story, including its financial aspects, has been well documented elsewhere,[26] and only highlights will be touched on here. By 1972 EC oil dependency reached high and dangerous levels--dangerous because of the single area and the single politicoeconomic organization on which that dependency rested. Coupled to this was the almost publicly imperceptible significant increase in U.S. oil imports from the same area. Almost 97 percent of all crudes came from OPEC, representing some 58 percent of total EC energy use. Even worse politically, 72 percent of total oil imports came from OAPEC, tying up 43 percent of EC energy demand in the Arab-Israeli conflict. Table 10 shows this oil dependency. Western Europe remains dependent on this oil in the near and medium term.

For the medium to long term, massive development of offshore finds is forecast, first in the known North Sea fields, later from new exploration there, then from the Irish Sea expectations, and finally from the Bay of Biscay hopes. The North Sea basin alone is expected to provide 75 percent of EC indigenous oil between 1980 and 1990, some 550 million tep annually by 1985.[27] There are two sets of problems associated with these prospects. The first centers around offshore technology, which in spite of earlier developments is fraught with major environmental problems that have been played down or put off. Although environmental concerns are being taken into account, experience with the technology is still not yet fully matured. Additionally, the full forces of nature on the seabed are not adequately known, especially in relation to the deep drilling that will be required as present fields are played out. The costs of the technology that is needed exceed the ability of single EC nations to exploit the Western European offshore oil fields; thus multinational consortia are needed.[28]

TABLE 10

Petroleum Import Dependencies of the
Economic Community, 1973

Geographic Area	Percent from Source*
Organization of Petroleum Exporting Countries (OPEC)	97.1
Middle East and North Africa	87.6
Organization of Arab Petroleum Exporting Countries (OAPEC)	73.2
Middle East	69.9
USSR	2.2

*Does not add to 100 percent because some countries are in more than one grouping.

Sources: Compiled by the author from "The European Community and the energy problem," European Documentation (Commission of the EC) 75, no. 2; "Les problèmes de l'énergie, perspectives d'avenir," Documentation européene (Commission of the EC) 74, no. 1; Prospects of primary energy demand in the Community (1975-1980-1985) (Luxembourg: Commission of the EC--Office of Official Publications of the EC, 1972); Selected Figures: Energy in the Community (Brussels: Commission of the EC--Eurostat, 1974, 1975).

This leads to the second and more important problem, which is primarily structural and functional rather than technical. Major difficulties have been encountered with local and central authorities in the United Kingdom (especially Scotland) and Norway with regard to licensing of particular sectors, taxing schemes, production limitations (Norway), and siting of coastal service facilities. The British North Sea programs have been designed to secure better public control over U.K. oil and gas to ensure that an equitable share is assigned to British needs. The same is true of Norway. The United Kingdom has set up a majority taxing regime (12.5 percent royalty, 45 percent Petroleum Revenue Tax on cash flow, 52 percent corporate profits tax) that will give the government about a 70 percent take of gross profits, leaving the firms a 20 to 25 percent return on investment. The sheer magnitude of the costs requires considerable political compromise as well as governmental facilitation of the financing necessary to ensure production. The government cannot exploit the North Sea without the producing consortia; and therefore it has compromised somewhat by allowing a 175 percent deduction for capital costs. The issue causing the greatest conflict is the British government's effort to renegotiate the original licenses to get 51 percent control (changing the rules after the game has started).[29] This is a typical governmental move regarding oil firms that has grown out of OPEC experiences--negotiate an exploration contract that gives the consortium all the risks, then renegotiate once oil is located so that the consortium becomes a servicing and sales contractor. New participation agreements have been made by Gulf Oil and Continental Oil (U.S. firms) giving the British National Oil Company (BNOC) 51 percent of the formers' interests in their respective consortia.

In sum, oil is the EC's primary fuel in the near and medium term. It is expected to be 40 to 60 percent of total EC fuel consumption in 1985. Its immediacy places it at the heart of significant domestic, international, and transnational energy issues. There is sufficient oil for world needs, but its availability is a function of the investments made and the political climate in which they are made.

Summary

What these complex but incomplete relationships show is that there are adequate energy sources in the Nine, that there are problems in their distribution, and that these problems center around the policy choices concerning such distribution. There are other forms of energy that can be exploited, but these are in the R&D stage or are not yet commercially feasible. These include solar, wind, geothermal, ocean wave, tidal, proton pump, fusion, and hydrogen energy. These alternative forms are for the long term, although investment choices and incentives must be made at this time in order that the most suitable are developed in a timely manner. Energy infrastructures have long lead times, and any switchover to an alternative or new source requires considerable preparation.

What links these various sectors is the relative cost of the energy that can be delivered for effective use and the policy decisions

allowing for choice among sectors. In the EC the cost criterion as
traditionally applied excludes environmental and social externalities,
except possibly where to a limited extent social costs have been included in some coal cost forecasting. Clearly the wise use of marginal costs while accounting for externalities, the distribution of
wealth (not income), and the time dimension will lead to a rational
choice for energy systems with the lowest total cost over the systems' lifetimes. The problem for the rational actor is to identify
all costs over time, a difficult task at best in the face of current
energy uncertainties. The fourfold increase in oil prices stopped
the rate of growth in demand but did not add much to supplies because the near- and medium-term oil supply and demand equation
is relatively price inelastic. Cost criteria often tend to overlook
environmental costs and can even deny resource-specific criteria.
Energy resource use (rational use) as a criterion means the less
used in a particular way the better the system. Energy "impact
statements" attempt to couple the marginal cost criterion to resource
use criteria while excluding all externalities. Such an exercise has
been attempted by the EC Commission in its efforts to set energy
policy objectives. So far these efforts have fallen short, as physical
realities or technical considerations have been politically denied in
one manner or another for varying reasons, or else their efforts have
been overtaken by events.

The dynamic sectoral relationships suggest that problems in
one sector will lead to a major shift in another, as expressed through
the economic supply and demand principle. Furthermore, crises
should assist these shifts. Each shift that has been accentuated by
a crisis in contemporary energy affairs has led to greater external
dependencies and to balance-of-payments problems that exacerbate
EC efforts to choose rational policies. Price inelasticity and the
rigidity of national energy structures, relating to the economics of
energy production in a globally integrated market, are the root
causes for energy crises failing to achieve productive, timely shifts
to new sectors. Energy choice is thus a political economy question
rather than a physical problem.

ENERGY POLICIES

The energy policies chosen in the Nine and by the EC as a
whole supposedly reflect the efforts to solve their energy problems
by all participants and decision makers, using these political systems to allocate energy while supposedly taking into account environmental concerns.[30] Nevertheless, there are four general sets of
limitations in the choice of Community or common energy policies:

(1) geographic, geologic, and technical limitations; (2) limitations due to national structures and approaches; (3) the global energy market and the existence of other international forums in which the Nine can seek solutions; and (4) the EC context itself. Policy makers throughout the Nine are seeking to obtain sufficient stable supplies of energy at reasonable cost and with some degree of environmental protection; their policy statements reflect this.

Policies in the Nine

The hodgepodge of politicoeconomic structures and national policies was highlighted by the 1973 crisis. Energy has been an intractable domestic issue, with each government hoarding control over its own economy because of the political constraints under which it operates. The differing energy situations have led to different governmental responses, some relying more on the domestic market as it relates to the global energy market and others relying on governmental intervention, directly or through quasipublic corporations. These energy structures are highly oligopolistic; that is, a few elite decision makers operate in an interlocking fashion while excluding effective pluralistic economic or democratic influence. This oligopolistic structure stems not only from governmental interaction but also from demands for cheap energy, which push production of energy into large-scale complex industrial ventures because of the large capital requirements. Roughly 80 percent of the energy-industry assets in the United Kingdom, France, and Italy are state owned. Today only huge consortia are able to exploit energy resources, and often the only production ventures able to form such consortia are multinational and international in makeup.

The Belgian approach has been one of private production in all sectors, with governmental intervention used sparingly and as a last resort, reflecting the Belgian socioeconomic structure and political system as it has developed. The Danes have a closer public scrutiny over energy matters but leave the production up to private firms operating in consortia. Participation in NORDEL, a consortium of Nordic electricity-generating firms, is the main influence in Danish energy affairs. The Danes were able to keep their preferential arrangements in this highly effective power "bourse" upon accession to the EC. The policy of Luxembourg is tied to Belgium through the Belgium-Luxembourg Economic Union (BLEU). The Netherlands is free-market oriented but has made considerable intervention in the energy area for social reasons; its coal mines are now closed. The policy of the Netherlands is aimed at obtaining the cheapest supply, with security from indigenous natural gas, oil supply diversification

in North Sea ventures, and participation in European energy programs. The Irish have not yet articulated a clear policy but seem
to be aiming at cheap supply, with minimal security from indigenous
coal and oil supply diversification. These smaller members rely on
supply and sectoral diversification as well as multilateral and transnational cooperation. They are interdependent and cannot escape
the fact.

Of the four major partners in the EC, the French are the most
oriented toward market planning, with a strict hierarchic energy
structure the purpose of which is to intervene in the market to provide stability through "fine tuning." The French call this their
marché ordonné (regulated market). In this bureaucratic process
the financial view often dominates. The French energy industry is
mostly made up of public or quasi-public corporations, which are
lorded over by the ministerial hierarchies in spite of French industries' autonomous Administrative Councils. The French are trying
to drag EC energy policy along the line of their central planning
philosophy. They are seeking widespread nuclearization and through
this a degree of energy autonomy, at a cost they perceive as lower
than development of other sectors. Source diversification is secondary to their efforts to get preferential political arrangements bi-
laterally with traditional suppliers. Since 1973 cheapness of supply
has taken a lesser position in French policy.

The Italian response to energy problems has been based on
Italy's traditional lack of indigenous energy resources. Special
marketing trusts (ente) have been organized to expand exploration
globally and diversify sources of supply, with a policy of obtaining
the cheapest possible imports. These trusts, modeled somewhat
after the French energy corporations, are under Italian ministerial
supervision. Italy favors the general thrust of EC energy policy,
since the Italians perceive energy distortions in the Nine as causing
disruptive competition. Nevertheless the ente, as quasi-public
monopolies, tend to oppose effective EC action, which is seen as a
tendency toward dirigisme.

The United Kingdom follows in this trend of government intervention, having used a mixed approach until the North Sea gained
some importance for its hydrocarbons. Coal and electricity have
been monopolies of production and distribution and gas a monopoly
of distribution. Nuclear energy has been mostly a governmental
preserve because of the original weapons interest. Hydrocarbons
production and oil distribution were left to the private sector. With
the North Sea discoveries, the government has made it a policy to
seek 51 percent participation in all hydrocarbons exploitation ventures, and participating private firms are conceding reluctantly to
this desire. The British are becoming more like an oil-producing

country in their attitude toward Brussels and are opposing any effective EC action that might threaten their control over their new-found
hydrocarbon reserves. The British prefer transnational direct industrial cooperation on major energy projects rather than intergovernmental action. Their policy is to seek full control over all their
own energy sources, and so no strong central EC policy can be allowed to emerge prior to the full development of their own national
energy policy.

The Federal Republic of Germany has followed the approach
of minimal governmental intervention in energy production. Their
policy has been one of energy "cartelization," or rationalization into
large energy ventures, to take advantage of the economies of scale.
The preference for a private noncentralized structure reflects the
mixed FRG political system, but the units of production are very
large and can compare to the national units of other EC countries.
They have established what they call Marktordnung, which differs
substantively from the French marché ordonné, although the English
translations of both terms would be identical. The Federal Republic
of Germany has been much more hospitable to foreign energy firms
than has France; but at the outset of the oil crisis the FRG government was forced by public pressure to intervene in the oil sector to
preserve indigenous refinery capacity and to assist in creating a
national overseas firm not unlike the Compagnie Francaise de
Pétroles (CFdP) for exploration and production.

Bonn's policy in the EC has been to avoid overcentralization
and to preserve the FRG position of cartelizing energy industries
for economic efficiency. Like the United Kingdom, the Federal Republic of Germany prefers transnational industrial cooperation on
energy projects; and like the United Kingdom, it has made considerable use of the OECD for joint projects. The overall FRG policy has
been to seek economic supplies through diversification of sources.
The West German public has brought political pressure to bear on
the Bonn government regarding FRG financial support of the EC, and
so any energy action at the center in the EC must at least appear to
bring direct benefits to the Federal Republic of Germany or not cost
the West Germans any more of their wealth.

Policies at the Center: Brussels

Since the Nine have had varied policies, they have allowed no
effective central policies to evolve that would be binding on all. EC
policy has been possible only in narrow sectoral actions. Coal concerns under the ECSC must be seen as setting the stage for a sectoral approach to energy problems on the technical plane. Efforts

to secure a coal policy showed that a comprehensive approach was needed because of intersectoral dynamics; yet any ECSC High Authority efforts to take a comprehensive approach always bogged down in domestic squabbles.

After many years all the EC could do was get agreement on paradoxical guidelines: cheap and secure supplies at stable prices, with consumer freedom of choice among environmentally sound supplies, so long as no economic distortions occur. Sectoral action agreements such as the oil stockpiling rules came reluctantly and often so late as to be ineffective. Thus the Commission caucuses the members of the EC about energy and tries to come up with a policy that will fit the whole. Its "New Energy Policy Strategy" in 1974 only applied well-known energy concerns and agreed-upon principles to national forecasts in the changed circumstances following the oil crisis.[31] According to some officials this was done in the hope that the Nine could be "conned" into agreeing on an action policy. Unfortunately, at the center the need of the Commission to exercise its leadership, as well as the "community process" of engrenage, lead to policy making in this manner.

The governments of the Nine are hedging their bets about the validity of the EC arena for solving their energy problems. Through their nonagreement on the Common Energy Policy, they have affirmed that the EC shall only be able to issue objectives to guide nationally autonomous energy policies. The Nine have given an energy R&D budget on alternative sources to the Commission to administer, however, which shows that they do want these problems to be dealt with in a somewhat common European manner, in the hope that here the EC forum will give them the most benefits at the least cost.

Energy as a Means to an End

All too often overlooked in the energy-environment debate is the fact that energy is a means to an end, not an end in itself. Historically, energy use has improved somewhat over time, with a rise in the unit productivity capacity of energy, achieved primarily through technological advances.

Much pollution results from the production and use of energy; thus measures to save energy are in fact a means of improving the environment. Energy pollution is waste. Better resource use and recycling would result in considerable savings, as would a conservation program. An excellent technique here is to use energy budgets and energy "impact statements," the former to calculate the energy cost of any given project and the latter to analyze alternatives.[32]

The EC is assisting in the process of finding the best means through a stepped-up four-year R&D program in conservation, production of hydrogen, use of solar and geothermal energy, and systems analysis of energy supply models. A second program will look into coal liquefaction and gasification, fusion energy, and protection from the health hazards of all energy generation. These two sets of R&D programs are estimated to cost a total of $4.7 million. Critical in assessing energy environmental protection are ongoing R&D activities in desulphurization (fluidized-bed combustion) and nitrogen oxide abatement, with a view toward lessening the environmental impact of energy use.[33]

Central to the process has been the search for a more rational use of energy and better resource planning. Reduced energy consumption means reduced air and water pollution. Thus the rational use of energy contributes to a rational system of environmental protection. Energy programs and environmental measures are harmonized in this process to the greatest extent, but protection of the environment as a EC principle has "absolute" priority where serious damage to environmental quality is feared.[34] Rational energy use and environmental protection are seen as two sides of the same coin, regardless of member-state differences over particular policies.

ENVIRONMENT

Air, water, earth, fire--the basic "elements" of a prior era-- have become the focal points for environmental policies in Western Europe. Just as human welfare was thought to depend on the way in which these "primary qualities," the substances whose spatial and temporal relationships make up the physical environment,[35] were owned and used, so it is now. Abusing the environment is not new. Europe is considered to have used its environment better than many other areas, at least until the Middle Ages. Since its agronomy developed gradually, using primitive methods of cultivation that were well adapted to the soil and climate, and its population remained sparse until that time, it survived centuries of inhabitation and use with no real environmental degradation.

Changes in agricultural technology, followed centuries later by industrialization, changed all that. Population growth from improved agricultural methods, coupled with the industrial age, led to the emergence of broad environmental deterioration in Europe. The side effects of this were not noticed until the post-World War II population explosion further congested the urban centers. Technological advance permitted this, but by the mid-1960s what had previously been considered to be random cases of severe localized environmental

damage, such as the London "killer smog" of the 1950s, had seem-
ingly overnight become the focus of widespread concern, especially
at the middle-class and elite levels. The process of energy breeding growth breeding pollution, coupled with the greatly increased
output to meet consumption demand, led to the potentially greater
threat to the European populace.

Environment as an Issue

By 1968 Western Europe was gearing up for the first European
Nature Conservation Year, launched by the Council of Europe at its
1970 Strasbourg Conference. On its heels came the preparatory
work for the UN Stockholm Conference in 1972. Because of these
highly publicized events, the environment was more readily acquired
as an issue. What was seen, felt, and smelt locally had finally
worked its way up to and beyond the national level as a critical issue
demanding governmental officials' time and effort. The Strasbourg
and Stockholm conferences gave the issue considerable credibility
among the Nine, reinforcing the national efforts that were being
made. Some consider that the realization of the gravity of environmental problems had come earlier in the United States and had eventually, through media exposure, assisted in the Western European
mass concern; but it took the Strasbourg Conference and the Conservation Year to stimulate greater interest among Western Europeans, because only then did they identify the issue as their own
problem.

Environment as an overall issue has not aroused the same
pressing interest in the EC as energy. The governments of the Nine
felt the need to control energy in order to control their economies,
but they did not feel that they had to control their physical environment in order to maintain a degree of economic autonomy. This
contributes to the continued general perception of the environment
as a free good, external to production and consumption costs. Only
when an item such as water for industrial or agricultural purposes
is so scarce that it creates significant economic difficulties or
severe hardship does public awareness of the externalities relating
to production and consumption increase to the point that demands
are articulated to the critical elites that influence the situation.

Economists in the Nine generally regard pollution of the environment as a problem of "externalities," that is, of actual costs
not required to be taken into account in computing the cost of consumption or production. They recognize that treating the environment as a public good--the common-property resource that it is--
and internalizing the costs involved would result in changes in the

prices of goods and services. This in turn would change patterns of production and consumption. The real problem for the Nine is that the environment has not been treated as a public good, resulting in production and consumption patterns that contribute to a worsening of environmental quality.

Where the economic system cannot of its own volition change the assumption--from free to public good--under which production and consumption occurs, then a political reordering of social priorities must be obtained if the market system is to internalize costs when environmental limits are reached. For energy in the Nine, the crisis of cost and apparent scarcity has been due not only to technological mismanagement of energy, but also to mismanagement of energy economics. It is well known that energy prices have not fully reflected the social cost of the energy consumed. Neither the EC nor any of the Nine have required energy producers to internalize their pollution and resource depletion costs. This results in environmental degradation from excessive energy production and consumption, possibly one of the gravest long-term ecological threats in the Nine.

This is symptomatic of the larger debate over growth, which culminated in the exchange of notes with the President of the EC Commission in 1972. Vice-President Sicco Mansholt sent President Franco Malfatti and the other commissioners a letter listing the basic conclusions of the then forthcoming "Limits to Growth" report. He outlined four areas that he felt needed full simultaneous Commission attention: priority to food production, including investment in so-called nonrentable agricultural products; reduced per capita material consumption; significant lengthening of equipment and product lifetimes; and much tighter limitations on pollution and resource depletion. The solutions, he thought, lay in rigorous economic planning and in nonpolluting means of production, coupled with a program of recycling. This could be achieved through a "Central European Plan" and five-year plans to create a new infrastructure for nonpolluting industry, which would include a system of production certificates; modification of the value-added tax (VAT) to favor certified production; incentives for product durability; a European raw materials distribution system to prevent collapses; and a research program on environmental protection, ecological balance, closed production cycles, and economic consequences.[36]

Granted there was no consensus on, and few supporters for, such a radical revision of the infrastructure of the EC. The reply was framed by Raymond Barre in a note to Malfatti and the commissioners that was highly critical of the report to the Club of Rome on limits to growth. He stressed that the environmental fight was a financial and economic problem in which it seemed the general interest would be politically imposed on particular interests, to him a questionable practice. He was adamant that technology could solve the problems and that raw materials could be obtained through substitution, especially since no one knew what really lay beneath the oceans. Additionally, the Green Revolution had been successful and promised global food growth superior to population growth. Finally, Barre held that air and water were no longer regarded as free goods and had not been for some years. For him the argument was already academic and clearly ideological.[37]

Out of that debate it was seen that the environment was not fully perceived as critical to the industrial motor of the EC. In energy this meant that siting considerations such as land use and cooling needs, energy relationships with other sectors of the economy, and the failure to charge full costs for energy would not be squarely faced until after the 1973 oil crisis had put everything close to shambles. One thing persisted before and after: the tendency to shift environmental impacts and burdens to other regions. In effect, the concentration of political and economic influence in urban areas made it easy and attractive to shift energy production facilities to rural areas. In the face of such particular issues, no national government was strong enough to risk itself politically over the relatively radical Mansholt proposals or their implications for energy. This meant steering along the traditional course and publicly stating simply that the government was concerned.

It is the particular environmental issue that causes intractable problems in the Nine. Usually this stems from impacts at the local level, which are articulated to particular governmental agencies at the national and subnational levels. In one adversarial case, through direct action the citizens of the French town of Metz blocked the construction of an airport they very much wanted. They just did not want it near them, although all the other regional towns had also rejected it.[38]

Clearly, people are more willing to act when issues hit close to home. In the Nine this is at the local level, where citizen action on the environment has been having its greatest impact. Local people know their elected officials personally and have greater access to them than to those at the national level; yet local officials usually have limited authority and resources to deal with environmental issues, which all too often have little regard for the niceties of political units and boundaries.

Response in the Nine to environmental issues can also be, and has been, stimulated by international and transnational events. These stimuli have not necessarily been governmental. The Friends of the Earth (Australian branch), in their antinuclear campaign, precipitated a Western European response to something that was directed

at the U.S. nuclear program and industry. They provided documents
to the California State Energy Commission and Public Utilities Commission regarding uranium price fixing. The documents, sent to
the U.S. Department of Justice and Senate Committee on Foreign
Relations, resulted in the U.S. inquiry into alleged uranium cartel
activities that were contrary to U.S. antitrust laws. Ostensibly an
anti-U.S. action, it had great impact on the EC because of the great
influence the U.S. nuclear industry has had on EC markets.

Because of the impact on the EC, the Commission's Competition Directorate-General has been following this very closely. One
of the major protagonists in the dispute is the London-based Uranium
Institute, a direct follow-on to its predecessor, the Uranium Market
Research Organization (UMRO). If the allegations that leading
uranium producers (from Canada, France, the United Kingdom,
Australia, and South Africa) have met to fix prices and divide markets under the guise of market research prove true, then the EC
Commission will be required to take action under EC competition
rules against many of the Nine's firms in the nuclear area, such as
Kraftwerkunion of the Federal Republic of Germany; Electricité de
France; British Nuclear Fuels Ltd.; the Central Electricity Generating Board of Britain; Rio Tinto Zinc, which is based in the United
Kingdom; and Uranex, which is French and partly government owned,
among others.[39]

In this instance, the plans to greatly increase nuclear power
generation in industrialized societies in face of the energy crisis led
environmentalists everywhere to oppose such plans, which in turn
resulted in EC efforts to curtail certain fuel aspects, although not
for environmental reasons. What is critical in this dispute is that
without a relatively high and stable price for uranium, plans for
nuclear power become highly uncertain because of intersectoral economic relationships. If the plans become uncertain enough, it might
become too costly politically to push ahead with the massive investment needed. Thus in the EC effective opposition to actions perceived as environmentally degrading has not necessarily been direct.

Environmental concerns in the Nine have not been directed
abstractly. By 1972 there was sufficient consensus to describe the
particular areas in which action was needed on an EC as well as a
national basis. It was perceived that the quality of life was "men-
aced" because of the failure to account for environmental considerations in economic growth projections. It was perceived (and remains
so) that environmental degradation was directly linked to industrial
development and blind faith in economic growth. Responsive actions
had to be directed at industrial effluents and emissions as well as
solid wastes. Energy consumption was responsible for 60 to 80 percent of all atmospheric pollution, in addition to the significant thermal

pollution, which exacerbated the other contributions to water pollution. In addition to urbanization, Europe's most important problems were aggravated by rapid population growth, the use of pesticides, and the effects of consumption. Solving these problems would in effect mean going beyond any simple tradeoffs between policies and economic growth. The situation has been exceptionally complex and has involved the interaction of multiple factors ranging from the qualitative and quantitative aspects of technology to computation of social costs in pursuing full environmental protection. It was also recognized that pollution knew no frontiers. Governments would have to allocate significant funds to effect a suitable protection program and adequate research. Above all, it was explicitly recognized that in choosing national programs the results, if not worked out internationally, could mean significant economic barriers in the loss of comparative advantages for goods and services when different policies were chosen in different member states.[40] In effect, it was recognized by elites long before the 1973 oil crisis that Europe would back itself into an environmental "corner" if something were not quickly done.

Governmental recognition and response has not been the only action needed. Ordinary domestic energy usage has amounted to about half the total consumption in the Nine, primarily for vehicle propulsion and space heating. Many EC countries achieved a 10 percent reduction in motor fuel consumption, with a concomitant reduction in emissions, following the 1973 crisis. Granted, this resulted from the increased prices and slowdown in distribution. Space heating has contributed through direct stack emissions of fossil combustion products, and it has been cut back where energy costs drove consumers to insulate better, with savings of up to 30 percent.

On the commercial side, electricity generation has been the biggest culprit, from steam as well as gas turbines. The real problem here has been whether electricity is the best energy source to be used. If end-use strategies were determined from total energy systems analyses in the Nine, significant savings could be made. In particular, if combustible wastes could be used in small installations, such pyrolisis would save medium-level economies such as France and the United Kingdom about $28-42 million annually. In cases in which this has been done, the nature of emissions changed so much that a net reduction in atmospheric pollution was achieved because of the greatly reduced sulfur content. The promotion of this use of pyrolisis resulted directly from the increased price of oil in Europe. In the United Kingdom, where North Sea oil has not yet displaced imports, a projected $3 billion balance-of-payments deficit from future oil supplies prompted commercial consideration of and research on this method.

Environmental Policies

Although environmentalists have criticized the Nine for their insufficient efforts to provide proper environmental protection, the issues have been sufficiently salient to produce environmental policy programs in each of the Nine. The effectiveness of these has varied from country to country and has been a direct reflection of each country's political, economic, and social systems. The cultural history of each of the Nine has marked its individual approach. If anything, these approaches have remained unchanged through the energy crisis.

Before Stockholm, environmental matters were fragmented among many specialized sections, compartmentalized in various ministries. Each of the Nine had agencies addressing particular problems according to the particular geographic and economic situations that existed. This fragmented approach allowed little fruitful policy response to the ever-increasing environmental dangers arising out of increased consumption. In preparing for Stockholm, however, it was perceived that institutional means were needed, both politically and economically, to deal with the environment in a systemic rather than fragmented way. The results varied in each of the Nine, ranging from a simple interministerial coordinating committee to a superdepartment (or ministry).

Originally the Belgian government felt that only an interministerial committee was necessary in order to coordinate policy matters affecting the environment. The reasoning behind this was that the size and nature of the economy of Belgium did not require a separate ministry or special department. Moreover, it must be seen in light of the Belgian elite structure and the perceived necessity of keeping environmental issues on a technical plane, in the domain of professionals. Without a permanent ministry or agency there can be no "legitimate" pressure-group constituency. Pressures thus must be brought to bear on the prime minister's office and thus on the ruling party or coalition. Inasmuch as environmental issues tend to be fragmented and temporary in the eyes of many of the public, the government can retain control in these situations.

Programs and policies thus were dependent upon the established ministries: water quality on the Ministry of Public Health and air quality split between the same ministry and the Ministry of Labor and Employment. Local issues were distributed among the provincial councils. Suffice to say their general approach was insufficiently effective. Thus in early 1976 the appointment of a Secretary of State for the Environment was considered. This official would coordinate and monitor all environmental matters. At the economic regional level in Belgium, each Secretary of State for Regional Economy has had a Committee for Industrial Ecology, comprised of delegates from the various central ministries plus academic experts. Even with a number of good laws on the books regarding protection of the country-side, restrictions on air pollution and auto exhaust emissions, protecting surface and underground waters, preventing ground pollution, and so on, as well as institutions to deal with these issues, the dynamics have operated to produce questionable results. There have not been general environmental standards, but only specific rules put down in the operating licenses granted by the provincial authorities. In the future the advice and consent of the Secretary of State for the Environment would be necessary for all such licensing.

Environmental policies in Belgium have been implemented within the framework of the Management Plans for Land and Urbanization, an attempt to plan rationally and consider environmental needs in a total sense. Policy effectiveness, though, has rested on the degree to which environmental concerns have been written into particular plans. In spite of a good set of laws, Belgians have only been able to sue if the individuals bringing suit were directly affected. There has been no standing for class action as in the United States. More importantly, under Belgian environmental laws, governmental responses to the oil crisis could not be challenged, although, to be sure, the government's responses were directed toward the balance-of-payments losses and did not run in any real antienvironmental vein.

Denmark, which is comparable to Belgium in size but differs in many other respects, has taken a highly pro-environmental approach. (Denmark is treated in detail in Chapter 5.) Traditionally Danish politics has been consensual in nature, and this has marked the Danish approach to the environment. Denmark has been an industrial nation and has all the problems that advanced technologies bring. Traditionally there has also been great consideration for nature, but the advance into a highly industrialized status created tensions there. Denmark's response has been one of gradual legislative and administrative change to accommodate effective environmental protection. Starting from isolated proposals, Denmark proceeded through commissions and other intermediary stages to the creation of its Ministry of Environmental Protection. The policy chosen was to develop three key areas of environmental policy: to modernize and improve existing laws and institutions; to establish a research and information program and institute; and to specify action proposals.

The reasoning behind this approach was that all societies' activities were perceived to be related to environmental protection, and governmental coordination would be needed in order to deal with the issues. Poorly endowed in raw materials, the Danes have been exceptionally aware of using their resources with great efficiency.

Their propensity for coalition bargaining contributed to the lack of conflict in their response to the issues. Even industrial and commercial interests have shown positive attitudes, although their economic interests may have been diametrically opposed.

The immense cost of pollution control, however, has meant that the government must allocate its resources, and even in Denmark the environment does not always win everything it ought to have.[41] The estimated total investment cost to abate pollution as determined by the government was 4 billion kroner. Only some elements in the ruling coalition and in industry have been recommending a sizable nuclear program in response to the crisis; but the general Danish approach meant that the Danes did not lash back at environmental efforts when confronted with the 1973 oil crisis, even though their external dependence was above 99 percent.

The Netherlands has had a similar attitude toward the environment. Since 1965 it has had a forceful global framework that has taken the management and planning approach to environmental matters, reflecting a deep cultural and historical concern. Today's efforts trace back to land reclamation schemes. The Royal Land Management Service, Rijks Planologische Dienst (RPD), was a natural outgrowth of the fight to gain land from the sea. All environmental concerns stemmed from this, and thus institutional means were structured from it. The approach of the Netherlands has been global. It was tied into some 11 ministries of the government of the Netherlands through the RPD originally. Now a Ministry of Public Health and Environmental Hygiene accomplishes many of the same functions.

The largest environmental problem for the Netherlands has been water, not in quantity but in quality; there is even a section of the constitution on water. With increasing industrialization in the Netherlands as well as in neighboring countries, the major water problem has shifted from salt to heavy metals. For this reason the International Commission for the Protection of the Rhine has been an important institution.

Air pollution, especially transfrontier pollution from Belgium, has plagued the Netherlands from time to time. On one occasion workers walked off the job in Rotterdam to protest the truly unhealthy inversion that had trapped Belgian pollution in their location.

Because of its small size, the Netherlands is faced with a major solid waste management problem. This affects industry as well as domestic consumers in a major way. If solutions are not found soon, many industries will have to consider shutting down or shifting to other countries. This has been the one policy area sorely lacking in success.

Like Belgium, the Netherlands has provincial commissions and provincial management services. No part of its reaction to the

oil crisis was directed at the environment. To some extent the
Netherlands has opposed rapid nuclearization in response to the
crisis and has delayed somewhat on this issue. Dutch cooperation
in various nuclear projects does not mean this concern has been
false; they have been trying to ensure that no plants are located in
the Netherlands, although they are willing to buy nuclear-generated
electricity from their neighbors and cooperate in joint projects elsewhere. Public pressure has been against major nuclear plants in
the Netherlands due to its small size and the extreme pressures on
the land.

Of all the Nine, Italy has become the worst case environmentally. Since World War II its rapid industrialization has resulted in
almost irreversible degradation of its inland and coastal waters.
Until Stockholm and the airing of Antonioni's film "Red Desert"
there had been little overall concern for the environment. Clearly,
public and governmental concern has been heightened by the dioxin
(TCDD) cloud contamination of the entire town of Seveso near Milan,
where five pounds of gas has caused over $48 million in estimated
short- and long-term damage, killing almost all animal and plant
life plus at least six people outright. Even if there had been considerable interest, the Italian government system has been functioning
in such a way that the costs of any environmental protection program
would have been politically unacceptable in the struggle to get increased industrialization. The Christian Democrats and their coalitions have been shaky enough without having to justify allocations to
handle a problem created by industry and consumers. Just as the
Italian political culture is fragmented, so have been Italy's environmental protection "institutions."

Pollution abatement in Italy can only be described today as
utter confusion. With ten ministries holding various environmental
competences and no framework for environmental protection activities, all polluters have been claiming that no expenditures on abatement equipment and measures should be incurred until the national
government can promulgate hard and binding laws and priorities.
This has extended a "Catch-22" situation almost to the absurd. Provincial authorities use this state of affairs to propose illogical effluent and emissions standards and then enforce them in the mis-
placed belief that pollution can be prevented very quickly. It has
been estimated that $4 billion would be required immediately, plus
$200 million annually, to set up adequate water treatment facilities
and measures in order to bring the level of water pollution down to
that of the United Kingdom. The 1971-75 national five-year economic
plan placed priority on urban and tourist areas for water pollution
abatement actions as well as industrial air pollution abatement, but
no standards were set or means delineated. In 1971 the Italian

Senate set up a Steering Committee for Problems Relating to Ecology, which followed the Chamber of Deputies' establishment of its Commission on the Environment in 1969.

After the Stockholm Conference it became evident that this system would not work, and so an effort has been made to approach the problems in Italy in a more systematic way. Still, this was not a global approach, but sector by sector. By 1973 the Ministry of Scientific Research had responsibility for all studies of environmental pollution control in Italy, recapturing some of the inefficiently dispersed measures that had existed up to that time. The initial reaction had been one of throwing money in the name of high principles but not applying it in any logical manner. With time Italy's approach may be turned around to put things in their logical order. Granted, in such a situation there was nothing to delay or fight against following the 1973 oil crisis. As in most of the Nine, nuclear power was perceived as the panacea.

France has been the direct opposite of Italy with regard to institutionalizing environmental-issue responses; however, the French concern for the environment has not matched that of Denmark or the Netherlands. In typically French fashion, the issue remained under strict hierarchic control at the center. French environmental policy underwent four phases, starting with minimal protection from hazardous industry and ending with today's Ministry of the Quality of Life, which has a global approach in its functional responsibilities. In its previous form as the Ministry of the Protection of Nature and the Environment, it started to garner the various environment functions that were spread among nine other ministries. French logic dictated that these should be under one roof, and so the Ministry of the Quality of Life was created.

In France there has been almost a metaphysical notion of the state as the unified authority in society, a powerful symbolic value. Thus response to environmental problems necessarily stemmed from the government, which has been seen as the legitimate instrument of central power, apart from and almost in opposition to society itself. This centralization of the environmental bureaucracy means that it has been to a great extent isolated from parliamentary and external pressure group interference. This centralization has provided for concerted governmental action in the environmental sphere, allowing it initiative and the ability to intervene directly if it chooses to do so in a particular instance.

French policy stemmed from two general sets of regulations, the Law of December 1917 and Decree of April 1964, which cover dangerous and unhealthy premises, and the Charter of Environmental Hygiene of May 1963. In addition to this there have been numerous lois cadres, or framework laws, handling the various environmental

sectors, including noise. In their sixth economic plan the French
estimated that they needed a $1.5 billion investment in pollution con-
trol equipment and other measures over the life of that plan in order
to meet their policy objectives. The state portion ($300 million)
would in part be drawn from license and discharge fees paid by those
using the waterways for effluents. In French economic sense, this
has been a valid attempt to internalize the cost of using public goods.

Water has been the main problem, with only one-fifth of French
resources usable. The sixth plan attempts to improve on this. Notable in the French system have been the Agences de Bassin, six hy-
drographic basin agencies created in 1964 to administer water programs. These determine policies based on priority and the user,
using the pollueur-payeur, or pollutor pays, principle and taking
into account the various rivers' self-purification factors. Charges
have been levied on users by computing the pollutants discharged on
one normal day during the 30-day period of maximum activity. The
committees controlling the basin agencies have had a broad makeup
but have been effective for the most part. The one area in which they
have failed has been with respect to certain frontier areas, notably
along the Rhine. It has taken considerable external effort trans-
nationally and intergovernmentally to get the French to do anything
about the large volume of tailings dumped into the Rhine from their
potash industry. The volume has been so large that it requires
enormous land space to store one year's discharges (8 million metric
tons). Since the effluent fees are ridiculously low, it has paid the
French potash industry to dump its tailings into the Rhine rather
than pay land costs.

The French have clearly been concerned about the ability of
their rivers to cope with the enormous nuclear power program they
have proposed. This was their response to the energy crisis, and
it has incorporated environmental concerns into the process. Their
major concern has been the siting of nuclear plants. They have
pushed closed cooling loops with wet towers to save water, but the
fact remains that they have yet to address the nuclear-nonnuclear
question squarely. Coupled to this has been their concern with
energy conservation. In late 1974 a number of laws (some with
fines) were enacted, ranging from heating maximums for buildings
to speed limits to the creation of the Agence pour les économies
d'énergie. [42] Again the government deemed it necessary to intervene in the economy in order to maintain control, but not for environmental reasons in spite of the environmental good done by reduced energy consumption.

The Federal Republic of Germany has been possibly the most
impressive with respect to its contemporary environmental programs. It has had major environmental problems, but at the same

time has been acutely aware of them and thus has made comprehensive efforts to combat the degradation involved. Additionally, its
geographic position and its participation in the EC have given it
greater awareness of the international dimensions of environmental
protection. In 1970 the Willy Brandt government, having conferred
with environment experts from other nations, launched an all-
inclusive domestic program. That this step was taken must be seen
in light of the historical FRG situation, in which the postwar aim
was to rebuild as quickly as possible. Consequently industry has
gotten every advantage to facilitate this, and a residual pro-industry
attitude has remained. Generally, pollution abatement has not been
a politically sensitive subject, and the public has been unmoved by
the mounting dimensions of the problem. This indifference had its
roots in the general deference shown to the needs of industry. Concern for the environment has existed at the industrial and academic
levels, however, and also within the various governmental agencies;
but there has been no effective public pressure group pursuing efforts to impress politicians with the need for environmental protection. Nothing short of a major catastrophe, like the one involving
the chemical destruction of the entire Italian town of Seveso, could
get the German public to bring the whole of FRG ability and strength
to bear on the problem. Even where minor catastrophes have occurred, the reaction lasted only until the problem had been corrected.
This approach has also been true of the FRG reaction to the 1973
crisis.

Problematic to the FRG situation has been its federal structure. The federal government can only create "enabling" legislation.
Implementation of that legislation, an executive power, rests with
the 11 Länder, which zealously guard their autonomy. Also, the
varying climatic conditions and demographic situations across the
Federal Republic have meant that the environment has been perceived differently in each of the Land. This, coupled to the constitutional constraints, has not facilitated coordination of environmental protection measures. In spite of this, so far the FRG government has done an admirable job of coordination. It has had no environment ministry but has pulled together the federal supervisory
functions into the Ministry of the Interior. Some Länder have had
ministers of the environment, led by the Hessian example. Overall
coordination has occurred in the chancellor's office in the interministerial committee for Raumordnung, or urban and rural development.

Because of the type of structure set up for dealing with environmental issues in the Federal Republic of Germany, its federal
environmental program takes on great significance. It has been the
catalyst for all response and of necessity has been required to take

on comprehensive scope and some depth. Some 19 working groups
were involved in preparing the original report submitted to the
Bundestag. Opposition to the program came only from the Christian
Democratic coalition in the federal parliament. This was not merely
partisan opposition but a reflection of the lower priority that coalition
has had for federal intervention in this area. The program adopted
has had five main objectives: long-term environmental planning; enforcement of the "originator" principle (that is, pollueur-payeur);
achievement of umweltfreundlische (environmentally sound technology); introduction of environmental education; and effective international cooperation. [43] The government had hoped to cover damage
prevention and include all current as well as potential sources of
danger; but efforts to make whomever causes environmental damage
bear the costs of countermeasures have fallen mainly on the various
municipalities. It has been estimated that a $1 billion investment
over the next 15 years for waste disposal and $5 billion over the
next five for water pollution abatement would be required. Hesse
alone spent $1 billion on water pollution in the past 15 years and
$120 million annually for overall pollution abatement.

In spite of difficulties in coordinating environmental programs,
the West Germans have had considerable success in the activities
they have undertaken, more so than some of their neighbors. Exemplary among these has been their coal strip-mining program. The
lesser dependence of the Federal Republic of Germany on external
energy supplies has stemmed in part from its deposits of brown coal.
Nevertheless, reclamation efforts begin before any mining is allowed
to start. This involves detailed impact plans on resettlement of
homes and establishments, evacuation relocation, land restoration,
and postrestorative land-use planning. Thus mining operations have
been tailored to fit full restoration, social as well as physical. This
program has operated since 1948, and by 1974 over 33,000 acres had
been fruitfully used and restored. The cost of restoration to full
agricultural productivity has ranged from $3,500 to $4,500 an acre. [44]
Through this program the Federal Republic of Germany has achieved
the type of environmental benefits envisaged (but never achieved) in
U.S. urban-renewal-type programs, while getting needed energy
supplies.

As early as 1970 the FRG government stressed the need to reduce air pollution from auto exhausts. By 1972 it set standards for
gasoline lead content, in effect the first in the European Communities
to do so. This policy was the political brainchild of the Interior Minister, Hans-Dietrich Genscher, who used this issue to develop his
own political base independent of Brandt and to create a responsibility for lead content within his ministry. Immediately he ran into opposition from the Commission of the EC, which protested that this

action violated EC rules on free competition, since it changed the
comparative advantage for the engine industry right in the midst of
EC efforts to negotiate new nonpolluting engine designs with the industry. Furthermore, it placed the cart before the horse because
it came before exhaust standards as a whole could be determined.
In addition to the objections of the Commission, it would cost FRG
refiners more than $1 billion in investment to achieve the minister's
policy objectives.[45] The uncertainties involved generated considerable ill feelings. The 1973 oil crisis was used by industrial and EC
opponents to pressure the FRG government into changing the details
of implementation of the requirements, thereby nullifying the effect
until quality standards could be determined within the EC framework.
The target of this opposition, however, was not the environment but
infractions of EC competition rules.

In the energy-environment area, the major problem for the
Federal Republic of Germany has been ensuring sufficient water for
cooling waste heat. Water has generally been its largest environmental problem, and its rivers have been strained to the limit. Historically, water cooperatives have been used to allocate scarce water
resources on a local basis. For example, the purpose of these
genossenschaften (or verbund) has been to design and operate a generally efficient system of stream specialization and collective abatement measures so that maximum water use could be made. The
most notable have been those of the Ruhr river area, which in spite
of the Ruhr's 0.8:1 effluent discharge ratio has provided adequate
municipal as well as industrial supplies. The Rhine has been the
major problem, and in view of the number of major nuclear plants
planned along its path, drew considerable attention at the 1972 Interministerial Conference of the Rhine River States. This meeting set
a requirement that all future power plants would use closed cooling
systems.[46]

Constraints against nuclear power have grown since the 1973
crisis in the Federal Republic. Since the method of incorporating
environmental concerns generally precludes much public participation, the public has been taking to direct action to force environmental issues into the courts. In one instance, concerned citizens in
Whyl stormed and occupied a nuclear plant building site, pitching
tents and erecting temporary structures. This "sit-in" lasted almost a full year in 1975, with neighbors from some 21 other nearby
towns assisting in manning the site until the issue could be decided
in the courts. A stop-work order was issued, and the basic issues
of whether work could continue and whether Whyl could be eliminated
as a site were taken up by the court, an unusual procedure.[47]

In contrast, in the Markelsheim case in France, involving a
sit-in on a hazardous-chemical producing plant site, which included

transnational participation by concerned West German neighbors, the issues were handled politically. The basic issue of whether or not to have the plant was twisted by the French government into a question of how much compensation was due for potential degradation. In the course of this direct action protest the municipal government changed, the Franco-German border was closed by the gendarmes (an action expressly forbidden by the EC treaties), and the French national government pressured the local citizenry instead of vice versa.

These two cases were exemplary of the changing public moods, especially as they relate to nuclear power. The FRG government has felt that specific decisions not to allow construction of particular plants would not bar others from being built but would make industrial and governmental authorities take environmental and citizens' concerns into account. In the Federal Republic of Germany the environmental movement has been growing, and pressure groups, once fragmented and locally oriented, have been seeking common ground and an umbrella organization. If anything, the 1973 crisis created greater environmental awareness in the Federal Republic of Germany and no backlash against the environment.

The United Kingdom has long had concern for the environment and rampant industrial degradation, side by side. Its contemporary efforts have stemmed from the reports of the Royal Commission on Environmental Pollution, an autonomous body advising the government. The commission determined that population per se was not the main issue facing the United Kingdom but rather the concentrations in certain cities and geographic areas. The first report dealt with this as well as with governmental organization, and the second went on to deal with pollution from industrialization. The third dealt with coastal waters, and the fourth reviewed all efforts to that date, focusing on the failure to clean up certain industrial areas.[48] These set the tone in which governmental efforts were directed and policies were debated.

The environment has remained a peripheral issue in the United Kingdom, however. It took the 1967 wreck of the Torrey Canyon for the environment to shoot its way onto the government's agenda. The Heath government created the first national cabinet-level ministry dealing with environmental issues, the Department of the Environment, which brought under its aegis housing, transportation, and public works as well as traditional environmental functions. Nevertheless, the British dilemma remains. Even though the United Kingdom has been ahead of most countries in environmental awareness and response to degradation, the issue of environmental quality never garners ideological or electoral predominance.

A major problem has been the need to advance and redevelop the decaying U.K. industrial system. Thus the hazards of growth have been suppressed in the debate, and a system of bureaucratic review has kept the issue from becoming politicized over and over again, in spite of the nonhomogeneity of British society. Environmental issues have been deliberately placed on the periphery by the political system. This has stifled public participation.

Environmentalists have seen three conditions exacerbating this suppression: the paternalism of the civil servants dominating the governmental departments; local government weakness and citizen apathy because of the mismatch of local authority structures to the provision of the services the public wants most; and discontent with the two primary parties. Coupled to this have been restrictions on access, since many environmental bodies have not been considered legitimate by public officials. The structure of access at the national level has meant that business groups have had great influence through the Confederation of British Industries. Until the myriad environmental groups have created a similar umbrella organization that is moderate in nature, it is unlikely that environmentalists will lose the label of troublemakers and become legitimate in official eyes.[49]

The United Kingdom's own energy crunch came before the 1973 oil crisis and pushed Britain into a multiple strategy to ensure needed supplies. In addition to the quest for newer-generation nuclear systems, a major push for North Sea oil and gas was made. The tradeoffs between energy and the environment were fully investigated in the collectivist manner described above. The Committee on the Environment established by the Oil Development Council for Scotland found that local as well as central government provisions were grossly inadequate for protecting the environment while conducting oil operations. It pushed for a global approach to the problems, which eventually resulted in communications intended to educate all concerned and liability insurance for operators.[50] All this transpired while the 1973 events were occurring.

On the nuclear side, for both economic and environmental reasons, efforts were made to put off and stop U.K. purchases of LWR technology from the United States. Environmentalists played no major role in either instance. Furthermore, with environmental policy focusing on urbanization, the highly professional civil service did not deem it necessary to react to the 1973 crisis in any anti-environmental way, since it was widely perceived that all environmental concerns were being taken into account. It has been due to the professionalization and centralization of the British government that environmental issues have seen significant response and have been incorporated into long-range planning in the United Kingdom.

In sum, the Nine have developed unitary constitutional institutions to deal with environment, with the exception of the Federal Republic of Germany. In all cases, however, the central governments retain supervisory control over environmental and energy matters. In the Federal Republic of Germany and in Denmark, local authorities have had the preponderance of power to deal with these issues. In the others, the preponderance has rested with the central authorities and in some cases has been delegated to a great extent to subnational regional bodies. Over time in each of the Nine, there has been a greater effort to approach environmental issues with a global view and to bring this into the policy-making process so that environmental costs can be properly internalized. As a result, reactions to the 1973 oil crisis were not directed heavily against the environment but rather at the true causes of that crisis and toward solutions that would consider all factors. In many respects the various reactions to the crisis by the Nine may have brought greater environmental benefits because they perceived the crisis in terms of scarce resources and the need to cut back consumption rather than in terms of a need to find new abundances for greater consumption.

Policies at the Center: Brussels

In marked contrast to energy policies and policy making at the EC center, until late 1975 environmental policy had been created with much more success. Whereas energy policies predated the EC, environmental policy was its own creation and involved all nine members, not just the Six at first and then the three new members at a critical juncture (the energy crisis). None of the treaties have had anything explicit to say about any Community environmental programs; but all three have referred to taking actions necessary to contribute to continued growth and the raising of living standards. Specific treaty articles have allowed the Council of Ministers, acting unanimously, to take any action necessary to harmonize laws and practices in the EC so that distortions of trade are avoided and the maintenance of a common market is achieved. All environmental activities in the European Communities have originated implicitly from these ideas and rules.

Again, it was external activities that triggered a response at the EC level. Following the European Conservation Year and in the face of the preparations for Stockholm, Commissioner Altiero Spinelli decided that it was necessary to have a Community approach to environmental issues so that the EC could deal with the implications of possible coherent national programs and the impact these would have on the functioning of the internal market. He set up within

the Industry Directorate-General of the Commission a section on environmental matters that, with the enlargement of the EC to nine
members in 1973, became the Environment and Consumer Protection Service (ECPS), an autonomous department. It was not given
the status of a directorate-general, in order that the environment
as an issue would not get too much priority. The commissioners as
a collegial body did not want the environment to have a higher level
of importance than any directorate-general. To keep jealousies
among the directorates-general to a minimum, a "service" was
created.

Although this game of bureaucratic politics was played to diminish the power of environmental policy making within the EC, the
opposite has occurred. Because it is not a directorate-general, the
ECPS has been brought into each department's policy-planning process and cannot be excluded on questions involving actual or potential environmental impact. Also, the personality of the head of
ECPS has played an important role. Michel Carpentier has been
husbanding EC environmental policy efforts from the start and has
been called "Monsieur l'environnement" in many European circles.
He has applied himself with considerable insight and some forceful-
ness to almost all environmental issues. Gallic logic and style have
marked his approach. Because he has been willing to nurture his
contacts with all the environmental policy makers of the Nine and do
his homework in a timely fashion, he has been one of the best Eurocrats in the Communities and has been able to foster the desired
environmental policies.

This has not meant that the ECPS has always gotten what it
wanted when it wanted it. On two significant occasions, the ECPS
was blocked. It was considered by some to be a fly in the ointment.
The Energy Directorate-General set the stage for bureaucratic conflict following its introduction of the "Guidelines and priority actions
under the Community energy policy" in response to Commissioner
Henri Simonet's explicit concern over what might happen in any energy crunch. These guidelines referred to the impact of power-
plant environmental damage and had gone through the process of
ECPS staff input. When the 1973 oil crisis hit a few months later,
the Nuclear Directorate within the Energy Directorate-General
started its bureaucratic push for nuclearization. At the commissioners' cabinet meeting on this latter proposal, it was maintained
by the Energy Directorate-General that nuclear energy would do no
harm to the environment. When pushed in questioning on the environmental impact issue by the cabinet of the commissioner responsible
for environment, the Energy Directorate-General insisted that the
environment people did not know what they were talking about. Yet,
with all its responsibility for knowing about power stations, the

Energy Directorate-General seemed to know nothing itself by stating there was no harm involved. Finally the escalating costs of nuclear power stopped the EC Commission proposals in their tracks.

In the second case, the ECPS sought external research on the approaches other nations outside the EC were using in their fight against pollution. Included in this were questions about how other industrial countries determined particular effluent and emission standards, whether ambient condition approaches were suitable, how cultural and political factors bore down on environmental problems, and so on. A U.S. research firm was to get the grant, but one commissioner felt that it should go to a European university with which he still had links, and blocked it. Finally it went through as desired, when resubmitted in terms of the commission's "written procedure." This particular study subsequently proved important to continuing EC work on the environment, since it permitted more pragmatic and far-reaching action proposals to be prepared.

With this view of the EC process in mind, it should be noted that there has been an ongoing environmental program, based on harmonization of economic activities rather than on any altruistic concern. The first program was proposed in 1971 and finally adopted in 1973. A second program, which was passed in 1975, supplements the first. The first communication stated the general EC position, taking into account the desire for continuous improvement of the conditions of life and employment of the populace, and it focused on distortion in trade and competition and the need for EC action because pollution did not respect frontiers. The formal program was presented in 1972 after the statement on principles had been accepted, and in 1973 the details of a two-year action program were approved. These laid out seven priority lines of action: (1) prevention, reduction, and elimination of the harmful effects of pollution; (2) sound management of natural resources; (3) protection of the balance of nature; (4) protection of the biosphere; (5) application of quality-of-life requirements to development in the EC; (6) location of development to reduce urban concentration; and (7) cooperation with third nations to find common solutions to environmental problems. Eleven principles were laid out, and three priority groups were chosen for EC action: reduction and prevention of pollution, improvement of the environment and quality of life, and EC activities in other international organizations. The purpose of the program was to establish a common base for evaluating the facts, then establish a list of pollutants, and finally choose the most serious areas to work on in particular priorities. The second program is an extension of this.[51]

Although the program has been defensive in nature, its conception includes a necessary broad sweep, and it has been moderately well staffed. In recent years there has been a shift toward encouraging environmental impact assessment, so that all planning decisions can properly take environmental concerns into account. Additionally, conservation of resources has received new emphasis. The second program has also drawn attention to the global aspects of environmental policies. Most importantly, there has been more emphasis on the relationship between energy production and the environment. In 1974 a preliminary report on the pollution problems stemming from energy use was presented. It stressed widespread use of wet cooling towers and closed circuits, development of dry cooling towers, desulphurization programs, and nitrogen oxide research and monitoring.[52]

When all has been said and done, one can point to the success of the European Communities in being able to hammer out a general overarching environmental policy in the face of diverse national policy structures dealing with the issues as well as differing perceptions among the Nine, even within certain of the member states. Upon occasions the Dutch have called "reservations" on particular EC environmental policy actions, not to disagree, but by doing so to make the less-concerned neighbors pay more than lip service to the policy proposals. Even a number of specific action policies have been agreed upon, especially in the realm of water quality.

The second EC environmental program almost foundered on the British reservation in 1975 with regard to ECPS championing of effluent and emission point standards. The U.K. government has desired to maintain its ambient-conditions approach to pollution control. Anthony Crosland, as U.K. Minister of the Environment, stated a U.K. belief that overly rigid harmonization would only create economic distortions of the kind the European Communities were trying to eliminate. For the British to be required to make every industry conform to identical standards wherever located without taking into account local circumstances would in effect cause the overnight remaking of the British industrial structure.

Clearly implied was the cost necessary to achieve this aspect of the EC program, but the argument was placed in the context of a member state being able to choose its own means of effecting a general EC policy and not be locked into a detailed limiting policy. One U.K.-seconded ECPS official has felt that it would be politically difficult to allow any member state to set a policy differing too greatly from any other member's policy. Differences in comparative advantage would accrue to the one allowed to pollute more. Besides, it was felt that "any sort of patchwork policy--with one type here, another there--would be hellish to administer." Even though this important portion of the EC program has not yet been fully implemented, the momentum of the program has not been significantly slowed.

Environment as an End in Itself

If one accepts the environment and its effect on the quality of
life as an end in itself, then it must be recognized that environmental policy efforts in the Nine have been means to that end. Throughout the analysis, cost factors and the political decisions regarding
economic variables have come to the forefront, with good reason.
All the national economies of the Nine have been mixed private- and
public sector capital markets, even though considerable socialist
presence and concern exists in the policy making in these countries.
The crux has been, and continues to be, how best can the activities
and events previously treated as external be internalized into the
economic policy process. This has clearly been the thrust of the
political process in the Nine. Even EC policy making has followed
this thrust because of the manner in which EC treaties have put
these concerns forth.

Environment as an end has been reflected in the fact that environmental policy making has entered virtually every other area of
policy making in the EC process and throughout the Nine. In spite
of policy disagreements, no one in the Nine has wanted the "silent
spring" to come to Western Europe. With the propensity for increased regional planning in the Nine, the EC environmental program has played an important catalytic role linking many diverse
objectives with a single purpose--the improvement of the setting,
the quality of life, and the surrounding living conditions of the EC
populace.

CONCLUSIONS

What all this shows is that energy and environmental issues
have remained within the domain of the Nine's governments and the
EC Eurocrats. The enlargement of the European Communities of
the Six to that of the Nine made policy prospects in these two areas
even more difficult. The Six were in basic agreement on environmental issues and were pursuing parallel paths in energy affairs.
Environmental policy suffered to some extent because of the coupling
of enlargement to the energy crisis.

The energy crisis in the Nine also allowed industrial and other
lobbies to attack environmental programs, and lobbying took place
in every capital. Many industries whose cost margins were at stake
saw the opportunity to have their complaints heard. In most cases
this opportunity was seized but resulted only in lobbying. No real
setbacks in any environmental sector resulted from this because of
the preponderance of governmental and bureaucratic control over the

issues. The only positive results came through the price increase, which cut back consumption and heightened the awareness of scarcity of resources.

Out of the crisis also came the hastening of an umbrella public pressure group for environmental matters. The formation of the Bureau Européen de l'Environnement/European Environment Bureau (BEE) in Brussels in 1975 created an effective organization that will assist this environmental movement greatly through its informational and advisory functions. The International Union for the Conservation of Nature (IUCN) has considerable influence through its Environmental Law Centre in Bonn, but runs into problems of effectiveness in national and EC advocacy roles. The BEE has already gained legitimate access to the ECPS and has established a credible voice for the public interest. Additionally, the emergence of a focused European debate in the periodical Forum E (put out by the Junge Europaische Föderalisten, a youth federalist group) on nuclear energy; of public "hearings" by Agenor, a liberal left review; and of special information groups that have dealt with the subject, such as Press-Environnement in Paris and EuroEnvironment in Brussels, has contributed to greater public knowledge and awareness, which many Europeans feel have been lacking until recently. In turn this will lead to more public pressure and greater interest-group effort in this area.

The continuing energy crisis is, of itself, the environmental crisis. Prosperity and affluence have been seen as the great polluter; yet the way in which energy is used in any industrial society is what causes the crisis, rather than the gross amount consumed. If the industrialized nations of Western Europe continue to rely on rapid expansion of highly centralized supertechnologies to give them needed energy, especially electricity, it can be anticipated that the capital costs of such systems will be prohibitive--over 100 times greater than those of traditional direct-fuel technologies. Furthermore, approximately half the energy produced will never reach the consumer because of its loss in elaborate stages of electricity generation and transmission, wasting as much as 70 percent of the fuel used to generate the electricity.

The rational objective is to get maximum energy utilization for the least pollution generated. This, however, can only be achieved through an end-use strategy, matching renewable energy resources in scale and quality to particular end uses. What are thought of in generally esoteric terms, including solar, wind-hydraulic, and organic conversion energy systems, may be the only saving options of the Nine. This strategy uses transitional hydrocarbon fuels to move from the present-day traditionally centralized energy economy to a decentralized end-use energy economy.

What ought to hasten this choice should be the estimated $1 trillion needed during the coming decade to develop and maintain the current energy systems and plans of the Nine. Since this burden is not temporary, considerable potential exists for political backlash against the Eurocrats who jockey energy policy in the EC.

The 1973 energy crisis made people think hard about how they could best obtain cheap but stable supplies; but since there were few real shortages then, Western Europeans let the issue slip from their grasp, back into the graveyard of nonfunctioning EC policies.

In sum, the minor assaults made on environmental policy in the Nine and at Brussels following the 1973 oil crisis have not been able to deflect or greatly slow down the basic EC programs for protecting the environment. True, the reaction in Europe was much more positive than in the United States. It was not so altruistic for environmental concerns, but rather conceived out of the necessity of handling the political and economic problems of the energy crisis.

Both energy and the environment point to the highly pluralistic nature of the EC system and to the difficulties in coordinating the issues between these two areas and among nine differing sociopolitical economic systems. The EC context has meant that the Nine must come away from bargaining in that framework with concrete results that can be carried to their publics to show that something has been done. A very large amount of time and consultation goes into the engrenage of the EC policy-making process. Thus considerable time has had to be given to evolving legislation to meet the varying needs of the member states in the areas of energy and the environment. The three principles of security, economy, and environment have always involved tradeoffs that policy makers must face, and they require political decisions. The era of cheap and secure sources in advanced industrialized democracies has vanished and will not return until the end-use strategy of a fusion-hydrogen-solar economy arrives in the distant future.

NOTES

1. E. F. Murphy, Governing Nature (Chicago: Quadrangle, 1967), pp. 1-8.

2. General statements of EC energy policy are found in Energy and Europe (Brussels: Commission of the EC--Press & Information, 1972) and in later restatements with amendments, such as "The European Community and the energy problem," European Documentation (Commission of the EC) 75, no. 2.

3. This struggle is analyzed in Harald H. Bungarten and Josef Fullenbach, International Dimensions of Environmental Problems in

Europe (Bonn: Forschunginstitut der Deutschen Gesellschaft für Auswärtige Politik, forthcoming); this is an English translation of the German title.

4. D. H. Meadows et al., The Limits to Growth (New York: Universe Books, 1972).

5. Selected Figures: Energy in the Community (Brussels: Commission of the EC--Eurostat, 1973); John Bradbeer, "Energy in the EEC," European Studies (London) 18 (1974). See also Prospects of primary energy demand in the Community (1975-1980-1985) (Luxembourg: Commission of the EC--Office of Official Publications of the EC, 1972); Financing of the energy policy by the Community, COM(75)245 final (Commission of the EC, June 11, 1975); Energy and Europe, op. cit.; Europe + Energy (Luxembourg: ECSC High Authority--Spokesman & ECIS, 1967).

6. See "Nuclear Energy: The Dragon Is Dead, Long Live the Dragon?" European Report 294 (January 21, 1976).

7. This has been debated in a number of forums, including U.S. Atomic Energy Commission, An Assessment of Nuclear Risks in U.S. Commercial Power Plants, WASH-1400 (the Rasmussen Report) (Washington, D.C.: Government Printing Office, 1974), which is one of the best known on the probability and causes of system failures. This report receives a balanced critique in K. H. Hohenemser, "The Failsafe Risk," Environment 17, no. 1 (January-February 1975). The Colgate Hypothesis and its implications were put forward in August 1974 in an unpublished geophysics paper by Sterling Colgate; Colgate put forth the Krakatoa effect in Nature, August 1973; its implications for nuclear energy systems are treated in Kevin P. Shea, "An Explosive Reactor Possibility," Environment 18, no. 1 (January-February 1976): 6-11, and in Sheldon Novick, "A New Dimension of Nuclear Hazard," Environment 18, no. 1 (January-February 1976). An industry-oriented appraisal of the problems is found in T. Alexander, "The Big Blowup over Nuclear Blowdowns," Fortune, May 1973. The British proponents of the advanced gas-cooled reactor (AGR) maintain that no accident releasing major amounts of radioactivity could occur with this design. The Germans remain skeptical and continue to test reactors for failure dynamics; see W. Baier, "Battelle Institute investigates reactor pressure chambers," The German Tribune, December 21, 1975.

8. D. C. Leslie, "Nuclear Energy as an Effective Competitor" (Paper presented to the Institute of Petroleum summer meeting, London, 1973), which compares engineering designs and the relative costs of reactors. See also M. Grenon, "Nuclear Energy as an Alternative to Imported OPEC Oil" (Paper presented to the Colloquium on Energy Policy Planning in the EC, John F. Kennedy Institute, spring 1974), which compares the economics of differing systems, including fueling.

9. Policy data from Federal Republic of Germany, Federal Minister of Economics, First Revision of the Energy Policy Programme for the F.R.G.--November 1974 (Bonn: Ministry of Economics, 1974); J. Pagès, rapporteur, "Les Problèmes de l'énergie en France à moyen et long terme," Conseil Economique et Social Francais, July 3, 1974; "Nuclear Energy," Irish Independent, December 1975; "Fact Sheet--Energy in Denmark" (unofficial translation), Danish Ministry of Foreign Affairs (preliminary prepublication version, 1975); for the United Kingdom see "Nuclear Energy: The Dragon Is Dead"; Leslie, op. cit.; and Grenon, op. cit.

10. Strohm, "Billiger Atomstrom?" Forum E 2 (February 1975); B. Salchow, Nuclear power plant from the Federal Republic," The German Tribune, October 19, 1975; "Finanzierungslucken in Energieprogramm," Frankfurter Allegemeine Zeitung, December 3, 1974; "Vier Kernkraftwerblocke in Biblisgeplant," Die Zeit, April 16, 1975.

11. E. J. Sternglass at the Agenor hearings in Brussels, November 11, 1975; "Nuclear Energy: EEC's policy heavily criticised," European Report 277 (November 13, 1975).

12. See I. Fells criticism in the Agenor hearings. See also electrical sector data from Situation and Prospects, op. cit.; cost data from NEA/IEA Working Group, "Uranium Resources, Production & Demand" (preliminary unofficial 1976 report). CEC estimates are lower, at $216-45 billion; see Main foci of a policy for the development of energy resources in the Community and within the larger framework of international cooperation, COM(75)310 (Commission of the EC, June 11, 1975).

13. "Uranium: EEC enriched uranium imports in 1974," European Report 267 (October 8, 1975).

14. "Uranium: US enrichment price," European Report 243 (November 28, 1975), with estimates of $60-75/usw US commercial and governmental, $70/usw EURODIF, and $100/usw URENCO; see also European Report 252 (August 30, 1975) and "Uranium: Europe will be more than 50% self-sufficient by 1985," European Report 292 (January 14, 1976).

15. Uranium enrichment technology is compared in F. A. M. Alting von Geusau, ed., Energy in the European Communities (Leyden: Sijthoff, 1975), Appendix 2; data on EURODIF and URENCO is found in M. Grenon, "Nuclear Energy," in Alting von Geusau, op. cit., Chapter 6; system costs are projected from the data supplied.

16. Derived from Grenon, "Nuclear Energy"; and from "Research: Pause for thought on Jet site," European Report 305 (Februaty 26, 1976).

17. A thorough treatment of this is given in Roger Williams, European Technology (London: Croom Helm, 1973), pp. 78-88.

18. Data from "The European Community and the energy problem," op. cit.; "Energy in the EEC," op. cit.; World Energy Conference 1974 data cited in "Coal: still dethroned," The Economist 258, no. 6917 (March 20, 1976).

19. D. H. Broadbent, "Prospects for Coal" (Paper presented to the Institute of Petroleum summer meeting, London, 1973).

20. R. L. Gordon, The Evolution of Energy Policy in Western Europe: The Reluctant Retreat from Coal (New York: Praeger, 1970); "And now the coal mountain!" The German Tribune 712 (November 30, 1975); "Government plans to stockpile anthracite," The German Tribune 715 (December 21, 1975); Pol Carrewyn, "The Nine's Energy Policy after Two Years of Oil Crisis," European Report 270 (October 18, 1975).

21. Data and information derived from: "Energie: la Communauté dans le grand jeu mondial," Les Entreprises et le Marché Commun (Bruxelles: Europolitique, 1974), vol. 1, p. 23; Federal Republic of Germany, Federal Minister of Economics, First Revision of the Energy Policy Programme for the F.R.G.--November 1974 (Bonn: Ministry of Economics, 1974); Pagès, op. cit., and "Coal Technology: five agreements signed in IEA," European Report 280 (November 22, 1975).

22. Coal is best treated in Gordon, op. cit.; also summarized in R. Prodi and A. Clo, "The Oil Crisis: In Perspective--Europe," Daedalus 104, no. 4 (Fall 1975); the prospects for coal are treated in Schmitt, "Coal as a Substitute," in Alting von Geusau, op. cit., Chapter 5.

23. "The EC and the energy problem," op. cit.; P. R. Odell, "Indigenous Oil & Gas and Western Europe's Energy Policy Options," Energy Policy 1, no. 1 (June 1973); restatement of these data in Odell, "Towards Self-Sufficiency based on Indigenous Oil and Gas," in Alting von Geusau, op. cit., Chapter 4; see also P. F. Corbett, "Natural Gas--Growth of a World Market" (Paper presented to the Institute of Petroleum summer meeting, London, 1973).

24. Federal Republic of Germany, Federal Minister of Economics, op. cit.; "Teheran natural gas agreement," The German Tribune 710 (November 16, 1975); "Gas Agreement with Teheran," The German Tribune 713 (December 7, 1975).

25. Data from Corbett, op. cit.

26. See, for example, R. Vernon, ed., "The Oil Crisis: In Perspective," Daedalus 104, no. 4 (Fall 1975); Horst Mendershausen, Coping with the Oil Crisis: French and German Experiences (Baltimore: Johns Hopkins University Press--RFF, 1976); Alting von Geusau, op. cit.; Marc Ippolito, Contribution a l'étude du problème énergétique Communautaire (Paris: Librarie Générale du Droit et Jurisprudence, 1969); Danielle Blondel-Spinelli, L'Energie dans

l'Europe des Six (Paris: Cujas, 1966); Wolfgang Hager, Erdöl und Internationale Politik (Munich: R. Piper Verlag--DGAP, 1975); J. E. Hartshorn, Politics and World Oil Economics: An Account of the International Oil Industry (New York: Praeger, 1967); Neil Jacoby, Multinational Oil: A Study in Industrial Dynamics (New York: Macmillan, 1974); Z. Mikdashi, The Community of Oil Importing Countries (London: Allen & Unwin, 1972); M. Adelman, The World Petroleum Market (Baltimore: Johns Hopkins University Press, 1972).

27. Odell, op. cit.

28. Daniel Yergin, "Britain Drills--and Prays," New York Times Magazine, November 2, 1975; W. Günthardt, "Operation North Sea," Swiss Review of World Affairs 25, no. 10 (January 1976).

29. Derived from Yergin, op. cit.; House of Commons, Committee of Public Accounts, First Report (North Sea Oil & Gas), Session 1972-73 (London: Her Majesty's Stationery Office, 1973); U.S. Department of Energy, "Oil from the UK Continental Shelf," Fact Sheet N.1 (June 1975); U.K. Department of Energy, Development of the Oil and Gas Resources of the UK (London: Her Majesty's Stationery Office, 1975); Eric Varley, "The Place of N. Sea Oil in the UK Energy Scene," Wall Street Journal, May 5, 1975; Eric Varley, "British Secretary of State for Energy Outlines Basic Governmental Policy for Oil," Offshore, May 1975; "Financial Times Survey: Offshore Exploration," Financial Times (London), April 23, 1975; "For the Record," British Record (New York) 6 (April 12, 1975).

30. For a more detailed treatment, see Robert A. Black, Jr., "Plus ca change, plus c'est la meme chose: Nine governments in search of a Common Energy Policy," in Policy-Making in the European Communities, ed. Helen Wallace, William Wallace, and Carole Webb (London: John Wiley, 1977), Chapter 7.

31. See Energy and Europe, op. cit.; Bradbeer, op. cit.; "The European Community and the energy problem," op. cit.; Problems, resources, and necessary progress in Community energy policy, SEC(73)1481 final (Commission of the EC, April 19, 1973); Towards a new energy policy strategy for the European Community, Com(74)550 final/2 (Commission of the EC, June 26, 1974).

32. G. Leach and M. Slesser, "Energy Budgets," Energy Policy 2, no. 3 (September 1974).

33. Programmes of research and development actions in the field of energy, Com(74)2150 final (Brussels, January 8, 1975); Energy for Europe: research and development, SEC(74)2592 final (Brussels, July 17, 1974).

34. G. Hartkopf, "Environmental protection and safeguarding energy supplies have equal priority" (Statement before NATO Committee on Challenges to Modern Society [CCMS], April 8, 1975).

35. Alfred North Whitehead, Science and the Modern World (New York: Free Press, 1925), p. 54, as cited in W. A. Peterman, "Nature: A Democracy of Trees," Environment 18, no. 7 (September 1976).

36. Letter to Franco M. Malfatti from Sicco Mansholt, February 9, 1972.

37. Note to Franco M. Malfatti from Raymond Barre, June 9, 1972.

38. D. Harris, "Comments on the Strategy and Tactics of the Environmental Battle," in Vers une politique Communautaire de l'environnement/Towards a Community Policy on the Environment, ed. I. B. F. Kormoss (Bruges: de Tempel, 1975), pp. 265-79.

39. "Uranium: EEC eyes US anti-trust probe," European Report 351 (September 4, 1976); "Uranium: EEC, US anti-trust chiefs in private talks," European Report 359 (October 2, 1976); "Uranium: Westinghouse enters anti-trust fray," European Report 364 (October 20, 1976).

40. "L'environnement, problème Communautaire," Documentation européenne (Luxembourg: Commission of the EC--OOPEC, 1972).

41. The information here is derived from Joanne S. Wyman, "Environment Politics in Denmark: Conflict and Cooperation in Policy-Making" (Paper presented at the Northeastern Political Science Association, Saratoga Springs, N.Y., November 7-9, 1974).

42. See "Localisation des centrales nucléaires" and "Agence pour les économies d'énergie" (Ministère de l'Industrie et de la Recherche, 1974).

43. A programme for the protection of the human environment adopted by the Government of the Federal Republic of Germany (Bonn: Bundesinnenministerium, 1971).

44. M. Getler, "W. Germany Sets Pace in Reclaiming Strip-Mined Land," Washington Post, December 4, 1975; G. E. Dials and E. C. Moore, "The Cost of Coal: We Can Afford to Do Better," Appalachia 8, no. 2 (October-November 1974); E. A. Nephew, "Healing Wounds," Environment 14, no. 1 (January-February 1972).

45. "Germany: Jumping the Gun on Lead in Gasoline," Business Week, January 8, 1972; The Bulletin (FRG Press and Information Office) 9, no. 1 (December 10, 1974), archive supplement.

46. Allen V. Kneese, "Water Quality Management in the Ruhr Area," in Controlling Pollution: The Economics of a Cleaner America, ed. Marshall I. Goldman (Englewood Cliffs: Prentice-Hall, 1967), pp. 109-29; Harald H. Bungarten, "Transnational Problems of the Rhine River Basin" (Working paper presented to the International Studies Association, Toronto, February 25-29, 1976).

47. David Mutch, "Town protest halts German nuclear plant," Christian Science Monitor, August 6, 1975.

48. Reports of the Royal Commission on Environmental Pollution (London: Her Majesty's Stationery Office, 1971-74).

49. See Cynthia H. Enloe, The Politics of Pollution in Comparative Perspective (New York: David McKay, 1975), Chapter 8, for a detailed study of the British case from which this analysis is derived.

50. Oil Development Council for Scotland, Committee on the Environment, North Sea Oil and the Environment (London: Her Majesty's Stationery Office, 1974); North Sea Oil and the Environment--Pollution: An assessment of the risks and action to deal with incidents (London: Scottis Office, 1975).

51. Première communication de la Commission sur la politique de la Communauté en matière d'environnement, SEC(71)2616 final (Commission of the EC, July 22, 1971); A European Communities' programme concerning the environment, III/337/72-E (Commission of the EC, 1972); Programme of environmental action of the European Communities--Part II, Com(73)530 final C (Commission of the EC, April 10, 1973); "Environment programme," Bulletin of the EC (June 1976) Supplement; Initial reflections on the second action programme of the European Communities on the environment, COM(75)289 final (Commission of the EC, June 17, 1975).

52. Preliminary report on the problems of pollution and nuisances originating from energy production, SEC(74)1150 final (Commission of the EC, April 3, 1974); "Rapport sur le rapport préliminaire de la Commission . . . concernant les problèmes de pollution et de nuisances--et sur le projet de résolution du Conseil sur l'énergie et l'environnement," Documents de Séance 1974-75 320/74 (European Parliament, November 5, 1974).

7

JAPAN
Margaret A. McKean

When the October War broke out in the Middle East in 1973, followed by the Arab oil embargo to "unfriendly" nations and by OPEC price increases for exports of crude oil, it was widely predicted that Japan would be the most seriously affected among the industrialized nations. Japan is the largest importer of oil in the world, in terms of the percentage of annual oil needs that must come from imports, and is also the most dependent on oil, as opposed to other fuels, for its energy supply. Japan imported about 250 million kiloliters of oil annually, constituting 99.7 percent of its oil needs, and oil-derived energy provided for 78 percent of Japan's annual energy needs. Furthermore, 77.6 percent of Japan's oil imports came from the Middle East.[1]

In addition to the dubious honor of being the most oil-dependent industrial nation, Japan is also holder of several world records for pollution and environmental damage. Not only is its annual consumption of energy (and therefore presumably also of pollution output) per unit of area the highest in the world, but Japan also has the largest number of persons afflicted with pollution-related diseases. Japan's GNP per unit of land was four times that of the United States in 1970, and Japan's GNP per unit of level land was 12 times that of the United States. Its concentrations of industrial activities, oil consumption, and overall energy consumption are similar.[2] The numbers of victims of pollution disease are continually on the increase. By September 1975 there were 871 official victims, including 134 dead, of mercury poisoning in Kumamoto and Kagoshima Prefectures; 568 victims, including 28 dead, of mercury poisoning in Niigata Prefecture; 225 victims, including 100 dead, of cadmium poisoning in Toyama Prefecture; 191 victims, including 24 dead, of hexavalent chromium poisoning; and over 2,700 mercury poisoning

patients who were still awaiting final certification as victims. With
the rapid increase in the number of areas designated as critical air
pollution zones, there were over 30,000 official air pollution victims.[3]

The severity of these pollution problems, all concentrated and
thus highly visible in such a small country, eventually led to the
proliferation of environmental and consumer groups that turned pollution into an issue of national concern. In comparison to environmental groups in other industrialized nations, the Japanese movement appears to be fragmented and preoccupied with local mani-
festations of pollution rather than with legislation or lobbying at the
national level. Nonetheless, in Japan, where the conservative
Liberal Democratic Party (LDP) has maintained a substantial majority of seats in both houses of the Diet since 1955, the rise of so
many groups that are learning to articulate their complaints and
demands is unsettling. Although these citizens' groups have not
brought much direct pressure to bear upon the national government,
they have given the opposition parties a new lease on life by contributing to the rapid growth in the number of local governments that
are now dominated by the leftist parties.[4]

The new visibility of the environmental movement and the
possibility of a coalition among leftist parties, along with the fact
that the pollution problems are so severe that even those who are
dependent on the support of industry have finally grown alarmed
about them, have led the conservative party to produce an impressive array of antipollution legislation since 1967. Upon examination
many of the laws turn out to be quite toothless. They often lack
severe penalties for violations or delegate the actual calculation of
enforceable standards to agencies that have since delayed taking
action.[5] Nonetheless, this cluster of new laws includes the first
law (of any nation) that defines the act of pollution as a crime and a
set of automobile emissions standards that is even stricter than the
Muskie Clean Air Amendments of the United States. The oil crisis
of late 1973 created a great apprehension that the industrial pressure groups that had lobbied earlier to water down these laws would
now demand the suspension of enforcement and the modification and
delay of new standards. Presumably industry would argue that the
energy crisis had converted antipollution investment, long justified
by environmentalists and the opposition parties as necessary for
human survival, into a luxurious indulgence.

However, this widely predicted confrontation between business
pressure groups and environmentalists has actually been very re-
strained in Japan, despite the fact that the extreme vulnerability of
Japan to the oil crisis gave industry an opportunity to make a persuasive case for abandoning or softening enforcement of antipollution

regulations. Budgetary allotments for antipollution research and
technology continued to rise faster than other budget items in spite
of the oil crisis, and expenditures on pollution prevention equipment
began to subsume large portions of the operating budgets of some of
the major polluting industries.[6]

In a thorough survey of Japanese news coverage since the oil
crisis, I was able to discover only two obvious cases in which industry had successfully lobbied for a rollback of specific environmental regulations, though in neither case was the oil crisis itself
the major excuse used to justify the rollback. The real danger of an
environmental rollback appears to be in the choices Japan will make
about the diversification of energy supplies and the extent to which
environmental considerations will be given weight in evaluating the
alternatives. In June 1974 Prime Minister Kakuei Tanaka unveiled
one of his optimistic plans for the future, a Project Sunshine to develop alternatives to oil in the form of "clean" energy types of coal,
hydroelectric plants, geothermal exploitation, some solar power,
and of course nuclear fission, fast-breeder reactors, and eventually
fusion power.[7] This particular plan has since been shelved, but the
efforts of Japan to secure steady supplies of oil and simultaneously
to develop a variety of energy sources pose vital environmental
questions. In this chapter I will attempt to analyze the political and
economic forces that seem to have restricted the scope of industrial
pressure for a rollback and assess the effect of the oil crisis on the
general quality of environmental administration, with particular
reference to the development of energy supplies.

ECONOMIC IMPACT OF THE OIL CRISIS

After the October 1973 oil crisis, the economic forecast for
Japan, "an international resource pauper," was extremely grim.[8]
Although it never suffered from a total embargo, Japan did have to
endure the same monthly reductions as other importers. Because
of its extraordinary dependence on oil, these sacrifices were a much
greater economic burden for Japan than for other importing nations,
and because Japan's rapid postwar growth had been based on its already efficient industrial processes and high labor productivity,
there was very little fat to trim.

Japan was expected to be able to continue a high level of oil
imports, thus preventing the economy from coming to an immediate
standstill, particularly because the government encouraged direct
deals between exporting countries and Japanese oil refineries, to
guarantee a steady supply independent of the international oil majors.
However, the diversion of huge funds and foreign exchange reserves

for oil purchases, sometimes at higher rates than the prevailing
world prices, was expected to have disastrous consequences nonetheless. Economists expected to see a rapid contraction of the
economy, lower absolute levels of industrial production, negative
growth of the GNP, and serious deficits in the balance of trade and
balance of payments. All Japanese industries would be forced to
reduce investment, and many firms in energy-intensive industries
would probably cease operations for lack of fuel or declare bank-
ruptcy. Other industries would suffer from the resulting shortages
of semifinished goods and from inability to pay the higher fuel costs
passed down to them by the processors of oil and other fuels. Japan
was expected to experience massive unemployment, forcing its government to spend much more than before both on aid to firms in
trouble and on vastly increased welfare benefits for the newly unemployed. Paying these increased expenditures out of a steadily
shrinking tax revenue base would produce huge deficits in the government budget, also unprecedented. Bottlenecks in production and
slowdowns in transportation would lead to commodity shortages and
perhaps to consumer panic, further exacerbating inflation and the
decline in the standard of living. Finally, and of greatest concern
here, it was widely assumed that as a matter of course that in the
rush to develop energy alternatives, Japan would have to postpone
the enforcement of environmental regulations, abandon expenditures
on antipollution technology, and ignore environmental considerations.

However, viewed from the vantage point of 1976, it would appear that Japan has avoided the worst of these economic predictions
and has recovered from the oil crisis, although not without difficulties.[9] By some measures and forecasts, Japan was showing signs
of recovery as early as the spring of 1974. Japan did have a negative growth rate during 1974, but by 1975 it was once again experiencing positive real growth in GNP (see Table 11). Although the
monthly balance of payments and the balance of trade deficits did
indeed reach highs, toward the end of 1974 Japan began to experience
surpluses again. Whereas the balance of payments deficit for fiscal
1973 was the most serious in the postwar period, by fiscal 1975 the
deficit had dropped considerably, thanks in large part to unexpected
growth in exports, and the overall balance of trade remained a surplus even during fiscal 1973. Bankruptcies among firms also
reached record highs, but these were blamed on the government's
"overkill" policies after the oil crisis, which were intended to bring
about price stabilization, and on recession, rather than on the oil
crisis itself.[10] Unemployment increased but did not reach serious
proportions at all (2 percent) when compared to the levels considered
normal in other countries. The unemployment rate held steady at
about 2 percent throughout 1976. If the marginal "overemployed"--

those who continue to draw wages but whose labor is not being used
to maintain current production levels--are included, then Japan may
have a "real" unemployment rate as high as 7 percent. [11]

TABLE 11

Indicators of Economic Recovery in Japan

	1973	1974	1975
Growth rate of GNP (calendar year figures)	10.2%	-1.8%	2.0%
Balance of payments (fiscal year* figures in millions of dollars)	-13,407	-3,420	-1,760
Balance of trade (fiscal year* figures in millions of dollars)	803	3,978	5,880

*Japanese fiscal years run from April through March of the
following year.

Sources: Growth rate of GNP in 1973 and 1974 is from Japan
Times, March 8, 1975, and June 11, 1975; growth rate for 1975 is
from Japan Economic Review 8, no. 4 (April 15, 1976): 6; balance
of payments for 1973 and 1974 and balance of trade for 1973 are
from Japan Times, April 18, 1975; balance of payments for 1975 and
balance of trade for 1974 and 1975 are from Japan Economic Review
8, no. 5 (May 15, 1976): 5.

Consumer panics were frequent but restricted to a few commodities (soap, detergent, heating oil, kerosene, cooking oil, toilet
paper, mayonnaise, ketchup, bottled sauce, and seasonings). Once
consumers became accustomed to paying higher prices and controlling their own consumption levels accordingly, some prices began
to drop, and most consumer shortages had also disappeared by
mid-1974.

Japan did have the highest rate of inflation in the industrial
world during 1973 (19 percent in the consumer price index and 29
percent in wholesale prices), but this had tapered off considerably
by fiscal 1975, to 8.8 percent in consumer prices and only 4.5 percent in wholesale prices. [12] Although the 32 percent wage increases
granted to labor unions in 1974 were high enough to cause alarm in

many circles, organized labor appears to have adopted a cooperative
position in the effort to control inflation. It accepted wage increases
of only 15 percent in the spring of 1975 and an even lower 9 percent
in the spring of 1976.[13]

Overall, then, the Japanese economy seemed more resilient
in the face of the oil crisis than any of the forecasters had predicted,
and the downward economic spiral was restricted to a modest recession no more serious than experienced elsewhere. Vindicated by
these developments, proponents of the long-discredited strategy of
rapid economic growth emerged once again to condemn their col-
leagues' more pessimistic predictions as a melodramatic overreac-
tion and even to blame the government's cautious stabilization policies after the oil crisis for the subsequent recession.[14]

EMERGENCY PROGRAMS TO DEAL WITH
THE OIL CRISIS

Japan's response to the oil crisis was a complicated phenomenon; so here we shall confine ourselves to a discussion of the most
significant aspects of the emergency measures devised by the government as they bear on environmental questions.[15] Japan, along
with the rest of the industrialized world, had begun to feel the energy
pinch before the Arab oil embargo of October 1973. The Ministry
of International Trade and Industry (MITI) had already created a new
Natural Resources and Energy Agency, and in September 1973 it
announced a timely energy report advocating lower rates of economic
growth, diversification of energy sources to reduce Japan's dependence on imported energy, and greater emphasis on nuclear energy
and related research and development. It is noteworthy that in order
to solve the problem of constructing power plants in Japan, MITI
urged that more effort be made to reduce the pollution they generated.
A few years earlier MITI would probably have insisted that people
be educated to appreciate the urgency of Japan's energy needs and
to understand the necessity of tolerating the inevitable pollution
problems associated with power plants.

In mid-October 1973 MITI also produced a contingency program
for dealing with energy shortages through its regular policy of administrative guidance of the economy.* By mid-November, Arab

---

*Administrative guidance refers to business-government coop-
eration in devising and carrying out indicative economic planning.
MITI weighs the opinions of business, and in return business voluntarily complies with MITI's advice in price levels, inventory, investment rates, corporate mergers, and so on.

embargoes, production cutbacks, and price increases had created
consternation in Japan, and the government launched an emergency
program. Voluntary measures proved entirely inadequate, but the
passage of two laws late in December 1973 permitted the government
to declare a state of emergency and initiated a period of mandatory
controls on energy consumption by large users. The People's Life
Stabilization Law enabled the government to recommend levels of
prices for daily necessities, production, stockpiling, importation,
and sales of goods in short supply and to make emergency commodities available. With prior notification of the Diet, the government
would also be able to impose short-term rationing, quotas, and bans
on the use of certain goods. The government could suspend construction in order to restrain investment, ask firms to report their
costs and profits, and conduct spot-checks of inventories. A separate resolution also permitted the government to confiscate "ab-
normal profits" obtained through the sale of goods at prices higher
than the recommended ceiling levels. After six months the government would be obligated to report to the Diet on how efficiently the
law had been enforced, and the Diet would review the law again after
one year had passed. The Petroleum Supply Adjustment Law required oil dealers to report their plans for levels of production,
sales, and imports to MITI; in turn, MITI could set mandatory limits on the quantities of oil that could be used by larger consumers.
Finally, the law also granted MITI such powers as the ability to
order gasoline stations to curtail their business hours.

　　Together the declaration of a state of emergency and the
mandatory controls set a clear priority on economic stability and
public welfare. There were no provisions suggesting that environmental regulations might be suspended. Although many criticized
the laws because offenders would not face anything worse than embarrassment at being identified (no one expected the heaviest penalties for violations to be used--three years in jail and one million
yen fine), the particular industries that came under greater control
were quite worried about possible government intervention.

　　By mid-1974 the power companies and MITI found themselves
involved in a quiet confrontation with the Finance Ministry over
prices and the relaxation of emergency controls, which seems to
have deflected everyone's attention away from the relatively small
economic costs of environmental controls. MITI permitted a 62
percent increase in the price of petroleum products in March 1974
and wanted to approve price increases for the major utility companies as well (so that they could afford the petroleum products
they were now buying at higher prices) and to lift the emergency
controls in June. The Finance Ministry, concerned more broadly
about inflation and the health of the total economy and not about the

balance books of individual companies, argued that such a price increase would be dangerously inflationary and contrary to the government's tight money policy of reducing overall demand in the economy. Because the conservative party faced an election in the upper house of the Diet in July 1974, it also wanted to avoid the political risks inherent in granting any price increases to major industries. Thus the Conservative Party and the Finance Ministry won, and MITI continued the emergency controls until September 1974, after the election was safely done with.

Generally, then, we can see that Japan did not resort to any particularly innovative or strict measures to deal with the energy crisis. Only one set of controls, the consumption cutbacks for large users of power, was mandatory. MITI's preference for the conventional method of administrative guidance (to be ignored by many firms, as the Fair Trade Commission would reveal later) eventually led to accusations by the public that government-business collusion was permitting the serious problems of hoarding, panic, and artificially high commodity price increases to go unchecked. What is of particular importance here is that these arguments over prices and economic controls absorbed most of the attention of business and the economic ministries, thus preventing an environmental rollback from becoming a major issue.

ENVIRONMENTAL POLICY AFTER THE OIL CRISIS

An assessment of the environmental implications of the oil crisis is considerably more difficult than an economic analysis, there being no handy comprehensive indicators; but a reading of press reports on enforcement of environmental regulations from 1970 to 1976 indicates that both the severity and frequency of enforcement steadily increased over the entire period, with a noticeable acceleration after the oil crisis. It would appear that existing environmental regulations were maintained, standards protected, and the law vigorously enforced. Although the immediate effect of the oil crisis was to cause ordinary citizens to become much more concerned about inflation than about anything else, their concern about pollution problems did not sink below the protest threshold, and they remained quite prepared to mobilize on behalf of environmental protection. The number of environmental lawsuits continued to grow, with an increasing proportion of them preventive in nature (suits to stop factory operations or to prevent construction of industrial complexes, highways, and other projects that threatened to disrupt the environment), not merely compensatory (demands for monetary compensation after pollution had severely damaged health or livelihood).

The Environmental Disputes Arbitration Committee reported
a modest decline in the number of antipollution complaints in 1974,
but attributed this to a relative improvement in the physical state of
the environment itself rather than to relaxation on the part of the
citizenry. [16] Various environmental surveys in Japan have shown
that certain varieties of air and water pollution are actually clear-
ing up, [17] although pollutants not yet legally designated or regulated
continued to assure that even the familiar varieties of pollution are
still very serious problems in Japan.

The Rollback

As soon as the shock waves of the oil crisis reached Japan,
industry tried to suggest a rollback of standards. The first episode
was really a question of conflict of interest between two different
consumers of oil, and only secondarily an attempt (unsuccessful) to
roll back environmental standards. In November 1973 the oil refinery industry complained to MITI that strict environmental standards on sulfur oxides (SOx) has caused thermal power plants to
switch from heavy oil to the direct use of low-sulfur crude oil. Thus
the utility companies were consuming 40 percent of Japan's imports
of crude oil, shrinking the amounts of crude that the refining industry could process into petrochemicals (naphtha, kerosene, gasoline,
and so on). The solution, argued the refining industry, was to
loosen the environmental standards on SOx so that the utilities could
use heavy oil and the refining industry could use crude oil. Such
changes had already occurred in the United States, and MITI quickly
answered these pleas by prohibiting the use of low-sulfur crude as
industrial fuel oil by the utility companies. [18]
However, Environment Director-General Takeo Miki stood
firm and insisted that if the utilities used high-sulfur heavy oil,
they must also use advanced desulfurization techniques to prevent
the release of SOx into the air. Furthermore, he added that Japan
could not afford to abandon the hard-won emphasis on environmental
protection, regardless of the U.S. example, because pollution was
so much more serious in Japan. Indeed, Miki's reply to the refineries was a scathing criticism, not a humble request for for-
bearance by industry. [19]
In a thorough review of the press, I was able to find only two
cases of successful lobbying for relaxed antipollution regulations.
Both were due to pressure from the automobile industry, a vital
export sector that has had the sympathy of the economic ministries
in government. In the first case, MITI decided to postpone a comprehensive ban on the use of leaded gasoline from April 1974 to

April 1977, based largely on the argument that there were still 9.2
million vehicles on the roads that required high-octane leaded gasoline. The scarcity of light crude oil, which is more easily converted
into desirable by-products than is heavy oil, was indirectly related
to the delay on banning leaded gas, in that proponents of the rollback
argued that it would be a better use of resources to make leaded gas
from heavy oil than to make unleaded gas from crude, regardless of
the consequences for air pollution. Although the Environment Agency
quietly stood aside this time, during the extremity of Japan's panic
over the oil crisis, it should be pointed out that the ban on lead in
low-octane gasoline went into force as planned in October 1973. [20]

The second rollback involved a much more controversial decision to delay enforcement of 1976 automobile emissions standards
on nitrogen oxides (NOx) for two years, from April 1976 to April
1978. Although this postponement greatly disappointed environmentalists, the Environment Agency had earlier displayed surprising
obstinacy during the most critical period of the oil shortage by in-
sisting on enforcing the 1975 standards on time. Whereas the
United States decided in December 1973 to delay by one year its
1975 auto emissions standards, in January 1974 the Japanese Environment Agency decided to ignore that precedent by going ahead
with its own similar 1975 emissions standards as planned. These
standards called for a 90 percent reduction in hydrocarbons and
carbon monoxide and a 45 percent reduction in nitrogen oxides,
relative to 1973 levels. However, several months later automobile
manufacturers complained of serious technological problems in designing vehicles that would meet the April 1976 standards, which
called for .25 grams of NOx per kilometer run, or a 90 percent
reduction in NOx emissions relative to 1973 levels. Accordingly,
the Environment Agency began to hold hearings to deliberate the
1976 standards. [21]

Environmentalist and consumer groups, as well as the local
governments with the greatest need for concern about the role of
automobile emissions in air pollution, did press their wish for
timely enforcement of the 1976 standard. Citizens' groups held
rallies, visited the relevant agencies of government, and wrote let-
ters, but at this juncture they carried little weight against the insistence of the automobile industry that compliance was nonetheless
impossible. Local governments probably had a bit more influence,
particularly when they revealed a report prepared by their own
scientific experts arguing that the 1976 standards were not only
attainable but that some models already in use came close to meeting them. [22] The Tokyo Metropolitan Government conducted a public opinion poll that revealed, to the dismay of the auto industry,
that Tokyo citizens strongly favored enforcement of 1976 standards

on time, the use of tax credits to users of low-pollution cars, and limits on the numbers of high-pollution vehicles that could be manufactured. [23] Tokyo also announced that if the 1976 emissions standards were delayed, it would have no choice but to triple taxes on auto ownership in the city to maintain reasonable levels of air quality. [24]

The final decision in February 1975 to postpone the 1976 standards by two years and to enforce intermediate standards in the meantime was controversial for two reasons. First, due to the scientific report mentioned above, there was considerable confusion over how authentic the technological obstacles were. The fact that Tōyō Kōgyō (Mazda) and Honda were continually ahead of Toyota and Nissan (Datsun), which produce larger, and thus dirtier, cars, in progress toward meeting the standards, and consequently in their willingness to put up with more stringent interim standards, created jealousy within the auto industry and further compounded the controversy. Unexpected technological success had permitted the Japanese auto industry to meet 1975 standards on time, and now the Tōyō Kōgyō rotary and Honda CVCC engines demonstrated that it was possible to accomplish the allegedly inconsistent goals of reducing both NOx and hydrocarbons and carbon monoxide. It now appears that Toyota and Nissan will meet emissions standards by buying, quite reluctantly, patent rights and finished engines from their more innovative competitors.

Second, the Central Council on Environmental Pollution Control, which produced the recommendation to delay enforcement, apparently invited representatives of the automobile manufacturing industry to participate in its supposedly closed deliberations, thus casting doubt on the credibility of the Council and on the relationship between the auto industry and the Environment Agency. Nonetheless, the Environment Agency managed to hold firm on several points. The postponement was for two years rather than the three that auto manufacturers had hoped for; the interim standard adopted (.84 grams per kilometer run) was more stringent than the levels that Toyota and Nissan had said they could meet; and the final package included tax incentives and penalties to encourage production and consumer purchases of low-pollution vehicles instead of the high-pollution models.

In sum, then, the loosening of standards because of this rollback would have detrimental effects on the environment--the postponement of the ban on leaded gasoline and the decision to delay enforcement of the 1976 emissions standards--but this was not primarily a result of the oil crisis, but more directly of arguments that the automobile industry would have raised in any circumstances. Finally, the delays did not alter the fact that Japan's operating automobile emissions standards are nonetheless the most stringent in the world* and are likely to remain so for some time to come in view of the repeated postponement of stringent NOx standards in the United States.† Japan is unlikely to postpone final NOx standards beyond the current date of 1978, in view of the Environment Agency's conclusion of hearings with each of Japan's nine automobile manufacturers, all of whom report that they should be able to meet the strict NOx standards during 1978. As usual, Tōyō Kōgyō and Honda expect to meet the standards well ahead of the new 1978 deadlines. [25]

Enforcement

Although I have not done a systematic content analysis of the reports, it seems clear that the Environment Agency backed down on enforcement only in the instances mentioned above and that the emissions standards rollback was an exception within a larger pattern of tightening enforcement during the period since the oil crisis, a position expressed in the white paper on the environment released in April 1974. Particularly conspicuous was the Environment Agency's aggressive interest in dealing with air pollution apart from the question of automobile emissions standards, in spite of the temptation created by the oil crisis to ignore air quality in order to use all available fuel as economically as possible and to skimp on all nonproductive expenditures. In fact, in the midst of the aftershock, the Environment Agency set initial exhaust standards for diesel vehicles, heretofore unregulated whatsoever, because this dirty 7 percent of the vehicles in Japan was responsible for 40 percent of all automobile air pollution. [26]

---

*Michio Hashimoto, an Environment Agency official, said in June 1976 that Japan spends a larger portion of the GNP (2 to 3 percent) on environmental measures than any other country and that Japan has the most stringent standards for NOx and SOx pollutants. (See interview with Hashimoto, "Real Environmental Countermeasures From Now," in Ekonomisuto [Economist], June 29, 1976.)

†In September 1976, the U.S. House of Representatives voted to postpone final hydrocarbon and carbon monoxide standards until 1980 and to postpone final NOx standards from 1978 to 1982. A compromise with a slightly harsher Senate bill will be necessary before the delays become law, but there is every reason to expect a lengthy postponement. (See Prudence Crewdson, "House Votes Clean Air Bill After Weakening Auto Emissions Requirements," Congressional Quarterly Weekly Report 34, no. 38 (September 18, 1976): 2502.)

At the same time, the Environment Agency prepared a bill, which passed the Diet during the spring session of 1974, to regulate air pollution according to the total amount of pollutants rather than according to existing standards of concentration, since polluters could easily meet concentration standards by diluting their waste products. This new law drastically tightened air pollution standards in critical areas, and these standards have continued to be tightened every six months in order to achieve higher levels of air quality on the original schedule set in 1974. Despite the oil crisis, this legislation allowed prefectural governments to require major oil consumers to use low-sulfur oil and to install desulfurization and smoke removal devices. The penalties included six months in jail, although the accompanhing fines would be small (100,000 yen, or about $300 per count). This measure used a principle of designing environmental standards that environmentalists had long demanded, and it also enacted into law the verdict from the Yokkaichi air pollution case on joint and several liability, by which a group of firms is held responsible for pollution damage even if they each meet environmental standards when their effluents are measured separately.[27]

In August 1974 the Environmental Agency began preparing legislation to create what would become the first system in the world to provide relief (calculated rather generously on the basis of average national wages) on the polluter-pays principle by diverting funds obtained from automobile taxes and by collecting mandatory contributions from industries according to the quantities of pollutants they generate, with all industries releasing over 10,000 cubic meters of waste per hour into the air having to contribute funds. Because thermal power plants were the largest contributors to SOx pollution, releasing 34 percent of the total SOx in the air in 1972, the agency would levy a special tax against them of ¥15.84 per cubic meter of pollutants from firms in critical zones and ¥1.76 per cubic meter from power companies elsewhere, to add to the relief funds for pollution victims. Finally, in January 1975 the Environment Agency decided to augment the fund further by levying a surtax on imported crude oil (Japan is the only oil importer to maintain a tariff on oil, used to support the domestic coal industry).[28]

These are very illuminating examples of the Environment Agency's attitude toward the oil crisis. In essence, the users of oil are treated more harshly because of their role in contributing to pollution, rather than being treated leniently because of their increased costs. Additional examples of strict enforcement that is less directly related to the energy crisis are numerous. The Environment Agency continued to set aside wilderness areas, to create new national parks, to limit major construction projects by requiring impact statements, to set tighter standards of automobile and

airport noise, and to reduce drastically the level of mercury toler-
ated in bodies of water. Japan's first case involving violations of
the Pollution Crime Law began after the oil crisis, and the National
Police Agency conducted vigorous investigations of other offenses
against environmental laws during this period.[29]

Heightened environmental concern was also evident in new
land use legislation adopted in 1974. Prime Minister Kakuei Tanaka's
famed Kaizōron proposal to remodel Japan (environmentalists called
this a plan to disperse pollution all over Japan) was shelved by the
LDP in March 1974 and replaced with the National Land Utilization
Law, effective May 28, 1974, which emphasized severe environmental controls on land use and mechanisms to control land speculation,
rather than the emphasis on industrial development so predominant
in the earlier bill.[30]

In sum, then, it should be clear that the economic pinch produced by the oil crisis was not widely used as an excuse to relax
existing environmental standards, even though the cost of nonproductive investment in antipollution technology was precisely the
argument levied against environmental regulations when they were
first created. Japan's performance in environmental enforcement
seems especially impressive relative to my own expectation, based
on earlier research, that industrial pressure groups would take
advantage of every available opportunity to delay and defy environmental regulation.[31] Instead, in most cases the view that prevailed
was that of the Environment Agency, which regarded the oil crisis
as an opportunity to solve two problems at once--to reduce Japan's
dependence on oil as a source of energy and thereby to reduce a
major ingredient in Japan's pollution.

Energy Policy

Unfortunately, the impact of the energy crisis is not limited to
existing environmental policies, and in fact the most serious consequences for environmental quality may lie beyond the jurisdiction of
the Environment Agency. MITI and a variety of other agencies not
notably sensitive to environmental concerns have responsibility for
energy policy. Although there is little disagreement with the idea
that Japan needs to diversify its energy supply, environmentalists
are quite worried about the implications of a desperate search for
alternatives to oil.

Geothermal power, which is abundant and relatively unexplored
in Japan, attracted a lot of attention immediately after the October
War, and MITI promptly designated 30 sites for development. However, 80 percent of these were hot springs and volcanic areas in

national parks, giving the Environment Agency some authority over
the boring of geothermal wells at those sites. In November 1973 the
Environment Agency reluctantly authorized 14 wells, on condition
that heat damage to vegetation be avoided. A year later, after the
urgency of the energy crisis had passed, the agency decided not to
allow further boring. The environmental damage cuased by the six
existing geothermal plants included construction of extra roads and
facilities in otherwise natural areas, great damage to vegetation
and scenery, and serious pollution from literally tons of hydrogen
sulfide, sulfuric acid mist, and arsenic, all for a very low annual
kilowatt output.[32] The enthusiasm for geothermal power has been
dampened somewhat, but there is renewed interest in reviving coal
and hydroelectric power, which were once major energy sources
for Japan. The government is also promoting some research on
solar energy.[33] However, it will be many years before these
sources can begin to provide much electric power to Japan, so the
focus of attention for environmentalists is the much more substantial program for the development of nuclear energy.

Quite a few preventive lawsuits have been filed against both
conventional and nuclear power plants, to close them down or to
prevent further expansion.* The local opposition to nuclear power
plants has been so serious that no firm applied for a permit to build
a nuclear plant during 1973. Prime Minister Tanaka regarded this
as a pity, to be remedied with a more energetic effort to persuade
the public of the benefits of nuclear power.[34] Japan's nuclear power
program has turned out to be a rather dismal embarrassment to the
government, giving additional antinuclear ammunition to local protests, in spite of support for nuclear power from both the press and
the general public. The program has lagged far behind construction
schedules, continually being interrupted by a steady succession of
leaks, accidents, plant stoppages, and even a scandal involving the
falsification of safety reports, which led to the reorganization of
the atomic energy administration in Japan.[35] The Environment
Agency has almost no authority over nuclear power, since radioactive

---

*In August 1973, citizens of Ehime Prefecture filed the first
lawsuit to stop the construction of a nuclear power plant. Since then
other suits have been filed in Fukushima Prefecture, and complaints
have been lodged against both thermal and nuclear plants in Hokkaido,
Fukui, and Fukuoka prefectures. In April 1974 the first suit by an
individual was also filed against a nuclear plant in Fukui. (See
Japan Times, August 18, 1973; August 28, 1973; January 31, 1974;
April 7, 1974; and January 8, 1975; January 9, 1975; May 27, 1975.)

waste is not legally defined as a pollutant, but it has expressed consternation over this poor performance record and over the Japan Atomic Energy Commission's sloppy and irresponsible attitude toward safety and environmental considerations.[36] The government was finally forced to revise its projected energy development plans substantially, due to the current sluggish rate of expansion.* But environmentalists still have cause for alarm, since the government as a whole and the power industry are still devoted to the idea of going nuclear. The performance record of operating plants has not improved, and foreign technical observers suggest that Japanese safety precautions are the "flimsiest in the world."[37] In some instances the power companies involved have been able to reach compromises with local opposition, sometimes by signing pollution prevention agreements promising to obey the law and permitting periodic safety inspections, but sometimes by donating huge sums of money to the local communities. Henri Hymans provides several examples of the varieties of compensation the nuclear power developers have given to nearby communities to deflate opposition.[38] On the other hand, in 1974 Ibaragi Prefecture signed the first nuclear energy safety agreement with 14 firms and agencies.[39]

Thus far, then, several circumstances have combined to prevent Japan from embarking on an all-out race for the development of alternative energy sources. Local opposition, environmental lawsuits, negative publicity provided by the Environment Agency, and especially the poor performance on the part of Japan's nuclear program have managed thus far to stall further reckless or haphazard development of environmentally questionable energy supplies.

FACTORS UNDERLYING JAPAN'S RESPONSE

How can we explain the fact that Japan maintained its environmental policies with only a relatively small rollback rather than allow them to be eroded by industrial pressure groups? First, there are rather special circumstantial factors, which are the nature

---

*Japan now expects to produce only 16 million kilowatts per year by 1980, which is half of the target originally set in 1972, and only 49 million kilowatts, rather than 60 million, by 1985. In view of current snags and setbacks, even these goals may be impossible to meet. (See Henri Hymans, "Turning Off Nuclear Power," Far Eastern Economic Review 88, no. 15 [April 11, 1975]: 33-34; and Henri Hymans, "The Japanese March to Nuclear Power," Far Eastern Economic Review 90, no. 41 [October 10, 1975]: 38-41.)

of Japan's economic structure and the patterns of its oil consumption, but apart from these, it is also necessary to examine closely
the relationships among Japan's conservative government, powerful
business community, political opposition, and environmental and
consumer movements. Recent events indicate that the following
factors also helped Japan's environmental policies to remain intact:
the independence of certain enforcement agencies; the nature of
decision making and policy execution in Japan; the rift between the
conservative party and its usual supporters in industry due to a dif-
ference in their respective overriding objectives; the haunting
presence of environmental and consumer groups; the example set
by leftist local governments in Japan's congested urban areas; and
the persistence of several highly visible pollution controversies,
which served as reminders to all concerned of the hazards of ignoring environmental problems.

Economic Arguments

First of all, many observers would argue that the oil crisis
was a blessing in disguise, providing Japan with an opportunity, or
perhaps the necessity, of slowing down a dangerously overheated
economy. Criticism of the high-growth policies of the 1960s has
been widely heard in Japan since 1970, to the effect that the economy
cannot possibly grow at such rapid rates forever and that to induce
growth in spite of natural limits on the economy, such as pollution,
the shortage of energy and resources, and the constraints of geographic size and population density, would only lead to intolerable
social costs. The political opposition has long argued that the emphasis should be shifted from heavy industry, particularly the petrochemical and chemical industries, to service and information industries and to investment in the social infrastructure (sewerage,
transportation, housing, education, urban planning, and so on) to
improve the well-being and "daily living environment" of the Japanese people.[40]

Thus the oil crisis provided immediate material incentives for
the Japanese government to plan for such a slowdown in growth rates
and a shift in economic structure, for economic reasons that would
satisfy conservatives not persuaded by the arguments advanced by
antipollution citizens' movements and the leftist opposition. Rather
than sacrifice the investment in pollution prevention in order to prop
up a controversial industrial structure emphasizing highly polluting
and energy-intensive activities, then, the Japanese government used
the oil crisis as a much-needed opportunity and justification for
overhauling the unbalanced economic structure in favor of activities

less detrimental to the environment. This policy shift has been particularly evident in the flurry of White Papers that have been released by the government since summer 1974, all referring to the need to change the economic structure and maintain antipollution efforts.

In the same vein, the oil crisis also enabled Japan to maintain environmental protection policies through its antiinflationary policies, which included denials of loans to business for plant expansion and of permits for large construction projects. The government also canceled or postponed many of its own public construction projects. Similarly, the Environment Agency announced that an environmental impact study would be required before any major land reclamation or construction project could be permitted, thus halting land reclamation in the Inland Sea. [41] The government's efforts to keep a lid on inflation had the simultaneous effect of curtailing highly polluting industrial activities and making possible a continued effort in environmental protection.

The Pattern of Oil Consumption

Certain features of Japan's pattern of oil imports and consumption also explain why the oil crisis did not lead to a major rollback of antipollution standards. These are the fact that so much of Japan's oil is used by industry and not by private households, the fact that rising prices in the Middle East made low-sulfur oil competitive in price, and the fact that Japan is now cooperating to develop refining capacity in the oil-producing countries rather than in Japan.

First, 55.2 percent of Japan's oil consumption is directly for industrial purposes, either as a fuel or as a raw material for Japan's enormous petrochemical industry. [42] This is an unusually high proportion in comparison to other countries because of Japan's enormous oil-dependent manufacturing industries, which not only supply the domestic market but also engage in a vigorous export trade. Director-General Takeo Miki of the Environment Agency observed that for Japan to be deprived of oil would set automatic limits on the amount of pollution the economy could generate and would create immediate incentives for industry to move out of energy-intensive activities. [43]

Secondly, as a result of more stringent legislation to combat air pollution, major users of oil as fuel--heavy industries and utilities particularly--have been utilizing advanced desulfurization techniques and shifting gradually from the use of high-sulfur oil to an increased use of expensive low-sulfur oil in order to meet effluent standards on sulfur oxide pollution. [44] The rapid price increases of

high-sulfur Middle Eastern oil made the low-sulfur oils of China
and Indonesia, which were once considerably more expensive than
Arabian crude, competitive in price; these imports are certainly
not so subject to sudden production cutbacks.

Third, there is increasing interest among the underdeveloped
oil-rich countries to control not only the drilling and production
process itself but also the refining of oil. Due to the vitality of the
environmental movement in Japan in recent years, it has become
increasingly difficult for new oil refineries and storage facilities to
be built in Japan. The government has scrapped national economic
plans providing for the establishment of mammoth refinery complexes in several areas. The need for more facilities was made
even more urgent by the large number of refinery explosions during
1974. These accidents took place because storage tanks, insufficient
in number, were being kept dangerously full (not allowing for the
expansion of gases) and because the refinery facilities had been
built rapidly and in haphazard fashion. Given this serious problem,
the government and the oil industry have found it almost impossible
to plan for additional refinery capacity in Japan.

However, new demands by the oil-producing nations, arising
out of their strong sense of nationalism and their sudden acquisition
of petrodollars, have given Japan a solution. Underdeveloped oil-
producing countries are anxious to control more of the production
process, to reap more profit from the additional economic activity
taking place in their own countries and to further stimulate their
domestic economic development. Japan has readily cooperated
in concluding arrangements with oil-producing nations to provide the
technological expertise needed to build refineries near the drilling
sites, in return for a guaranteed supply of refined oil. Japanese
leaders made a flurry of trips to the Middle East and other oil-
producing nations during December 1973 and January 1974 in order
to conclude pacts by which Japan would offer some form of aid in
return for guaranteed oil supplies. Since early 1974 the economic
news has abounded with reports of such negotiations.[45] By this type
of cooperation, Japan hopes to avoid both the pollution and the danger
associated with the refining of oil.

Bureaucratic Professionalism

Certain elements in the central bureaucracy have acquired a
powerful combination of good leadership, favorable publicity, popular support, and newly delegated powers, and this has resulted in
the continuation of Japan's existing environmental protection policy.
The Environment Agency, created in July 1971, has had the good

fortune to have had among its several director generals two men
who happened to be rather independent of personality and relatively
liberal members of the conservative ruling party, Buichi Ōishi,
whose crusades to save wilderness areas in the national parks are
fondly remembered, and Takeo Miki, whose role as a major faction
leader in the party lent considerable weight to his statements on
behalf of Japan's beleaguered environment, and whose subsequent
role as prime minister has undoubtedly given the Environment Agency
additional self-confidence.

    The generally sympathetic coverage by the Japanese press of
the environmental cause and of the agency's more engaging person-
alities has also probably helped to give the Environment Agency a
good deal of popular support. The agency's officials, once criticized for retaining the values and policy goals they brought with
them from the economic ministries, which generally defend the interests of industry, have over time developed their own sense of
identity as guardians of the environment.

    Another factor in creating an atmosphere of bureaucratic pro-
fessionalism and devotion to the enforcement of environmental law
was the authority delegated to the Environment Agency. The agency
has been given increasing power since 1970 to enforce new legislation, much of which was created prior to the energy crisis without
thought to situations in which some groups might want to suspend
regulations to protect the environment. As we have seen, throughout the oil crisis the Environment Agency, then under Miki, persisted in utilizing its powers and in enforcing the law.

    Another agency that exhibited this strong professional spirit
of devotion to duty during the energy crisis, and that must be mentioned because it was so important in restraining the activities of
industrial pressure groups, was the Fair Trade Commission (FTC),
which exposed price-fixing agreements and cartels among whole-
salers and retailers who hoarded commodities during the energy
crisis and among oil refiners and producers of petroleum products
who indulged in price fixing to reap excess profits, leading to more
indictments of business for fraudulent practices than ever before. [46]
Using provisions in the Anti-Monopoly Law that had been ignored
for 25 years, the FTC filed the first criminal suit against a price-
fixing cartel charging 17 executives from 12 different oil firms and
the Petroleum Association. *

------

    *After intensive investigations in March and April, the FTC
filed charges against the oil industry in May 1974. The Public
Prosecutor's Office indicted the appropriate firms and executives
in the same month. On September 30, 1975, the Tokyo High Court

The popular support generated by these whirlwind raids on company files and the public disclosure of well-stocked warehouses during periods of consumer panic over commodity shortages also lent strength to the FTC argument, echoed by Environment Director-General Miki, that the Anti-Monopoly Law should be strengthened. This would have been the first time that revision of the Anti-Monopoly Law would have strengthened rather than weakened its provisions. [47] In spite of much complaint from business, the FTC created its own draft in September 1974, and out of sheer embarrassment the conservative party submitted the draft to the 1975 Diet. Opposition amendments were incorporated, and the bill passed the Lower House unanimously on June 24, 1975. Very quickly the LDP revealed the strategy behind this rare display of enthusiasm for an anti-business measure. On July 4, 1975, the LDP shelved the bill rather than bring it to a vote in the Upper House, thus ensuring that it could not become law unless it were revived in a later session of the Lower House all over again. This move was widely criticized, but it did not surprise observers who suspected that the LDP would never have accepted opposition amendments so readily in the Lower House if it had intended to allow the bill to be passed in the Upper House also. [48] Nonetheless, the public eye was riveted on the issue of business practices, and the industrial pressure groups that might have wanted to use the energy crisis as an excuse for an environmental rollback simply did not have the gumption to try. It is noteworthy that requests from business pressure groups for a softening of this or that environmental regulation, which had been feeble enough when they did occur in late 1973, dropped off entirely after the FTC activities began humiliating and indicting the pillars of Japan's industrial community. The revelations of industrial profiteering made it impossible for businessmen to argue that they could not afford to observe environmental standards. Indeed, as the utilities and the petroleum industry began requesting permission to raise their prices in 1974, there is some indication that the ruling party found it politically necessary to delay granting the increases so long that some firms really did begin to suffer real, not imaginary, deficits. [49]

---

delivered a verdict in favor of the FTC, compelling the oil industry to comply with FTC orders. (See Japan Times, March 29, 1974; April 16, 1974; April 17, 1974; April 19, 1974; May 4, 1974; May 29, 1974; September 30, 1975.)

Decision Making and Policy Execution

Japanese organizations make decisions very slowly because of
the importance of obtaining agreement among as many of the participants as possible (not merely a majority) but they execute them very
quickly once this vital agreement is reached. This painstaking
process of consultation to reach consensus creates a commitment to
the final decision among the participants.[50] This matter of style
has had a great deal to do with Japan's maintenance of environmental
standards during the energy crisis. Antipollution legislation had
been produced only with much haggling and delay, and there were
similar delays in the subsequent creation of administrative standards.
But by 1973 the earlier antipollution legislation acquired its own
momentum, and the bureaucracy, which had also been involved during the process of drafting the bills, was committed to enforcing it.
Allan Campbell, who has studied the implementation of environmental legislation in Japan both before and after the oil crisis, has concluded that a consensus was formed in 1970-71 in both the national
and prefectural bureaucracies that pollution control legislation must
be positively enforced and, since the 1973 oil shock and recession,
prefectural pollution control agencies have been enforcing the legislation more vigorously than ever.[51] It is not likely that either the
conservative party or industry wanted to become involved in the
political turmoil that would have resulted from trying to subvert
this decision-making process or reverse the decisions agreed upon
earlier with so much difficulty. Thus the Japanese style of incremental but virtually irreversible decision making by consensus may
have had a great deal to do with the absence of a rollback in environmental regulations.

Divergence of Objectives

Specialists have always argued that politics in Japan is generally characterized by a degree of cooperation and consultation between government and large-business pressure groups that is not
practiced elsewhere.[52] This pattern of decision making has persisted during most of the postwar period because there have been
times of steady economic expansion, broad social consensus on the
goals of growth and prosperity, and little political controversy over
bread-and-butter issues. However, the 1970s have brought a wide
array of divisive issues to Japan, including pollution, social welfare
benefits, urban planning, and industrial development in rural areas.
These issues have placed a great deal of stress on the conventional
"ruling triad" of Japanese politics, which is the conservative party,

the bureaucracy, and big business, and have produced a divergence of views and goals. This new confusion over objectives--how much pollution, how much development, how much inflation, how much government control over supplies during shortages, how much expenditure on social welfare, how much profit, and so on--has created an increasing number of situations in which big business has had to give in.

The oil crisis created an obvious divergence in priorities, in that the long-term economic interests of Japan as a whole (a continued supply of oil, stable supplies of materials in general, the prevention of hoarding or consumer panic, the control of runaway inflation, and so on) clearly ran contrary to what many businessmen would have defined as in their short-term interests, such as hoarding in order to induce inflationary price increases, speculation, and profiteering. Because of this, the conservative party clearly felt unable to take the political risk of permitting a sizable rollback in environmental controls.

Environmentalists and Consumer Lobbies

Another vital factor in the government's response to the oil crisis was the role of environmental and consumer groups. Although these groups have not been strong when compared to those in other countries, they were nonetheless capable of frightening the conservative party into producing policies to prevent pollution. Their vigorous activities in direct negotiations with enterprises and in the courts have obviously constituted a major nuisance to industry. Given the rise of leftist coalitions that have been victorious in local elections, the conservative party is anxious to second-guess the opposition and to appease the public, and the environmental and consumer movement poses a credible threat. Activists have had increasing recourse to the courts since 1973, particularly since they had favorable verdicts in the four first pollution cases to fall back on. There is also a vast array of new laws created since 1970 on which to base lawsuits.[53]

It may seem paradoxical that a relatively weak popular movement can inspire fear in an apparently permanent majority party; but small threats may loom large to such a powerful political party precisely because it is accustomed to having a great deal of authority and to wielding it with great ease. Furthermore, the conservative party consists of many factions that are held together by steadily eroding ties, so that each potential threat to its unity and each issue that could create a coalition among the opposition parties seems all the more alarming. It is also my impression that over time the

members of the party have grown increasingly concerned with ob-
serving the rules of parliamentary procedure and avoiding trouble.
The party often decides to give up on a point of policy or to shelve a
bill rather than abuse its power. Thus the environmental and consumer lobbies, though fragmented and active primarily at the local
level, had considerable effect on the conservative party's decision
to leave environmental policies relatively unmodified.

Consumer and environmental groups maintained their pace of
activity even after the oil crisis hit Japan. It is significant that they
mounted intense protest campaigns, including the first lawsuits to
stop the construction or operation of nuclear power plants and oil
refineries, despite the common knowledge that Japan needed to
diversify its energy sources and expand refinery capacity in order to
fulfill its obligation as a member of the OECD oil-consumers' group
to develop the capacity to stockpile a 90-day supply of oil.

The Example of Leftist Local Governments

Local governments in the largest cities have also influenced
the central government's environmental and energy policies. Of
course, the conservative party is quite worried about the potential
growth of its rivals on the left, and it is quite vulnerable when leftist
mayors and governors come up with ideas or policies that are more
popular with the public than its own programs. Leftist local governments, in addition to this mode of influence through example, have
also been able to use certain concrete powers granted to them in
recent antipollution legislation in order to influence the ruling
party's decisions on environmental and energy matters. For example, most of the new antipollution law provides that in certain designated areas where pollution problems are critical (inevitably the
major urban areas, which have leftist governments), local governors
and mayors have considerable freedom of action in devising their
own pollution-prevention plans, in setting standards more severe
than those of the central government, and in ordering compliance.[54]

Tokyo resorted to its emergency powers to fight air pollution
when the central government permitted the postponement of 1976
auto emissions controls. Tokyo also lobbied actively on its own for
an accelerated program of environmental protection. When a new
pollution scare erupted in the summer of 1975--the discovery that
certain companies had been dumping tremendous quantities of toxic
hexavalent chromium wastes--the Tokyo metropolitan government
was in the forefront of the investigations and ordered the offenders
to pay compensations to both the victims and the metropolitan government and to foot the bill for removing or neutralizing the

contaminated waste material.[55] Throughout the energy crisis, the
Tokyo metropolitan government was extremely active on its own in
reporting cases of hoarding or speculation and violations of administrative guidelines and prices. It also came up with many ideas on
energy conservation and offered solutions to many problems that the
central government had neglected. Other prefectures with large
urban areas, Chiba, Hiroshima, Kanagawa, and Okayama, also took
innovative steps to enforce environmental controls.

Persistence of Pollution

Finally, an extremely important reason for the maintenance of
the government's antipollution policies has been the persistence of
serious pollution problems and environmental lawsuits. Disputes
concerning arsenic contamination of milk, thalidomide, AF-2 (a
carcinogen used in the preparation of bean curd), noise pollution
along highways and train lines and from major airports, cadmium
contamination of rice reserves, red tides and industrial pollution
in the Inland Sea, and hexavalent chromium wastes, and the designation of mercury poisoning victims have continued to keep environmental problems in the public eye since 1974. In May 1976 the
Public Prosecutor filed criminal charges against Chisso Corporation, which was already paying large sums to mercury poisoning
victims on the basis of a civil suit that ended in 1973.

The checkered career of the Mutsu, Japan's first and perhaps
last nuclear-powered ship, immobilized for over four years because
of radioactive leaks, has also played an important role in sensitizing
the Japanese public to the dangers of nuclear energy.[56] A nationwide poll conducted in October 1975 showed that, in the abstract,
39 percent of the population would approve of increased efforts to
develop nuclear power, but that 27 percent would be opposed and
the remaining 34 percent were uncertain. When asked their opinion
about living near a nuclear power plant, 15 percent said that they
would be pleased, 18 percent said that they would oppose it, and
52 percent said that they would feel uneasy about the prospect but
wouldn't oppose it.[57]

Local successes and a virtually unbroken record of legal
victories, as well as the continually increasing size of compensations won by environmentalists, have strengthened the environmental
movement. All in all, continuing pollution crises have kept the issue
of environmental protection alive and have probably served to re-
mind both people and government that pollution in Japan is a life-
and-death matter, far too serious to permit any relaxation of the
rules.

The Energy-Environment Stalemate

The fact that the rollback after the energy crisis was restricted and that environmental activists have achieved many small tactical victories should not be interpreted as meaning that Japan is on the brink of solving its environmental problems. On the contrary, Japan remains the most polluted country in the world, and the return to a pristine state of environmental health is almost certainly impossible in such a highly industrialized, densely populated nation. It will probably require an immense effort merely to slow down the pace at which environmental disruption takes place. The energy crisis has not greatly changed Japan's pattern of energy production, and consequently it has not altered the environmental impact of such activity either. Despite Japan's acute awareness of energy scarcity, the alternatives to imported oil as an energy source are few and not terribly promising, and in any case they would still require much research and development before yielding practical results.[58] What is significant is that the Japanese government has come to appreciate this dilemma and thus to place some value on maintaining present environmental efforts.

NOTES

1. These figures were taken from the Japan Times, November 4, 1974; April 26, 1975; and May 9, 1975.

2. See John W. Bennett, Sukehiro Hasegawa, and Solomon B. Levine, "Japan: Are There Limits to Growth?" Environment 15, no. 10 (December 1973): 6-13.

3. See Japan Times, December 14, 1974; June 11, 1975; July 6, 1975; August 21, 1975; August 27, 1975; and September 3, 1975.

4. On the connection between citizens' environment groups and the rise of the left, see "Citizens' Movements," Japan Quarterly 20, no. 4 (October-December 1973): 368-73, as well as Hiroyoshi Yanaga, "The Rising Tide of Reformist Forces," in the same issue, pp. 397-406. See also Keiichi Matsushita, "Politics of Citizen Participation," Japan Interpreter 9, no. 4 (Spring 1975): 451-64. This phenomenon is discussed in Margaret A. McKean, "Citizens' Movements in Urban and Rural Japan," in Social Change and Community Politics in Urban Japan, ed. James W. White (Chapel Hill, N.C.: Institute for Research in the Social Sciences, 1976), and in Margaret A. McKean, "Political Socialization through Citizens' Movements," in Local Opposition in Japan: Progressive Local Governments, Citizens' Movements, and National Politics, ed. Kurt

Steiner, Ellis Krauss, and Scott Flanagan (Princeton: Princeton University Press, forthcoming).

5. For a discussion of the ways in which this legislation has been created, see Margaret A. McKean, "Pollution and Policy-Making," in Policy-Making in Contemporary Japan, ed. T. J. Pempel (Ithaca, N.Y.: Cornell University Press, 1976).

6. Japan Times, November 22, 1974. See also interview with Michio Hashimoto, "Real Environmental Countermeasures from Now," in Ekonomisuto [Economist], June 29, 1976; and Henri Hymans, "Reducing the GNP (Grand National Pollution)," Far Eastern Economic Review 90, no. 48 (November 28, 1975): 9-10.

7. Japan Times, June 25, 1974.

8. Periodicals emphasizing economic news were extremely preoccupied with disaster. See Nihon Keizai Shimbun [Japan Economic News], Japan Economic Review, Oriental Economist, Far Eastern Economic Review, or the business pages of any major Japanese newspaper from October 1973 on.

9. For a review of Japanese economic conditions after the oil crisis, see Takafusa Nakamura, "The Tarnished Phoenix," Japan Interpreter 9, no. 4 (Spring 1975): 403-19; and Yoshikazu Miyazaki, "A New Price Revolution," in the same issue, pp. 420-50.

10. Susumu Awanohara, "The Psychology of Recovery," in Far Eastern Economic Review 90, no. 48 (November 28, 1975): 5.

11. See Susumu Awanohara, "Japan Faces Labour Dilemma," Far Eastern Economic Review 91, no. 11 (March 12, 1976): 38.

12. Japan Times, January 26, 1974; and Tracy Dahlby, "Recovery on the Cards as Exports Rise," Far Eastern Economic Review 92, no. 26 (June 25, 1976): 52.

13. Japan Times, April 14, 1974; and "Shuntō" [Spring Struggle], Japan Quarterly 22, no. 1 (January-March 1975): 608; and "Wage Hike Limited to Less than 9 Per Cent," Oriental Economist 44, no. 788 (June 1976): 35.

14. For the pessimistic viewpoint in this squabble over how to forecast Japan's economic future, see "No Recovery Power to 1975 Economy," Oriental Economist 43, no. 771 (January 1975): 6-12; and "Outlook for Japan's Growth: Japan's Economy in Five Years, as Seen by Five Research Organizations," in the same issue, pp. 12-16. For the revival of optimism, see Hisao Kanamori, "Slow Growth Proponents Again Are Mistaken: Growth Potential of Japanese Economy and Policy Choices," Oriental Economist 43, no. 777 (July 1975): 22-28; and Ichio Takenaka, "Low Economic Growth Proposition is Sheer Fantasy: Thoughts on the Possibilities of the Japanese Economy," Oriental Economist 44, no. 783 (January 1976): 21-30.

15. The details mentioned in this section come from reports in the Japan Times and the Asahi Shimbun.

16. Japan Times, September 3, 1975; February 15, 1976.

17. Japan Times, April 18, 1975; June 2, 1975; August 23, 1975; and September 3, 1975, provide examples of some of these surveys. See also Kankyōchō [Environment Agency], Kankyō Hakusho 1974 [White Paper on the Environment 1974], (Tokyo: Ministry of Finance Printing Office, 1974), pp. 1-8.

18. Japan Times, November 4-16, 1973.

19. Japan Times, November 9, 1973.

20. Japan Times, November 16, 1973; March 20, 1974; March 21, 1974; March 26, 1974.

21. Japan Times, October 1974 through February 1975.

22. Japan Times, October 22, 1974.

23. Japan Times, October 21, 1974.

24. Japan Times, November 3, 1974.

25. See Japan Economic Review 8, no. 9 (September 15, 1976): 4.

26. Japan Times, May 11, 1974.

27. Japan Times, February 1, 1974; March 16, 1974; July 18, 1974; November 22, 1974; April 14, 1975; May 21, 1975.

28. Japan Times, February 9, 1974; August 13, 1974; September 4, 1974; September 14, 1974; January 29, 1975.

29. Japan Times, April 30, 1974; July 31, 1974; August 17, 1974; March 20, 1975; May 21, 1975.

30. Japan Times, April 24, 1974; April 25, 1974; May 29, 1974.

31. Industrial pressure group activity is discussed in Margaret A. McKean, "Pollution and Policy-Making," op. cit.

32. Japan Times, November 11, 1973; October 26, 1974.

33. On Japan's interest in returning to coal power with increased coal imports and a revival of the domestic coal industry and in enlarging present hydroelectric stations by rebuilding dams from scratch, see Japan Times, March 9, 1974, and February 13, 1975; Henri Hymans, "A New Sense of Direction," Far Eastern Economic Review 86, no. 47 (November 29, 1974): 15-16; Henri Hymans, "Japan's Search for Local Power," Far Eastern Economic Review 89, no. 30 (July 25, 1976): 41-42. On Japan's research on solar power, see Japan Times, January 1, 1974; November 23, 1974; May 26, 1975.

34. Japan Times, January 26, 1974.

35. Japan Times has published several series of articles on nuclear power by Yukihiko Ikenaga, on January 6, 1975; January 7, 1975; January 8, 1975; March 8, 1975; March 9, 1975; March 10, 1975; February 21, 1976; February 22, 1976; February 24, 1976. See also Henri Hymans, "Turning Off Nuclear Power," Far Eastern Economic Review 88, no. 15 (April 11, 1975): 33-34; Henri Hymans,

"The Japanese March to Nuclear Power," Far Eastern Economic Review 90, no. 41 (October 10, 1975): 38-41; Henri Hymans, "Tokyo on a Nuclear Bandwagon," Far Eastern Economic Review 92, no. 20 (May 14, 1976): 55-56.

36. Japan Times, January 8, 1975.

37. Hymans, "The Japanese March to Nuclear Power," op. cit., p. 38.

38. Ibid.

39. See Japan Times, December 17, 1974.

40. See Bennett, Hasegawa, and Levine, "Japan: Are there Limits to Growth?" op. cit.; "Indices of National Welfare," Japan Quarterly 18, no. 3 (July-September 1971): 260-62; Solomon B. Levine, "Japan's Economy: End of the Miracle?" Current History 68, no. 404 (April 1975): 149-53 passim; and Shigeto Tsuru, "In Place of Gross National Product," Area Development in Japan 3 (1970): 208.

41. Japan Times, September 30, 1973; May 11, 1975; July 1, 1975; August 3, 1975.

42. Japan Times, May 9, 1975.

43. Japan Times, November 9, 1973; November 14, 1973; November 15, 1973; April 27, 1974.

44. Hideo Nakanishi and Tsutomu Yamaguchi, "Pollution," Japanese Economic Studies 2, no. 4 (Summer 1974): 64.

45. See Japan Times, October 17, 1973; December 2, 1973; December 28, 1973; January 8, 1974; January 17, 1974; January 25, 1974; February 17, 1974; February 19, 1974.

46. Japan Times, December 21, 1974.

47. See Chitoshi Yanaga, Big Business in Japanese Politics (New Haven: Yale University Press, 1968), pp. 152-76.

48. See Japan Times and Asahi Shimbun, September 12, 1974; September 19, 1974; September 21, 1974; various dates in February 1975; March 1, 1975; March 6, 1975; June 25, 1975; July 4, 1975; July 15, 1975; and July 16, 1975.

49. See in particular Japan Times, March 4, 1974; March 17, 1974; March 21, 1974; April 4, 1974; May 14, 1974; May 15, 1974; and May 16, 1974.

50. This feature of Japanese decision making is frequently mentioned in the literature on Japanese politics. See Shigeo Misawa, "An Outline of the Policy-making Process in Japan," in Japanese Politics: An Inside View, ed. Hiroshi Itoh (Ithaca, N.Y.: Cornell University Press, 1973), pp. 12-48; Chie Nakane, Japanese Society (Berkeley: University of California Press, 1970), passim; and Ezra F. Vogel, ed., Modern Japanese Organization and Decision-Making (Berkeley: University of California Press, 1975).

51. Personal communication, October 9, 1975. See Allan Campbell, "The Implementation of Water Quality Legislation: A Comparative Study of the United States and Japan" (Ph.D. diss., Rutgers University, 1976).

52. This is the theme elaborated by Chitoshi Yanaga, op. cit.

53. For a discussion of the four major cases, see Margaret A. McKean, "The Potentials for Grass-Roots Democracy in Postwar Japan: The Anti-Pollution Movement as a Case Study in Political Activism" (Ph.D. diss., University of California at Berkeley, 1974), Chapter 2. Accounts of Yokkaichi asthma and Minamata mercury poisoning are also available in Norie Huddle and Michael Reich, Island of Dreams: Environmental Crisis in Japan (Tokyo: Autumn Press, 1975).

54. For a description of these laws and the issue of local control and initiative, see Kōgai Hakusho 1971 [White Paper on Pollution 1971] (Tokyo: Ministry of Finance Printing Office, 1971), pp. 169-88.

55. Japan Times, August and September 1975; "Pollution Irresponsibility," Japan Quarterly 23, no. 1 (January-March 1976): 3-6.

56. On the Mutsu, see Japan Times, October 22, 1973; August 1974; September 1974; October 1974; and August 26, 1975. See also "The Mutsu," Japan Quarterly 22, no. 1 (January-March 1975): 3-6.

57. See Sōrifu, "Genshiryoku Hatsuden" [The Generation of Nuclear Power], Gekkan Yoron Chōsa [Monthly Opinion Surveys] 8, no. 3 (March 1976): 27-35.

58. Kenneth R. Stunkel, "Energy Policy and Alternatives in Japan" (Paper presented at the annual meeting of the International Studies Association in Toronto, Canada, February 25-29, 1976).

CHAPTER

8

BRAZIL
Thomas F. Kelsey

Brazil is big. Surpassed in physical area only by the Soviet Union, the People's Republic of China, Canada, and the United States, its population is greater than the populations of all other developing nations with the exceptions of China, India, and Indonesia. Its area, which is approximately 3.3 million square miles, covers nearly half of South America, and its estimated 1975 population of 107.7 million accounts for half the total population of the continent. Its sheer size hints that Brazil is complex and highly variegated in all respects.

RECENT GROWTH AND DEVELOPMENT

In recent years Brazil has been viewed by many as a nation that has an excellent opportunity to move from its acknowledged position among the developing countries into the world's select group of "developed" nations. Becoming developed means improving the

This study was made possible through the cooperation and generosity of many individuals in Brazil and the United States. I would like to extend my appreciation to Jacques Schwartzman, Heinz Charles Kohler, Laura Lavenère-Wanderley, Jouve Camisassa, Alfranio Alves de Andrade, Roberto Messias Franco, and Charles Marsh. Of course, the author bears the sole responsibility for opinions expressed herein. Travel and research in Brazil during May and June 1976 was funded by the Center for Latin American Studies of the University of Pittsburgh Center for International Studies and the John G. Bowman Memorial Faculty Grants, University of Pittsburgh.

social, economic, and political quality of life of its people, and there are those who have little faith that such improvements will or even can occur. Indeed, a number of popular sayings, some originating within Brazil and others without, reflect this doubt: "Brazil is a country of the future--and always will be!" "Brazil has a great future--and always will have!" "Brazil progresses at night, while the politicians sleep." "Brazil grows at night, when the Brazilians are asleep and can't get in the way."

The actions and achievements of the four administrations that have followed the military takeover of Brazil's constitutionally elected civilian government in March 1964 have been both criticized and praised. The bulk of the criticism has centered on human rights, civil liberties, and the distribution of wealth, while plaudits have been heaped upon Brazil's spectacular economic growth since 1968 and the technocrats' innovative approaches to the simultaneous diversification and development of the economy, while they managed inflation. Terms such as "economic miracle," "the Brazilian miracle," and Brazil's "economic boom" had become commonplace in the early 1970s. Arthur F. Burns, Chairman of the United States Federal Reserve, in addressing a press conference at the U.S. consulate in Rio de Janeiro, characterized Brazil as "one of the great economic miracles of our time."[1]

Much has been written in recent years regarding the Brazilian economic success story. In nearly all cases, published works that support or refute the "miracle" do not cover the period since the dramatic price increase of crude petroleum (and subsequently its various refined products) in October 1973 and the accompanying onset of a world economic recession and, for some nations, depression. What follows is an analysis of Brazil's continuing quest to cross that wide chasm separating the less developed and the developed nations, to join the latter. Specifically, this chapter will address itself to the impact of the so-called energy crisis on the Brazilian strategies for economic growth and development.

The National Development Plan of 1972-74

The major objective of the National Development Plan of 1972-74 (a plan construed with no inkling of the imminent petroleum crisis) was to place Brazil among the world's developed nations within a single generation. This called for a doubling of per capita income between 1969 and 1980; an annual average growth in GDP of 8 to 10 percent up to 1974; a reduction in the overall annual rate of inflation to about 10 percent; and an annual increase in the employment level of 3.2 percent by 1974.

The list of steps to achieve these goals was long and ambitious. The plan called for the decentralization of economic decision making; modernization of local concerns, with particular emphasis on increasing competitiveness; a rise in incomes to develop and increase consumption through cooperation of state and federal governments with the private sector; further strengthening of the financial system and capital market; promotion of greater efficiency in all branches of government; increased financial support, especially for the expansion of small- and medium-sized firms; a national technological policy and the establishment of research centers for all basic economic activities; and programs involving the development and modernization of transportation, communications, electricity, mining, and the manufacture of steel, petrochemicals, and ships. There was a call to integrate regional development strategies, which included plans to establish new growth regions in the South, Amazonia, the Central West, and the Northeast while implementing measures to consolidate the development of the booming Southeast. To improve Brazil's position in the world economy, the plan urged the growth of exports, particularly of manufactured goods, mineral ores, and nontraditional agricultural products such as soybeans, in order to reduce the degree of dependence on coffee as a foreign exchange earner. Finally, a key to successful development was to be the human resource. This all-important resource would be enhanced through reduction of illiteracy, increased use of vocational training facilities, and educational reforms at all levels.

In the transport sector, it is significant to note that the first National Development Plan emphasized improvement and expansion of the highway system to promote efficient internal movement of commodities and people. The government chose to direct its limited capital resources more toward investment in highways than in railroads because investment in highways would create more transport capacity on a per unit basis. In the case of highways, the public sector invests in the route facilities, that is, the roads themselves, while the private sector provides the transportation equipment, in this instance trucks and service facilities. Railroads, a government enterprise, would require the allocation of public funds not only in the route facilities but also in the rolling stock and service facilities.

In general the National Development Plan required creation of, or improvements in, public and private institutions to promote economic growth and expansion, especially in secondary activities. Little was stated with respect to energy strategies. While it was recognized that Brazil was a rapidly growing consumer of petroleum and that its own known petroleum resources were meager, it was generally agreed that the import price tag for petroleum was an

acceptable bill to be paid for a meteoric rise to the goal of being an
economic superpower. [2]

To carry out all the steps for achieving the aforementioned
goals, the governmental planners and decision makers envisioned
two types of coordination or integration: (1) a coordinated relationship between government or state enterprise and private entrepreneurship (both domestic and foreign) and (2) a tie-in of Brazil's
domestic economy with the international market. The government
gave itself the role of formulating the overall strategy, that is, the
setting of goals, priorities, and means for action, in planning the
development of a sophisticated market economy. The government
would set specific and compulsory targets for its enterprises while
stating expectations and offering incentives for private enterprise. [3]

A major role of state and federal governments has been to
provide the infrastructure to support and nurture the drive for development. As such, governments have invested heavily in such
areas as energy, transport, communications, housing, water supply, and sanitation and in the enrichment of human resources
through programs in health, education, nutrition, and welfare assistance. State enterprises also dominate those activities deemed
necessary for "national security," such as mining, petroleum production and refining, petrochemicals, shipbuilding, and steel manufacturing. Most of these economic activities can be characterized as
requiring large amounts of capital and at least reasonably advanced
technology. According to government officials, most of them also
had received little interest from domestic and foreign private enterprise. The issue of the degree to which the state should participate
directly in the Brazilian economy is currently undergoing much debate. The feature article and theme of Veja (May 19, 1976) focused
on estatizacao (the act of government takeover of private enterprise),
and various politicians claimed that the government's ownership of
industries in Brazil ranged anywhere from 23 to 70 percent, depending on one's motive and point of view for saying so.

The Second National Development Plan, 1975-79

The Second National Development Plan, 1975-79 (II Plano
Nacional de Desenvolvimento), which was made public in September
1974, follows the basic strategy established under the previous plan,
but it also reflects the dramatic change in conditions brought on by
rapid growth and by the energy crisis. [4] The Second Plan puts forth
three major areas for attention: energy, urban development, and
the environment. Investments are to be encouraged in basic industry;
scientific and technological research; energy production (based on

hydropower, fossil fuels, and nuclear energy); transport and communications; education; and health. The Southeast will continue to
dominate economic output and will expand its production of import-
substituting basic goods. High priority is given to research and
further infrastructural development. While it may seem somewhat
contradictory (further discussion will clarify this), a policy of industrial decentralization will be followed as an attempt to maintain
a quality environment and make the best use of Brazil's basic natural
resources.[5]

In view of these plans, just how well has Brazil's economy per-
formed since 1972.* Table 12 reveals that in spite of the failure to
bring the annual rate of inflation down to a tolerable level of 10 percent, through 1974 the economy grew at the high rate projected in
the first national development plan. Notice, however, the abrupt
increase in inflation between 1973 and 1974 and the pronounced decrease in the overall rate of economic growth for 1975. Projections
by the Instituto Brasileiro de Economia placed growth for 1976 at no
greater than 4 percent. There was much evidence to indicate that
inflation would be greater in 1976 than it was in 1975.

The economy of Brazil is very complex and forever changing.
To say that the quadrupling of oil prices since 1974 has been the
reason for Brazil's slowdown in growth and increased rate of inflation
is somewhat true but too simplistic. The direct role of petroleum
is notably different from that in most other nations. Brazil is blessed
with one of the world's lowest degrees of dependence on petroleum
for the generating of electricity (less than 10 percent). More than
80 percent of its electrical power is derived from an extensive and
expanding network of hydroelectric generators.[6] Given its temperate
to tropical climate, there is little demand for household heating.
Even so, petroleum remains crucial for the development of transportation, for industrial processes requiring heat, and as a raw material
input for the chemical industry. Petroleum is most significant in
that it is currently the source of approximately half the energy consumed in Brazil. By late 1975 it was calculated that energy was provided by various sources in the following proportions: petroleum,
49 percent; wood and charcoal, 25 percent; hydroelectricity, 21 percent; coal, 3.2 percent; and other sources, 1.8 percent.[7]

---

*Owing to constraints of space and time, it is not feasible to
present a highly detailed, sector by sector, topic by topic account of
Brazil's economic performance since 1968. Nevertheless, one is
strongly encouraged to consult the outstanding monthly publication
Conjuntura Economica, published in Rio de Janeiro by the Instituto
Brasileiro de Economia of the Fundacao Getúlio Vargas for a complete view of the workings of Brazil's economic and financial systems.

TABLE 12

Annual Rates of Growth and Inflation of the Gross
Domestic Product of Brazil, 1969-75
(in percent)

Year	Growth Rate of GDP	Average Rate of Inflation*
1969	9.0	22.3
1970	9.5	19.8
1971	11.3	20.4
1972	10.4	17.0
1973	11.4	15.1
1974	9.6	28.7
1975	4.0	27.7

*The figures cited in this column represent an average of several measures of inflation, including such indices as cost of construction and construction materials, wholesale and retail food prices, agricultural products, industrial products, cost of living in Rio de Janeiro, and raw material costs. The more frequently cited general price index yields somewhat higher figures. For example, the rises in the general price index for 1973-75 are 15.7, 34.5, and 29.4 percent.

Source: Conjuntura Economica 30 (March 1976): 89, 111.

BRAZIL'S PETROLEUM SITUATION

While Brazil has frequently been described as a vast storehouse of basic natural resources, it has been rightfully acknowledged that this nation suffers from a lack of abundant, accessible fossil fuels, especially petroleum.* The discovery of petroleum in Brazil

---

*While Brazil's known oil and gas reserces are low and its Santa Catarina coal deposits rather unsuitable for use as an efficient fuel, the nation is blessed with one of the world's largest reserves of oil shale, concentrated in the states of Paraná and Sao Paulo. Since 1961 research has been continuing in order to develop a technology capable of producing petroleum and gas from these deposits, and the effort has been intensified since the 1973-74 oil crisis. Even so, economically feasible large-scale production still appears to be only a distant possibility as a solution to Brazil's petroleum supply problem.

dates back only to 1939, when commercially exploitable quantities were located in the Bahia Basin.[8] By the end of 1947 total annual production had reached only 15,348 cubic meters (or 96,539 barrels, given that one cubic meter is equivalent to approximately 6.29 barrels). This, of course, was far short of the supply needed to satisfy a growing national demand.

Between 1951 and 1952 there was a significant increase in domestic production (53,849 to 119,278 cubic meters), and public opinion in Brazil called loudly for the nationalization of all foreign petroleum interests. Legislation enacted in late 1953 created a state enterprise, Petróleo Brasileiro, S.A. (better known by its acronym, Petrobrás), which came into existence in 1954 and took control over all exploration and production and, for all practical purposes, came to dominate all but the retail sales in the petroleum sector. To this day Petrobrás is commonly referred to as the "state oil monopoly." Throughout the 1950s and 1960s and into the early years of the present decade, Petrobrás has continued to search Brazil's land base and, more recently, its continental shelf for petroleum and natural gas deposits. In the mid-1960s significant discoveries were made in Sergipe and Alagoas, followed closely by offshore finds in nearby areas on the continental shelf. In 1960-71 domestic production more than doubled, from 4.7 million to 9.9 million cubic meters. However, since then production has not increased significantly and in fact has tended to fluctuate.

The announcement of recent offshore discoveries off Sergipe in Rio Grande do Norte and especially in the Garoupa field off Campos in Rio de Janeiro placed many Brazilians in a near-euphoric state by early 1975. With respect to petroleum production, a page-one statement in the January 1975 issue of the forever optimistic Brazilian Bulletin blared out, "Brazil's major oil find in the Campos field off the coast of the State of Rio de Janeiro has sparked optimism throughout the country. Brazil's self-sufficiency in this field has been fully guaranteed."[9]

Nevertheless, Petrobrás officials estimate that total production for 1976 will reach 10.4 million cubic meters, 80 percent coming from land-based wells concentrated in Bahia and the remaining 20 percent from offshore platform wells.[10] This is not surprising, given the time lag between initial discovery and subsequent on-line production. Even though a number of new discoveries do hold promise for future increased production, Petrobrás itself has made no claims to self-sufficiency in crude petroleum for the near future. Based on the most current evidence, if all new discoveries were brought into full production by the end of the decade, the total domestic output of crude petroleum could reach an annual output of 40.62 million cubic meters. On the other hand, by this time domestic demand could be expected to reach some 75.44 million cubic meters annually. What this implies, then, is that all the successful efforts of Petrobrás would merely serve to hold imports at or near current levels.[11] On the positive side, however, this would significantly reduce its present 75 to 80 percent degree of dependence on foreign supplies, as shown in Table 13.

TABLE 13

Crude Petroleum Consumption, Brazil, 1972-75

Year	Domestic (in cubic meters)	Imported (in cubic meters)	Total (in cubic meters)	Imported (in percent)
1972	9,711,705	28,459,000	38,170,705	74.6
1973	9,876,154	41,030,000	50,906,154	80.6
1974	10,294,782	38,342,157	48,636,939	78.8
1975	9,978,880	40,996,160	50,975,040	80.4

Sources: Conjuntura Economica 27 (February 1973); 28 (February 1974); 29 (February 1975); 30 (February 1976).

To fuel the drive for broad economic development, Brazil has come to rely increasingly on petroleum and natural gas, especially in the transport and industrial sectors. Rising personal incomes, greater accessibility to consumer credit, substantial increases in automobile production, and a vastly improved highway system have made the automobile the most desired form of transportation to the individual Brazilian. Furthermore, prior to the 1973-74 petroleum price increases, the government's strategy for the improved efficiency of moving commodities was to concentrate development capital on building roads rather than railroads. This dramatic rise in the consumption of petroleum derivatives can be seen in Table 14.

Between the end of 1962 and the end of 1975, Brazilian consumption of gasoline (excluding aviation gasoline) increased 179.2 percent, that is, 2.79 times, or nearly threefold. The consumption of diesel fuel and petroleum gas increased even more dramatically, 226.9 percent and 233.7 percent respectively, reflecting industrial growth and an expanding truck transport system. In 1972-75, a

period that included the drastic petroleum price hikes, consumption
of these three products continued to climb. For this particular
period, consumption of gasoline, diesel fuel, and petroleum gas
increased by 21.7 percent, 47.2 percent, and 22 percent respectively,
giving evidence of the increased role of truck transportation.

TABLE 14

Consumption of Selected Petroleum Derivatives,
Brazil, 1962–75
(in thousands of cubic meters)

Year	Automobile Gasoline	Diesel Oil	Petroleum Gas
1962	5,231	3,603	970
1963	5,594	3,860	1,139
1964	6,074	4,344	1,332
1965	6,040	4,178	1,355
1966	6,639	4,522	1,502
1967	7,247	4,898	1,701
1968	8,220	5,534	1,894
1969	8,748	5,932	2,027
1970	9,705	6,515	2,225
1971	10,617	7,157	2,400
1972	12,004	8,004	2,654
1973	13,928	9,641	2,945
1974	14,343	10,608	3,120
1975	14,603	11,779	3,237

Sources: Conjuntura Economica 30 (January 1976): 93;
30 (February 1976): 58.

Comparing Tables 13 and 14 makes it obvious that Brazil continues to face an adverse situation with respect to its petroleum
supply. The various strategies of Petrobrás and the federal government for dealing with these problems warrant close attention.
While the long-range goal of lessening the degree of dependence on
imported petroleum has remained intact before, during, and since
the petroleum supply crisis of 1973–74, the strategies of Petrobrás
have changed markedly.

Petroleum Development Strategies Prior to
the Crisis of 1973-74

Even though opportunities for decreasing Brazil's dependence
on foreign oil appeared rather gloomy in the short run, a number
of measures were undertaken by Petrobrás to ease the import bill
while simultaneously stimulating development within Brazil. Because the cost of imported refined petroleum products is much
greater than that of importing crude petroleum, Petrobrás has made
a concerted effort to increase domestic refining capacity. When it
entered the refining business in 1954, Brazil's total refining output
which was only 8,711 cubic meters (or 54,800 barrels) per day,
came from a single refinery in Mataripe, Bahia, that was close to
the producing fields. By the end of 1971 production of refined
products had reached 65,500 cubic meters per day, 28,300 from
domestic crude and 37,200 from foreign sources.[12] Refinery output exceeded 100,000 cubic meters per day in 1972, with approximately 85 percent refined by six Petrobrás refineries located in
Bahia, Rio de Janeiro, Minas Gerais, Sao Paulo (two), and Rio
Grande do Sul. The remaining 15 percent was produced by six
privately owned installations.

The effort to increase refining capacity has been carried on
through the 1973-74 petroleum crisis. Domestic capacity for 1973
was 126,036 cubic meters per day; in 1974 it was 157,190; and in
1975 it was 170,700. Because of purchases of privately owned refineries, construction of new refineries, and expansion of existing
facilities, Petrobrás now accounts for more than 98 percent of the
total refining capacity, while two private refineries, Refinaria de
Manguinhos and Refinaria Ipiranga, produce less than 2 percent.
During 1976 Petrobrás was expected to bring two more refineries on
line: a new refinery in Manaus that would have a daily capacity of
4,770 cubic meters (or about 30,000 barrels) per day, which would
be nearly four times greater than the capacity of the already existing Refinaria de Manaus; and the Refinaria de Araucária, with 20,000
cubic meters (or about 125,800 barrels) daily.[13] The latter was
viewed as a major addition, since it was expected to serve as the
nucleus of an industrial complex in Paraná and its refined products
were also to be distributed to nearby demand points, thus eliminating costly surface shipments from refineries in Rio de Janeiro
(Duque de Caxias), Sao Paulo (Paulínea), and Rio Grande do Sul
(Canoas). What this meant to Brazil, then, is that while it might
be necessary to import 75 to 80 percent of the total crude oil demanded by Brazil's pulsing economy, Brazilian installations would
already account for more than 95 percent of the total amount of

refined products, and this share was expected to increase in the near future.*

That portion of the Petrobrás annual budget allocated to exploration and development of crude petroleum had been increasing steadily prior to the crisis. Search efforts were conducted both on land and in the offshore basins, but emphasis was placed on the latter. The level of technology and the skilled manpower and equipment needs of petroleum exploration and development per se, especially in offshore locations, have grown to be highly sophisticated and astronomically expensive. At this point it is important to note that Petrobrás, as opposed to other state petroleum monopolies in Latin America and in other developing regions of the world, is credited by many as having moved far beyond the stage of having been charged with a given responsibility but not having the human and capital resources to carry it out. Many Brazilians point with pride to the fact that Petrobrás is staffed by an abundance of highly competent Brazilian petroleum engineers, geologists, and geophysicists. Increasingly these technicians and scientists have received their formal educations within Brazil. Janet D. Henshall and Richard P. Momsen have asserted that after a painful initial period of mismanagement owing to inexperience and the appointment of unqualified political hacks to top positions, Petrobrás has become one of South America's largest and most efficient enterprises.[14] For the year 1975 Fortune places Petrobrás twenty-first on the list of the 500 largest industrial corporations outside the United States.[†] Of the 50 largest industrial corporations in the world, Petrobrás ranked thirty-eighth. Of the top 60 firms, only Brazil and Iran (National Iranian Oil) were listed as having industrial enterprises within this category while being considered developing nations. The remaining 58 are found in Europe, Anglo America, and Japan.[15] That it is one of the largest firms is not disputed, but its degree of efficiency

---

*The increased refining capacity has been accompanied by a series of developments to insure that imported crude oil could move quickly and efficiently to inland refineries. Port facilities were modernized, large-scale storage facilities were constructed, and pipelines were built. (For details of these undertakings, see Janet D. Henshall and Richard P. Momsen, Jr., A Geography of Brazilian Development (London: G. Bell and Sons, 1974), pp. 201-04.

†This ranking was based on 1975 sales of $6.626 billion. In addition, Petrobrás held assets worth $6.77 billion, had a net income of $703.59 million and $3.365 billion in stockholders equity, and employed 51,044 people.

is a constant subject of controversy, as subsequent discussion will reveal. The point here is that rather than simply issuing general directives to foreign firms working under service contracts, Petrobrás was primarily using its own personnel and equipment.

Realizing that Brazil would require foreign petroleum for a substantial number of years to come, in April 1972 Petrobrás created a subsidiary organization, Petrobrás Intercional, S.A., better known as Braspetro, to send its expertise abroad. This firm was given the responsibility of participating directly or indirectly through its own subsidiaries in the exploration, development production, transportation, and marketing of petroleum in other developing countries. In that same year Braspetro signed exploration contracts with Colombia, Iraq, the Malagasy Republic, Egypt, and Algeria. By engaging in overseas petroleum ventures, Petrobrás would develop a more secure foreign supply and at the same time develop a market for Brazilian industries that manufacture products used in the various phases of the petroleum industry, such as steel pipe, and crude-oil tankers.

Since large volumes of crude petroleum had to be imported, Petrobrás implemented plans to order high-capacity oil tankers in order that Brazilian ships would move the oil, thus saving valuable foreign exchange while stimulating Brazil's shipbuilding industry. Modern terminal facilities were constructed at Sao Sebastiao (near Santos), and channels were dredged that were deep enough to permit Petrobrás to utilize the efficient supertankers (150,000 tons deadweight and more). Prior to the petroleum crisis, besides ferrying crude oil to its own shores, Petrobrás had reached an agreement with Venezuelan authorities to carry Venezuelan crude to the United States.[16]

In summary, then, prior to the 1973-74 crisis the strategies of Petrobrás to ensure Brazil a plentiful, affordable petroleum supply were to increase domestic refining capacity and provide an efficient infrastructure to acquire crude petroleum and disseminate refined products; expand domestic exploration efforts; increase overseas connections and exploration through Braspetro; and increase its international ocean shipping capacity. As October 1973 approached, it appeared that these coordinated measures would indeed assure Brazil of a continued supply of petroleum that could keep pace with the demands of one of the world's fastest growing economies. However, as can be seen in the following discussion, the drastic price hike in crude petroleum and the supply uncertainties raised by the Arab oil embargo have caused Petrobrás to reassess its strategies and its role in Brazil's path to development.

Altered Petroleum Development Strategies
Since 1973-74

The drive to create adequate domestic refining capacity has
continued since the crisis. Comparison of 1974 and 1975 data for
the importation of refined petroleum products in Brazil appears to
show that this strategy is beginning to pay off. In terms of quantity,
imports fell from 2,004,113 cubic meters in 1974 to 687,415 cubic
meters in 1975, a decrease of 65.7 percent.[17] This resulted in a
net savings of foreign exchange of nearly $150 million. It may be
suspected that this decrease was the result of the slowdown of the
economy rather than of increased refining capacity. To refute this,
Brazilian consumption of the principal refined products in 1975 exceeded that of 1974, ranging from a slight increase in automobile
gasoline (.6 percent) to sizable increases in liquefied gas (3.8 percent), kerosene and jet fuel (6.4 percent), and diesel oil (11 percent).[18]

A Petrobrás strategy, which was begun before the crisis but
which has since been intensified, has been to influence the level of
consumption of certain petroleum products through the use of a
discriminatory pricing system. Table 15 illustrates the timing and
the nature of a series of Petrobrás price hikes since the beginning
of 1973. In late 1975 it was announced that, for 1976, gasoline
prices would be raised by 25 percent to discourage increased consumption, while diesel and fuel oil prices would rise 10 percent.
The anticipated additional revenues would be directed toward projects
for transport improvement and expansion of energy supplies.[19] By
July 1, 1976, regular gasoline at the pump retailed for 4.34 cruzeiros
per liter (about U.S. $1.54 per gallon). Since December 31, 1972,
the price for gasoline had been raised no less than 13 times. From
January 1, 1973, when the price was 0.745 cruzeiros per liter, to
July 1, 1976, when the price reached the level stated above, there
had been nearly a sixfold increase.[20] At the beginning of June 1976
the Minister of Mines and Energy, Shigeaki Ueki, announced that the
policy of high gasoline prices was showing the desired results: consumption of automobile gasoline had been relatively stable since 1974
in spite of the fact that there was a growing number of vehicles in
operation.[21]

Another step to curb consumption was the issuance of Decree
76703 of December 2, 1975. This decree limits purchases in 1976
of liquid fuel (primarily gasoline) for the motor vehicles of government ministries and agencies to 80 percent of the volume purchased
in 1975.[22]

TABLE 15

Petroleum Price Increases, Brazil, January 1, 1973,
to September 19, 1975

Date	Products Affected	Percent of Increase
January 1, 1973	gasoline	8.0
	all others	4.7
May 1, 1973	average of all products	3.0
January 1, 1974	average of all products	14.0
April 1, 1974	average of all products	32.3
August 23, 1974	average of all products	11.0
January 1, 1975	gasoline	10.9
	fuel oil	9.2
	liquid gas	8.2
May 21, 1975	average of all products	14.5
September 19, 1975	average of all products	10.08

Sources: Bank of London and South America, Bolsa Review, various issues.

Much of the gasoline burned in Brazilian automobiles is approximately 2 percent anhydrous alcohol; this is still another measure that has been taken to stretch each precious barrel of petroleum. In November 1975 the National Alcohol Plan was made public and set forth an ambitious annual production goal of 3 billion liters (approximately 80 million gallons) of alcohol by 1980 for use in fuel mixing and industry. [23] Today it is thought that the ideal mixture of gasoline and alcohol is 85 to 15 percent but that it is feasible to have a mixture containing as much as 25 percent alcohol. For Brazil to achieve a mixture having 15 percent alcohol, it would be necessary to have an annual production of no less than 1.5 billion liters. Brazil's annual output of anhydrous alcohol now stands at approximately 200 million liters. [24]

As might be expected, the announcement of the plan to produce so much alcohol triggered fears that the consumer price for refined sugar would rise drastically, owing to this sudden increased demand for cane sugar as a source for anhydrous alcohol. The plan requires substantial investment in cane planting and processing, storage facilities, and so on. The Banco do Brasil (Bank of Brazil) will finance projects once they have been presented to and approved by the Institute of Sugar and Alcohol (IAA). The IAA will maintain its monopoly by determining unit prices for production; making the actual purchases; and, in turn, selling the alcohol to Petrobrás and other industrial consumers. Sugar will not be the sole source of alcohol, however. An item in Veja (June 9, 1976) announced that a contract had been signed between Petrobrás and Veragro (Veredas Agropecuaria, S.A.) to provide 38,000 tons of mandioca per year, beginning in 1978, for four years, to supply 30 percent of the raw material needed by a Petrobrás processing plant to be constructed at Curvelo, in Minas Gerais, 110 miles north of Belo Horizonte.

The effectiveness of the consumption-curbing measures of Petrobrás is difficult to discern. Imports of petroleum for the first quarter of 1976 totaled 12.4 million cubic meters, a 14 percent increase over the comparable period in 1975.[25] However, this did not necessarily mean that total imports for 1976 would exceed those of the previous year. When OPEC price increases are anticipated, imports tend to be stepped up prior to the actual price rise, and quarterly import figures vary considerably as a result.

Before the petroleum crisis Petrobrás purchased its foreign petroleum through the huge transnational petroleum companies, but it is important to note that since that time it has sought to deal directly with the governments of the producing countries to secure a long-term supply. This has been especially true in obtaining oil from Saudi Arabia. Accompanying this trend, Petrobrás is striving to increase its overseas service and marketing activities through yet another subsidiary, Interbrás, which is penetrating the African market by providing various services to oil-rich Nigeria.[26]

Within Brazil Petrobrás has greatly intensified its efforts to find and develop its own petroleum supplies. Petrobrás spent some 3.3 billion cruzeiros (approximately U.S. $400 million) in 1975 to explore and develop its domestic petroleum resources, and that effort was to be nearly doubled for 1976, in the amount of 6.1 billion cruzeiros (approximately U.S. $540 million, the rate of exchange having changed because of frequent minidevaluations of the cruzeiro in 1976).[27] This activity is occurring so rapidly, on such a large scale, and requires such sophisticated equipment, that Petrobrás must purchase or lease outside help. For instance, the semi-submersible offshore platform Blue Water III arrived at its location some 60 miles off the coast of Santa Catarina in early June of 1976, having been shipped from the North Sea area the previous March. Petrobrás is leasing this platform and another from the United States firm Santa Fe International at a daily cost of approximately $18,000.[28]

By far the most controversial measure undertaken by Petrobrás to speed up the search for Brazilian petroleum was the decision, first announced by President Geisel in October 1975, to invite transnational petroleum firms to participate directly in the exploration for petroleum on Brazilian territory under a new "risk contract" system. The efficacy of this move is still being hotly debated in Congress, and journalists are constantly criticizing Petrobrás officials for the latter's refusal to release details of the tentative contracts.

Those who continue to oppose foreign participation in Brazil's search for domestic petroleum resources argue their case on the basis of two major points. First, Law 2004 of October 3, 1953, sets forth the condition that all petroleum in Brazil, whether below or above ground, is the property of the state. It is feared that the foreign private firms that would undertake the risk and expense of searching would have to be given a share of production if exploitable reserves were located or, at the least, these firms would expect payment in kind if production were established. In effect, this would endanger the sovereignty of Petrobrás over Brazilian petroleum resources. The second point made by the opponents of risk contracts is that the recent offshore discoveries by Petrobrás indicate that a significant breakthrough has been made by the state enterprise and that self-sufficiency in petroleum is just around the corner. Therefore there is no need for outside participation.*

Supporters of foreign participation argue, with convincing data to back them up, that there is a need for altering Law 2004 if Brazil is to carry out its ambitious economic and social development plans, but this does not mean that Petrobrás must relinquish its decision-making control over exploration and development matters. The state entity would dictate the terms for private participation (national or foreign), while the contracted firms would be under direct Petrobrás control. Any crude petroleum produced by these firms would remain in Brazil until such a time as the country's annual requirements were fully satisfied. It is accepted that some form of payment would have to be made for the transnational company's share

---

*In its accelerated drive to develop Brazil's petroleum resources in the late 1960s and early 1970s, Petrobrás did in fact purchase, lease, or contract for foreign equipment and personnel to aid in exploration efforts. For example, U.S. firms provided supply ships, captained by Americans and crewed by Brazilians, to Petrobrás to ferry men and supplies to offshore drilling platforms. A Canadian firm was under contract to Petrobrás to furnish a rig and a toolpusher to drill test wells in the westernmost portion of the Amazon Basin. This was not contrary to the stipulation of Law 2004, which established the Petrobrás monopoly, since the decisions regarding the use of these foreign technicians, equipment, and supplies remained with Petrobrás.

of production, but it seems far preferable to purchase crude petroleum within Brazil from firms operating in the country and, presumably, over which the government could exert some price control,
than to be forced to buy it overseas. This way Brazil would be
protected from the supply controls exerted by petroleum-exporting
countries, such as those of the Arab oil embargo of 1973.

In spite of the continuing debate, Petrobrás produced a list of
40 transnational petroleum companies it deemed "qualified" to undertake exploration in designated areas and invited them to submit contract proposals by March 16, 1976.* Because of the adamant refusal of Petrobrás to make public the details of a typical risk contract, an environment of adversity and suspicion surrounds its
current dealings with the foreign firms. Nevertheless, it is possible to state the general conditions of a contract as follows. (1) The
contracted firm executes all operations of exploration and field development in the stipulated area. (2) All costs and investments of
exploration and production are the total responsibility of the contracted firm. (3) Reimbursement of these expenses will occur only
if the petroleum discovery comes into commercial production.
(4) The conditions of remuneration for services rendered, considering the risk taken by the private firm, are set forth in each specific contract, whether in the form of direct repayment of capital
or participation in the production of oil. (5) All programs and investments are subject to prior approval by Petrobrás, which will
continue to be the sole owner of the reserves discovered, the
petroleum obtained, the areas developed, and the installations
constructed. [29]

Bitterness, pessimism, and suspicion of the Petrobrás risk
contracts are highly visible in Brazilian newspapers and magazines.
For example, Veja, which is a weekly news magazine similar in
format to Time and Newsweek, reported in its May 12, 1976, issue
on the visit of Walter Link, a petroleum geologist who had come as

---

*While the precise concession areas have not been made public,
it is generally agreed that there are some ten areas to be offered for
foreign exploration. Three are in the North, one inland close to the
Venezuelan border and two in the extensive delta region at the mouth
of the Amazon River adjacent to Petrobrás test well sites. The
remaining seven lie along the central and southern continental shelf,
as follows: two off Espírito Santo; one off Rio de Janeiro; two off
Sao Paulo (near Santos); one off Santa Catarina (near Laguna); and
one off the coast of Rio Grande do Sul. Note that this excludes areas
near producing fields and discoveries off Bahia, and none of the
concessions will lie in deep waters beyond the 200 meter contour.

chief of a technical mission sent by Exxon to negotiate for the right
to explore one of the ten areas open to search by foreign firms
under risk contracts.[30] Link had served as chief geologist for
Petrobrás from 1954 to 1961 and had helped prepare a series of
geologic maps now being sold by Petrobrás for a fee of $0.4 million
to companies considering entering into a risk contract. He had become a controversial figure in 1958 when he publicly issued highly
pessimistic opinions about the existence of petroleum in Brazil
while simultaneously urging that the U.S. Secretary of State, John
Foster Dulles, speak to Brazilian officials about terminating the
Petrobrás monopoly on exploration and production. The account of
a connection between Link and the U.S. Secretary of State is popular
among many Brazilians who fear loss of control of Brazil's petroleum resources to the huge transnational petroleum companies. The
scholarly investigation of Petrobrás and foreign interests by Peter
Seaborn Smith does not reveal a direct contact between these two
parties.[31]

The mere presence of Link in Brazil set off a series of re-
marks by various politicians. An apparent defender of Link,
Senator Luiz Cavalcanti of the Alianca Renovadora Nacional-Sergipe,
or National Renewal Alliance (ARENA-SE), stated that the U.S.
geologist had not been deceptive in his 1950s opinion of Brazilian
petroleum prospects because he had been referring only to land
areas, not what may lie beneath the sea. Now Link urged, and
Cavalcanti agreed, that the areas subject to foreign exploration
should be expanded. Deputy Getúlio Dias of the Movimento Demo-
crático Brasileiro-Rio Grande do Sul, or Brasilia Democratic
Movement (MDB-RS) issued an acrid retort: "Link has nothing more
to say. He has already said that there is no petroleum in the country. Now he should be considered persona non grata."[32]

The response to the Petrobrás invitation has been neither
rapid nor widespread. The closing date for contract proposals had
been pushed back from March 16 to July 15, 1976. By mid-May
Petrobrás officials indicated that only nine foreign firms had purchased the sedimentary basin data packets upon which exploration
proposals were to be made. When it was publicly acknowledged in
early June that British Petroleum (BP) had acquired an information
packet, an air of optimism arose. It was pointed out that BP has a
rather distinguished record of successful petroleum exploration.
It was a pioneer in the North Sea discoveries, and its Alaska finds
occurred at a time when most firms were seriously considering
halting exploration efforts there.[33] The sketchy initial reports are
that BP is interested in exploring an offshore region at the mouth of
the Amazon River, applying its deep-water exploration expertise.

It is much too early to anticipate the results of this new and
highly controversial policy, since the risk contracts have yet to be

let. First Petrobrás must review all the proposals, and then it must negotiate with each firm or consortium. Meanwhile, the frustration and criticism generated by the paucity of substantive information released by Petrobrás continues to grow. For example, in May a congressional debate over the risk contract policy between Senators Jarbas Passarinho (ARENA) and Roberto Saturnino (MDB) was suspended owing to a lack of official information.[34] An editorial in the Jornal do Brasil, a Rio de Janeiro newspaper, states that Petrobrás has failed to produce the results it has promised and that its rates of efficiency are among the lowest and its wages per man-hour the highest in the petroleum and petrochemical industries of the world.[35]

In the review of Brazil's petroleum situation for 1976 in World Oil, the expressed opinion is that the terms of the Petrobrás risk contracts are generally perceived as "onerous" by the companies.[36] This was seen by many as an indication that Petrobrás did not really desire this particular type of foreign assistance, while those who make decisions for Brazil as a whole, who in 1976 were faced with $4 billion in petroleum imports (primarily from Saudi Arabia), would have to take measures to remedy and improve a stagnating, perhaps sagging, domestic production. This leads one to suspect that there have been continuing differences of opinion between President Geisel (himself a former president of Petrobrás) and his executive staff and the officials of Petrobrás that are reminiscent of those described by Peter Seaborn Smith with respect to Petrobrás during 1954-70.[37]

THE RELATIONSHIP BETWEEN INCREASED PETROLEUM PRICES AND THE STATUS OF BRAZIL'S ECONOMY

As stated previously, to say that the increased price of petroleum and its uncertain supply is the reason for Brazil's reduced rate of economic growth is rather simplistic. There are many who assert that even if the petroleum crisis of 1973-74 had not occurred, Brazil's rate of economic growth would have declined nevertheless. If one analyzes the world economic situation for 1968-73, a period of rapid expansion in Brazil, it can be seen that for the most part the world was experiencing an economic boom. Prices for agricultural products and raw materials had risen sharply in response to high aggregate demand, and the productive capacities of the industrialized nations were at their peaks. Inflation was a major world problem.

The accelerated rate of GNP growth in Brazil through 1973 was bound to taper off. Brazil does not possess the full spectrum of industries and services typical of a developed nation, and it was only a matter of time before those economic activities that did account for domestic growth would encounter difficulties as a result of bottlenecks and lack of development in complementary sectors. The surfeit in the balance of trade, which had accrued through massive exports of raw materials, especially iron ore, and agricultural products (thanks to favorable weather conditions) at a time of very high world prices, and the high growth rates in certain economic sectors, including mining, steel, and shipbuilding, created an environment of high demand and inflationary pressures. The GNP declined slightly in 1974, but this was tempered by an exceptional output of agricultural export products. The various bottlenecks that arose by the end of this six-year period of high growth brought on the inevitable run on imports, and Brazil experienced a tremendous increase in its annual import bill, from approximately $6.2 billion in 1973 to $12.6 billion in 1974.

Petroleum in Relation to Other Imports

This sudden doubling of the value of imports, plus a worsening in the overall balance of payments, has been directly attributed to the increase in petroleum prices. Import statistics, however, show that this really accounted for only half the increase. While the value of petroleum and its derivatives accounted for 11.5 percent of total imports in 1973, this share increased to 21.5 percent in 1974, even though the price of petroleum had quadrupled.[38] While the total quantity of petroleum and its derivatives actually declined slightly between 1973 and 1974, the quantities of other imports increased significantly. For example, the percentage increase in imported tonnage of the following items for 1974 over 1973 was as follows: wheat, 17 percent; alloyed steel and steel shapes, 131.2 percent; fertilizers, 27.9 percent; copper, 43.9 percent; aluminum, 76.7 percent; zinc, 18.4 percent; electrical equipment, 33.4 percent; and transportation equipment, 49.7 percent.[39] It became necessary to purchase foreign products that could not be produced in Brazil because of the inelasticity of domestic supply. Since inflation existed in the developed countries where the products originated, Brazil, like so many developing nations, not only incurred domestic inflation but also imported it in the form of higher prices for increased purchase of foreign goods.

Priorities of Concern for Economic
Recovery and Advancement

Brazilian policy makers now describe their situation as an "economy in transition (economia em transicao), in preparation for a later return to a showing of higher growth rates. It is not difficult to understand the decision of the National Development Council (Conselho Nacional de Desenvolvimento), as taken in January 1976, to push for the development of those industries that produce capital equipment and intermediate goods. A key sector for this is the steel industry, which while fully capable of producing large volumes of steel plate, currently does not produce the alloyed steels and steel shapes needed by already existing industries. The result is the necessity to import large quantities of products having high value-added content. To illustrate, Petrobrás purchases as much equipment as it can from domestic sources. However, as a major purchaser of steel products for its petroleum exploration, production, and transportation efforts, it finds itself faced with the necessity of importing no less than 75 percent of the value of its steel needs.[40]

In the process of developing and diversifying the economy, the balance of payments is bound to suffer. The amount of foreign capital, technology, and goods required to develop efficient (in terms of economies of scale) productive capacities in such areas as steel specialties, fertilizers, petrochemicals, and nonferrous metals is enormous. When the rate of growth of the economy declined sharply in 1975, foreign observers began to grumble about the credit rating of Brazil, the IMF's largest customer. Massive amounts of private foreign credits had been extended to Brazilian projects prior to the petroleum crisis and economic recession, thus contributing to a favorable balance of payments, but as a result of subsequent financial outflows as interest, profit remittances, royalty and technical assistance fees, transportation costs, and foreign travel, Brazil has had since 1974 an adverse balance of payments situation. Nevertheless, a concerted effort was made by the Geisel administration, and by President Ernesto Geisel personally, to restore foreign faith in Brazil's economy even during its state of transition. Apparently the effort was successful. As a result of a visit to Great Britain by Geisel; Mario Henrique Simonsen (the Minister of the Treasury); and several other high-ranking officials representing federal, state, and private enterprises a complex $1 billion accord was reached between European credit suppliers from Great Britain (at 40 percent),

West Germany (at 30 percent), France (at 25 percent), and Italy (at
5 percent) and officials of Acominas, a new Brazilian steel venture
in Minas Gerais whose production is scheduled to come on stream
in 1979.[41] This credit will enable Acominas to produce a variety of
steel shapes for the domestic market that currently must be imported.*

One of the measures taken to achieve the foremost immediate
goal, the improvement in the balance of payments, serves to illustrate the government's very serious intention of improving its economic position. While increased wealth resulting from economic
growth has not accrued to the whole range of economic classes, the
absolute numbers of people who have experienced this is very large.
One result of this has been increased foreign travel, primarily for
purposes of tourism. For the year 1974, the precious foreign exchange consumed by Brazilians in foreign travel totaled $395 million.
By the end of 1975 the figure had reached $482 million, an increase
of 22 percent. According to a newspaper statement attributed to
Minister of the Treasury Simonsen, if no changes were made in
foreign travel policies for Brazilians, foreign exchange paid out for
travel in 1976 for tourism alone would reach $708 million.[42]

To stem this outflow of capital, Decree-Law 1470, effective
June 4, 1976, burst onto the scene without prior warning. This law
requires Brazilian tourists traveling out of the country by air to
deposit 12,000 cruzeiros per person, regardless of age, in the Bank
of Brazil in order to receive an exit visa and the right to purchase
$1,000 in U.S. currency. The deposit must remain in the bank for
one year, at the end of which a refund will be made without interest.[43]
The purpose of this law is twofold, to stem the outflow of capital and
to create a fund to be used for the development of tourism within
Brazil. Needless to say, the outcry from travel agents, international
airlines, and certainly Brazilian tourists was loud, but as of the time
of this writing the law still stands.

-----

*It is most encouraging to note that as Brazilian entrepre-
neurs, both state and private, import the equipment and technology
for the production of capital and intermediate goods, they also import the most recent techniques and equipment for the control of
pollution, the recycling of water and gases, and so on. Much of
the pollution control technology being adopted has recent origins in
the heavily industrialized areas in Japan and Western Europe (much
more so than in the United States).

DEGRADATION OF THE ENVIRONMENT AS A
TRADE OFF FOR RAPID GROWTH

Since 1968 the major metropolitan areas of Brazil, especially Sao Paulo, Rio de Janeiro, and Belo Horizonte, have experienced spectacular growth in terms of total population, numbers of fabricating and processing industries, and intensity of vehicular (car, bus, truck) traffic. It has become blatantly obvious that the overall quality of life in terms of the physical environment has suffered in the face of rapid economic growth. Monumental congestion, high noise levels, and intolerably polluted air (both in terms of particulate matter and noxious gases) and water have become commonplace. These developments have not gone unnoticed. Almost daily the newspapers carry harrowing accounts of traffic accidents, pedestrian fatalities, landslides, water main breaks, water shortages, unbearable air and noise conditions, and on and on. There are articles, interviews with politicians, and editorials crying out for solutions to these problems. These unfortunate conditions are not complacently accepted as an evil necessary for achieving growth and development.

Evidence of Federal, State, and Municipal Concern
for a Quality Environment

Federal Decree 73030 of October 30, 1973 created SEMA, Secretaria Especial do Meio Ambiente (Special Secretariat for the Environment), an autonomous agency within the Ministry of the Interior charged with the overall responsibility of assuring a quality physical environment and the rational use of Brazil's natural resources.[44] Among its myriad duties SEMA was charged with the task of establishing acceptable levels of air, noise, and water pollution; working directly or cooperating with other agencies in the control and financing of the work necessary to establish such norms; promoting, at all levels, the training of a body of skilled, technologically competent personnel to deal with environmental matters; and energetically promoting on a national scale, the education of Brazil's population with respect to the efficient use of natural resources and the need to maintain a quality environment.

The details of the workings of SEMA, its relationships with other agencies, and the environmental legislation it has recommended are extremely complex and pass far behond the scope of this study. Suffice it to say that the current situation in Brazil is much like that of the United States, where debates rage between industrialists and the environmentalists about who is to blame for the degradation of the environment, which parties should bear the cost of cleaning up the already polluted areas, and so on.

In Brazil the environmental programs in metropolitan areas are only in a nascent state of being, but they do in fact exist. Greater Sao Paulo, with its nearly 10 million people, millions of vehicles with no pollution control devices, and 30,000 industries, has come to experience conditions that truly test a human's ability to survive. In October 1975, under the auspices of the State of Sao Paulo Agency of Basic Sanitation Technology and Environmental Protection, or Companhia Estadual de Tecnologia de Saneamento Básico e de Defesa do Meio Ambiente (CETESB), a project to map the distribution of the industries that pollute the air and water of greater Sao Paulo was begun. By April 1976 some 19,440 plants had been visited, but only 10,550 had been analyzed with respect to their patterns and volumes of pollution. A goal of this inventory, which was expected to be completed by December 1976, was to provide reliable data for constructing a mathematical model that would anticipate pollution patterns under varying weather conditions. It is hoped that such a model can be available by the end of 1977.[45] A related program, Operation Winter (Operacao Inverno), has already been designed to recommend the various actions to be taken during times of very heavy air pollution, depending on the nature and intensity of local air conditions. It is unfortunate that Sao Paulo suffers so many temperature inversions during its winter months. The various stages of alert (Attention, Alert, and Emergency) call for differing degrees of action, such as voluntary degrees in use of automobiles and progressive cutbacks in industrial operations. Needless to say, the opposition from industrial associations such as the State of Sao Paulo Federation of Industries, or Federacao das Industrias do Estado de Sao Paulo (FIESP) is intense.

The greater Rio de Janeiro metropolitan area, encompassing 15 municipalities, also is undergoing change with respect to intolerable air, water, and noise conditions. On June 5, 1976, a $2 million contract was signed between the Development Foundation for the Metropolitan Region, or Fundacao para o Desenvolmimento da Regiao Metropolitana (known as Fundrem), and the State Foundation for the Management of the Environment, or Fundacao Estadual de Engenharia do Meio Amhiente (FEEMA), to conduct a study similar to the one undertaken in Sao Paulo by CETESB for essentially the same purposes.

In 1975 the government of Minas Gerais charged its principal research and planning agency, Fundacao Joao Pinheiro (FJP, a state version of the federal Fundacao Getúlio Vargas), with the responsibility for establishing a multi-faceted program to deal with air and water pollution, soil erosion, and mining problems.

Formulation of the <u>Programa de Meio Ambiente</u> (Environment Program) began in April. In August 1975 a special commission was created by the governor, within FJP, to systematically study the environmental conditions in the greater Belo Horizonte metropolitan area and recommend a plan of action to the governor by August 1976.

At present there are no state regulations with respect to air pollution, and attempts by local government officials to take direct action to reduce air pollution have met with little success. In 1975 Newton Cardoso, the mayor of Contagem, a heavily industrialized suburb of Belo Horizonte, gained national attention when he ordered the Itaú cement plant closed down after its officials refused his requests that they place filtering equipment on their stacks. Cardoso's order was hastily overruled by a federal decree permitting the Itaú plant to remain in operation with the promise that the stacks would receive filters within one year. Federal authorities viewed the mayor's move as a dangerous precedent. If all mayors issued orders for major polluters to clean up or shut down (in election years, it seems), in all likelihood Brazil's expanding industrial base would come to a screeching halt.

Critical Shortage of Skilled Environmentalists and Concomitant Resources

Although public concern abounds, those working in FJP Environment Program find themselves having to begin at ground zero. Industrialists feel threatened by rumors that the Special Commission on the Environment will recommend environmental legislation to the governor that would regulate mining, removal of vegetation (many blast furnaces still use charcoal), the use of water, and the types and amounts of factory waste allowed into the air. Those designing the most basic studies, which are sorely needed for policy recommendations, are feeling the plight of a developing nation. There are not enough skilled people available to serve the needs of industry <u>and</u> the government agencies who try to improve the environment. Brazil's efforts to increase its educated, technically skilled labor force have produced a large number of highly capable people, but given the massive scale of the nation, it is not nearly enough. Business and industry, with their high salaries, attract most of the very able. While federal and state agencies now offer higher salaries than in past years, if such agencies as Fundacao Joao Pinheiro do attract capable, dedicated individuals (and indeed they do), those individuals then find their earnest efforts thwarted by the lack of support personnel, research facilities, equipment, and operating capital. [46]

In the competition for highly trained people, the biggest losers are the universities, the very ones that should be the winners in order to train an ever greater number of people capable of serving the needs of industrial and environmental agencies. Soon after a bright young individual returns from overseas with an excellent education or graduates from one of a handful of outstanding programs in Brazilian universities and begins teaching and training others, he or she will hear from a friend or colleague that the rewards (especially material, but also of accomplishment) are far greater in industry, in governmental planning and research, or in business than in academia. The result: one less capable person to train others. This is the situation in Belo Horizonte, as it is throughout Brazil.

CONCLUSION

The policy makers of Brazil are well aware of the differences between growth and development. They agree that the relevant goal of development is improvement of the quality of life and that increasing the outputs of goods and services is a means of achieving that goal rather than a goal in itself. The differences in the two national development plans, 1972-74 and 1975-79, are notable. While the first plan emphasized the expansion of output and accumulation of developmental capital and technology, the second focuses on a more equitable distribution among the people of economic gains and promotion of the general welfare.

Unfortunately, the immediate future seems ominous. To succeed in its planned domestic programs, Brazil must be highly successful in the world economy. The particular goal of expanding semimanufactured and manufactured products for the export market will be difficult to achieve, since foreign demand is most likely to be constrained by the present recessed (depressed?) state of most other nations. Furthermore, if Brazil does manage to accomplish its export expansion, its perception by other nations as a new major supplier rather than a minor participant in the foreign markets will bring on adverse reactions. As a major economic power Brazil would undoubtedly encounter new trade barriers (witness the reaction of U.S. shoe manufacturers to the sudden influx of Brazilian-made footwear on the U.S. market) and find itself the target of protectionist attitudes in nations concerned about their own development plans.

Stefan H. Robock, in his most recent assessment of Brazil's road to development, raises a very important point that bears repeating here.[47] One particular strategy for gaining a greater role

in world trade is to rely heavily on the many transnational enterprises now operating in Brazil to increase their exports as suppliers
to other parts of their systems overseas. This may reduce the risk
of encountering protective barriers while at the same time creating
a favorable trade balance. It is plain to see, however, that some
rather sensitive issues would (or in fact do now) place these types of
Brazilian exports in a precarious position. Ford Motor Company of
Brazil exports engines to the United States for its Pinto model. How
does this affect its Sao Paulo operations when Americans are not
buying subcompact models? Brazil's largest and busiest shipyard,
Ishikawajima do Brasil Estaleiros, S.A. (ISHIBRAS), a joint venture
with the Japanese corporation Ishikawajima Harima Heavy Industries,
has orders to fill through 1980. Japanese shipyards have received
no major orders for the coming years, and as current construction
of ships is completed, the labor force is becoming unemployed.

If Brazil is to succeed in improving the welfare of its entire
population, it must accomplish several goals, simultaneously at
home and abroad. To do this Brazil must rely heavily on the world
economic order and quickly increase the number of highly educated,
technically skilled people available for its social and economic development programs. One unique problem that must be dealt with
in these programs is that Brazil's population, which is rapidly
growing, has a high dependency ratio (2.2 dependent persons to
share the income of each one gainfully employed) and an age struc-
trure dominated by the "less than 15 years of age" group (42.5 percent in the 1970 census). This places tremendous strain on the
infrastructure and absorbs capital that might otherwise be used to
expand directly productive activities such as manufacturing and
agriculture.[48]

To conclude, given the present chaotic world energy situation
and the sluggish performance of the world economy, Brazil's chances
of vaulting into membership among the developed nations are indeed
slim. While the attitude of the Brazilian populace toward concern for
the natural environment and the overall quality of life is increasingly
positive, allocation of resources to combat deteriorating environmental conditions does not yet receive top priority.

NOTES

1. Lewis Beman, "How the Brazilians Manage their Boom,"
Fortune, December 1972, p. 110.
2. Bolsa Review (Bank of London and South America) 5 (November 1971): 658-59.

3. "Dez Anos de Economia Brasileira (1964-1973)," in A Economia Brasileira e suas Perspectivas XIII (Rio de Janeiro: APEC Editora, S.A., 1974), p. 142.

4. Projeto do II Plano Nacional de Desenvolvimento (1975-1979) (Brasília: República Federativa do Brasil, 1974).

5. Bolsa Review 8 (September 1974): 600-01.

6. For a thorough understanding of the evolution of electrical power in Brazil and its regional distribution, see Judith Tendler, Electric Power in Brazil: Entrepreneurship in the Public Sector (Cambridge: Harvard University Press, 1968), and Janet D. Henshall and Richard P. Momsen, Jr., A Geography of Brazilian Development (London: G. Bell and Sons, 1974), pp. 187-98.

7. "Petróleo: A Situacao Mundial e o Brasil," Fundacao Joao Pinheiro 5 (October 1975): 21.

8. Peter Seaborn Smith, Oil and Politics in Modern Brazil (Toronto: Macmillan of Canada, 1976), p. 37. This book is an excellent description of the emergence and evolution of the Brazilian petroleum industry, a most sufficient background for understanding the various points of view with respect to current development strategies for petroleum in Brazil.

9. Brazilian Bulletin, January 1975, p. 1. This is a monthly English-language publication of the Brazilian Government Trade Bureau, a department of the Brazilian Consulate General in New York. Its reports tend to present a very rosy picture.

10. "Indústria--Retrospecto de 1975," Conjuntura Economica 30 (February 1976): 46.

11. "Brazil Considers Private Help," The Petroleum Economist 43 (October 1975): 383.

12. Henshall and Momsen, op. cit., p. 202.

13. "Indústria--Retrospecto de 1975," op. cit., p. 59.

14. Henshall and Momsen, op. cit., pp. 198-99.

15. "The 500 Largest Industrial Corporations Outside the U.S.," Fortune, August 1976, p. 232.

16. Henshall and Momsen, op. cit., p. 200.

17. "Indústria--Retrospecto de 1975," op. cit., p. 58.

18. Ibid.

19. Bolsa Review 9 (November 1975): 637.

20. "Petróleo: Reducao no Consumo Mundial," Conjuntura Economica 30 (July 1976): 83.

21. "Gasolina Tem Consumo Estável," Jornal do Brasil (Rio de Janeiro), June 8, 1976, p. 16.

22. Bolsa Review 10 (January 1976): 22.

23. Indústria--Retrospecto de 1975," op. cit., p. 59.

24. Ibid.

25. Bolsa Review 10 (June 1976): 331.

26. Aloysio Santos Filho, "O Alto Preco de uma Desaceleracao Economica," Negócios em EXAME, May 26, 1976, p. 23.

27. "Indústria--Retrospecto de 1975," op. cit., p. 46.

28. "Petrobras Diz que Descrobriu Óleo em Poco," Jornal do Brasil, June 8, 1976, p. 16. This same notice appeared in World Oil, August 15, 1976, p. 76.

29. "Indústria--Retrospecto de 1975," op. cit., p. 46.

30. "Link de Volta," Veja, May 12, 1976, pp. 87-88.

31. Smith, op. cit., pp. 122-32.

32. "Link de Volta," op. cit.

33. "British Petroleum Compra os Mapas do Contrato de Risco," Jornal do Brasil, June 3, 1976, p. 12.

34. "A Alma do Negócio," Veja, May 19, 1976, p. 96.

35. "Energia por Hipótese," Jornal do Brasil, June 8, 1976, p. 10.

36. World Oil, August 15, 1976, p. 76.

37. Smith, op. cit. See especially Chapters 5-7, pp. 102-87.

38. Marcelo Piancastelli de Siqueira and Paulo Roberto Haddad, "A Crise Economica Mundial: Tentativa de Avaliacao dos Efeitos sobre a Economia Brasileira e, particularmente, a Mineira," Fundacao Joao Pinheiro 6 (May 1976): 16.

39. Ibid.

40. Filho, op. cit., p. 23.

41. Evandro Paranaguá, "Acordo Garante U.S. $1 Bilhao para Acominas," O Estados de Sao Paulo, May 6, 1976, p. 14.

42. "Governo Impoe a Turista que Sair Depósito de CR$ 12 Mil," Jornal do Brasil, June 5, 1976, p. 1.

43. "Decreto-Lei 1470," Jornal do Brasil, June 5, 1976, p. 13.

44. "Secretaria Especial do Meio Ambiente," Conjuntura Economica 27 (December 1973): 9. This eight-page article reproduces the official decree in its entirety, together with a listing of all previous key federal environmental legislation and a representative list of federal, state, and municipal entities concerned in some way with regulation of the use of the environment.

45. "Assembléia Recebe Críticas," O Estado de Sao Paulo, April 29, 1976, p. 34.

46. Personal conversations with several officials at Fundacao Joao Pinheiro, Belo Horizonte, Minas Gerais, May and June 1976.

47. Stefan H. Robock, Brazil: A Study in Development Progress (Lexington, Mass.: D. C. Heath, Lexington Books, 1975), pp. 171-72.

48. Ibid., p. 88.

9

IRAN: THE POLITICS OF
POLLUTION AND
ENERGY DEVELOPMENT
Cynthia H. Enloe

One nation's "crisis" may be another nation's opportunity.
Certainly this is the standard interpretation of the 1974 energy
crisis, which left the industrialized capitalist nations struggling to
cope with a severe oil shortage and an imbalance of payments while
it simultaneously enriched the treasuries of oil-producing countries.
The political repercussions for environmental protection were not
confined to the former; oil producers as well as oil importers experienced environmentally relevant political consequences as a result
of the crisis. Furthermore, since the nations worst hit by the oil
boycott and price inflation included both highly industrialized states
such as France and Japan and economically strained states such as
India and Tanzania, one cannot make easy generalizations about the
precise nature of these environmental impacts.

Among the nations that appeared to reap the greatest benefits
from the crisis, namely the OPEC member states, there also is
considerable diversity. The variables that seem most salient in
determining the environmental consequences of the oil crisis in oil-
rich nations are (1) the extent to which the regimes identify pollution
with foreign exploitation, (2) the extent to which the regimes feel
that the benefits derived from oil may be short-lived and thus feel
compelled to maximize growth while the advantageous conditions

---

This chapter could not have been written without the generous
assistance of two specialists in Iranian politics, Professor Ann
Schulz and Masood Abolfazli. Senator Jahansha Saleh and officials
of the Department of the Environment of Iran were also very helpful
in furnishing current information. Naturally, the interpretations
found in the present paper are solely the author's.

last, (3) the amount of authority and autonomy granted to the bureaucratic agencies mandated to implement environmental controls, and
(4) the degree to which environmental hazards are linked directly to
the countries' petroleum industries, thus confronting the regimes
with a direct choice between environmental protection and promotion
of their countries' principal asset.

The environmental politics of Iran are conditioned by the fact
that it is a leading oil producer; but as the following analysis suggests, that is not to say a great deal. What becomes clear is that
the way in which oil production shapes Iranian environmental policy
is determined by the particular character of the Shah-dominated
political system and by the regime's perception of itself as a third-
world leader, at the same time that it assiduously courts overseas
investment for the sake of rapid economic growth.

Elsewhere I have tried to ascertain what conditions heighten
or dampen a third-world government's concern about the issue of
environmental deterioration.[1] It is increasingly apparent that the
fact, as opposed to the issue, of environmental deterioration is not
found solely in highly industrialized societies. In addition, it has
become more and more necessary in political analysis to overcome
a tendency to lump third-world states together in a single analytical
category. Third-world countries are growing more diverse among
themselves. They include high-growth industrializing nations such
as Brazil, South Korea, and Jamaica, as well as overwhelmingly
agrarian and often marginally economically viable countries such as
Nepal, Haiti, and Upper Volta.

In my earlier investigation of the environmental issue in underdeveloped nations, what stood out at the end was the extent to which
the issue varied in the political saliency it could command, even
among the most rapidly industrializing and urbanizing nations. Although Singapore, Brazil, and Taiwan could be categorized as high-
growth members of the third world, their governments' approaches
to environmental protection differed significantly. What seemed to
be most crucial in explaining those differences was the degree to
which the current leadership was intent upon limiting foreign penetration and saw the environmental hazards flowing from oil drilling, the
Green Revolution, or new manufacturing plants as an integral part
of the broader hazards of foreign penetration. When, on top of this,
the specific pollution condition threatened an industry that the regime
was sensitive to, such as tourism or fishing, environmental protection advocates and environmental bureaucratic officials found that
they could command the attention of political leaders where their
counterparts in other developing nations were frustrated or fired.[2]

In this context Iran holds a rather ambiguous place in the third
world--an ambiguity reflected in its governmental activities to

preserve environmental quality. Since the ascendancy of the current Shah, the Iranian government has assigned top priority to national economic development. The "White Revolution," the core of the regime's development strategy, has devoted government resources to land reform, urbanization, and industrialization. Recent benefits derived from OPEC leverage in the international oil market have not basically altered this strategy. Along with its domestically initiated reforms and consolidation of power in the hands of the Shah, the strategy called for capturing greater amounts of foreign investment. While the Shah and his advisors have stepped up their pursuit of overseas capital, enterprises, and technical assistance, however, they have begun to fashion a role for Iran as a principal spokesman for not only the Persian Gulf region but for the third-world nations in general. In this expansive role, the regime plays not the dependent suitor but the confident pursued, warning developed nations that they can no longer operate in international relations according to their own interests alone. [3]

In its first role, that of a regime playing catch-up with other people's equipment and expertise, the Iranian government does not give environmental concerns great attention. In its second role, by contrast, environmental issues prove highly compatible with the regime's major goals and thus attract more serious political attention.

The pivotal and all-pervasive power of the Shah himself must be taken into account in evaluating Iranian policy formation and, more important, policy implementation. Unlike other members of the royal family, the Shah does not have defined spheres of policy interest, but is presumed to speak for the government on all issues. The extent to which the Shah is perceived by government officials as the key to legitimizing not only their authority but the very issues they are supposed to be coping with is reflected, for instance, in their repeated references to the Shah's environmental concern. There is a tendency to preface even the mildest criticisms of current environmental programs with extended reassurances to the reader that the Shah is personally committed to environmental preservation. On the other hand, in a recent interview with the New York Times, the Shah made scarce mention of the environmental problems that can accrue from uncontrolled industrialization but noted that Iran had to maximize the opportunities now available, as follows:

> In the life of a nation you have only a few periods
> where everything gathers to make it [swift progress]
> possible. This is one of those periods. We have
> got to take the fullest advantage of that. . . . And
> the only negative thing existing in the country are

just the terrorists, which are manipulated by international subversion so this is not a problem.[4]

The Shah has predicted, furthermore, that by 1988, when
Iran's seventh five-year plan is accomplished, the nation will have
become one of the world's five richest countries.[5] To symbolize
this objective, the Iranian government has not only pushed land
reform and literacy drives but has sought to acquire those technological trappings that distinguish great powers from merely
second-rank states. To this end, for instance, the Shah has contracted to purchase two Concorde supersonic jet aircraft for Iran's
national airline, to go into service in 1977, despite the serious
doubts voiced by environmentalists about the effects of SSTs.[6]

Where the Shah does appear to take explicit note of environmental issues is in those realms that touch on Iran's national sovereignty or on its role as an international and especially a regional
leader. In that spirit, for instance, in the spring of 1975 the
Iranian government hosted an international seminar in Ecological
Guidelines for the Use of Natural Resources in the Middle East and
Southwest Asia. In his speech marking World Environment Day,
the Shah asserted that a country could become fully industrialized
"without any loss to its natural beauties," but that this would require other ministries and private firms to cooperate with the Department of the Environment. In the same speech, however, the
Shah selected for special mention the necessity of protecting
Iranian offshore waters and called on the other nations sharing
those waters to cooperate.[7] In the Caspian Sea, Soviet oil-drilling
operations have been particularly polluting, to the point of jeopar-
dizing Iranian fishing enterprises. In addition, the government
estimated that about 2 million fish had been killed in the Caspian
Sea by pollution from a Japanese-Iranian appliance factory. The
government took stern action, jailing the managing director of the
Pars-Toshiba plant.[8] Nonetheless, at least one informed Iranian
official outside the environmental agency has concluded that "there
is no environmental agency. It's all merely tokenism--symbolic
gestures for the sake of immediate effect and international ap-
pearances."[9]

In a political system in which access to the Shah is the chief
measure of political influence and prestige, the current role of the
Empress, Farah Pahlevi, as principal spokesman on the environmental issue is interesting. Each member of the royal family
appears to be assigned an issue-area in which he or she serves as
spokesman, though not necessarily policy maker, for the government. This not only permits the expanded use of symbolic resources
but reinforces the public's (domestic and foreign) sense that all

issue-areas ultimately depend for their legitimacy upon the personal
sanction of the Shah.

The Empress has spoken to groups in Iran and abroad about
the government's official commitment to preserving environmental
quality while at the same time achieving its economic development
objectives. In Aspen, Colorado, she warned her American audience
that "the environment is being rapidly degraded by the thrust of an
unbridled technology" and went on to urge that "the concept of 'gross
national happiness' should stand beside that of 'gross national
product.'"[10] In Iran she told the Medical Congress of Iran that
industrial growth would have to be fashioned so as not to undermine
the quality of air and water. She encouraged Iranian professionals
to take care that Iran did not repeat the mistakes of the already industrialized countries.[11] In 1975, at a meeting of Iranian academics
at which the disfunctional consequences of Iran's economic change
were discussed with unusual candor, the Empress was seen as
lending legitimacy to the airing of such concerns in her address in
which she acknowledged that Iran was "traumatized by the conflicting winds of tradition and change."[12]

Protected by the cloak of legitimacy woven by the Shah's
general though somewhat ambiguous statements of environmental
concern and, more specifically, the Empress's frequent speeches
calling for economic progress that is compatible with environmental
quality, concrete steps have been taken legislatively and adminis-
tratively to reduce pollution. It is interesting to examine where
those steps appear to be most effective and what fundamental dynamics of Iranian politics in general curtail that effectiveness.

THE TALE OF TWO CITIES' ENVIRONMENTS

The efforts of two cities are worth examining, because they
reveal some of the positive conditions and their limitations. The
city of Isfahan, with a population of 730,000, is Iran's second-
largest municipality. It is also one of the most prized for historical
importance and cultural and architectural heritage. This legacy
has provoked more environmental concern than is evident in Iran's
largest urban center, Tehran. The Empress herself has paid
special attention to the preservation of Isfahan in her role as
guardian of Iranian culture and quality of life. This has been an
asset for Isfahan's otherwise relatively weak city planning officials
when they have tried to make the burgeoning new industries around
the city conform to environmental needs.

The Empress, however, while she can be called on occasionally to step in to save a historical site, can only give assistance on

an ad hoc basis. This leaves those in charge of fundamental, long-
term environmental planning still politically inadequate to meet the
challenges of the developmental entrepreneurs. The latter can cite
the Shah's goal of dispersing industrial growth away from Tehran to
lesser-developed regions such as that around Isfahan; in 1976,
1,800 of the country's total of 5,000 industrial units were located in
Tehran province.

Not only are the Isfahan planners faced with often-conflicting
central government priorities, but the municipal structure within
which they operate is in many ways ill-equipped to handle the demands placed on it by the new central policies.

A part of the Shah's overall plan for Iran's political development has been decentralization of administrative operations. This
should give environmentally sensitive officials in cities like Isfahan
added resources with which to fight polluting industries. In reality,
as Ann Schulz has noted, the conflicting guidelines of the national
ministries, as well as the ties of local elites to national power centers and the dependence of many locally posted administrators (including army officers) on the capital for career rewards, all serve
to undermine that theoretical local initiative. Schulz describes the
effect of this on city planning as follows:

> Isfahan's city planning head also recognizes his
> subordinates' sensitivity to external influences.
> He complains that it has been difficult to enforce
> the growth patterns outlines in the city plan. . . .
> Municipal policies are often ignored, the planner
> argued, because if we insist on enforcing zoning
> requirements, the parties subject to them will
> exert pressure on municipal officials and avoid
> the restrictions.[13]

In 1975 the mayor of Isfahan was jailed for illicit dealings in
construction bricks, an indication of the strains that rapid, few-
holds-barred growth puts on political integrity. In his place as acting mayor was appointed a London-trained Iranian architect. Himself a planning expert, the acting mayor took steps to overcome both
the economic and the political dynamics that were thwarting environmental controls in his negotiations with the U.S.-based multinational
corporation, DuPont. In a joint venture with Iranian investors,
DuPont was launching construction of an artificial fiber manufacturing plant 26 miles from Isfahan. It was to be one of the country's
costliest development projects and was expected to employ 2,000
Iranians, some of whom were to be trained in the United States.
Despite the environmental precautions that DuPont and the U.S.

building contractor, Brown and Root, said they were taking in designing and siting the plant, the acting mayor told reporters he feared that local water might be polluted by the effluents from the fiber processing. He thus suggested that DuPont relocate the plant well to the east of Isfahan. The acting mayor also voiced fears that the new installation would exacerbate the city's overcrowding and its proliferating American community. Echoing those anxieties, a prominent local private architect said that in the old days when it was the royal capital people claimed that "Isfahan is half the world." Now, he said, "I hope in trying to be the whole world Isfahan will not lose the true one half that it used to be."[14]

The Empress has also spoken out about the awesome air pollution problem now facing the capital, Tehran. The mayor of Tehran does not have the cultural legacy and delayed growth of Isfahan to draw upon in his environmental campaign. Moreover, he is operating at the very center of Iranian politics and thus does not enjoy even the minimal autonomy that geographic distance provides for his counterpart in Isfahan.

Air pollution in Tehran can be traced to several sources, but the most publicized is automobile exhaust, perhaps because it symbolizes most graphically the double-edged character of Iranian modernization. At present the city copes with an estimated 0.4 million passenger cars and some 0.3 million trucks and buses. One local observer compared driving downtown in the capital to smoking a full pack of cigarettes. The mayor of Tehran, Gholam Reza Nikpay, has acknowledged the problem, but he links air pollution with traffic in a way that may blur the environmental importance of the problem. In October 1975 Nikpay asserted that he could solve the city's traffic problem if the central government would only provide his requested $221 million. To push for that allotment, the mayor met with officials of the important Plan and Budget Organization and aides to the premier. The result was a grant to the city for $74 million, to be used in developing bus and subway projects. There was no specific mention of antipollution measures.[15]

Similarly, when the role of the automobile in Tehran became a major debating point in the Majlis, the lower house of the national legislature, it was not in terms of the environment but in terms of revenue. The press reported that a bill imposing new auto taxes "caused no debate." In conclusion, as the controversial bill passed, it was agreed that although the new taxes were burdensome, the Tehrani were already so dependent on their cars that they would pay the new tax rather than switch to mass transit.[16]

One of the reasons Tehran's automobile problem is being dealt with chiefly as a revenue-on-traffic issue rather than as a pollution issue could be that the automobile industry is one of the largest manufacturing sectors in the Iranian economy. In the private sector, car manufacturing is the largest single industry in the country, employing close to 20,000 workers. Total investment in the combined car, truck, and bus industry amounts to over $3 billion. It is not just the size of the private sector, which is mainly U.S. and British corporations, that gives the car industry its ability to resist pollution controls: the Iranian government is heavily involved in car manufacturing, both directly and indirectly. First, the government sees this sector as a "leading contributor to the development of home-based technology."[17] Second, the government gains considerable revenue from the industry. Third, more and more Iranian investors hold shares in the locally based manufacturing operations.

According to 1975 estimates, the country's vehicle industry will be producing 750,000 units annually by 1980.[18] General Motors has announced its intention to build, in a joint venture with Iranian businessmen, one of the world's largest auto and truck manufacturing plants, on the outskirts of Tehran.[19]

BUREAUCRATIC INSTITUTIONALIZATION

This is the sort of economic momentum and private-public collaboration that is almost impossible for even a well-established, strongly mandated environmental agency or powerfully entrenched municipal regime to curtail. In Iran this kind of momentum and collaboration faces a newly created national environmental agency just feeling its way through the bureaucratic maze and a city administration that enjoys little political autonomy in terms of either support constituency or budgetary resources. Nonetheless, the director of the national Department of Environment's Air Pollution Group went further than the mayor of Tehran in confronting the problem of pollution from the heavy car-production schedule. The director announced at a press conference in May 1975 that Iranian automobile producers and importers would soon have to observe special emission and pollution control standards. He went on, however, to assure his audience that his group would recommend standards that met Iran's own particular conditions; they would not be merely a carbon copy of those of the U.S. Environmental Protection Agency. The standards, once announced, would first be applied in Tehran and then gradually be spread throughout the country, because auto emissions had now become the primary source of air pollution in the capital. The department and the mayor's office would form a joint council to implement the standards.[20]

The real test of the efficacy of environmental controls, and thus of the political influence of an environmental agency in any country, is of course in implementation. It is yet to be seen whether the Air Pollution Group and the mayor will have the resources to not only promulgate but enforce their new standards.

The year 1973 marked the beginning of Iran's serious efforts to legislate and institutionalize governmental concern for environmental protection. The official Fifth Plan, setting forth the government's objectives and projected expenditures for the period 1973-78, was the first such plan to explicitly include environmental conservation as part of development planning. While in terms of total investments, those earmarked for environmental projects are relatively modest--6.1 billion rials--their separate inclusion in the plan at least indicates governmental commitment.

Total long-term investment and current expenditures on environmental protection between 1973 and 1978 should amount to 13.8 billion rials. As Table 16 shows, fixed investment will account for 6 billion rials, nonfixed investment for 5.8 billion rials, and current expenditures for 2 billion rials. [21]

TABLE 16

Credits for Environmental Conservation, Iran,
Fifth Plan (1973-78)
(in billions of rials)

	Current Credits			Development Credits	Total Credits
	Total	Fixed	Nonfixed		
Environmental conservation	1.0	2.69	2.64	5.33	6.33
Research	0.5	1.95	2.00	3.95	4.45
Administration	0.5	1.46	1.11	2.57	3.07
Total	2.0	6.1	5.75	11.85	13.85

Source: Kayhan Research Associates, A Guide to Iran's Fifth Plan, 1973-1978 (Tehran: Kayhan Group, 1975), p. 38.

The Department of Environmental Conservation came into existence in 1971, two years prior to this budgetary commitment, but it gained its real administrative significance with the passage of the 1971 Environmental Protection Act and the expansion of that act in May 1974. Other ministries in the central government still have authority and responsibilities that overlap those of the

Department of the Environment. For instance, in dealing with the increasingly worrisome pollution of the Caspian Sea, the department had to submit its proposals to the Ministry of the Interior. Since 1974, however, the department has grown in mandates, functions, and organizational elaboration.

In an arrangement that appears similar to that in the United States, the act created both a High Council for Protection of Living Environment and the Department of the Environment. As with the U.S. Council on Environmental Quality and Environmental Protection Agency, the Iranian High Council is responsible for coordinating environment-related policies throughout government, while the department focuses on specific standards and their enforcement.

The chairman of the High Council is appointed by the Shah, and the council membership includes the ministers of Finance, Agriculture and Natural Resources, Health, Cooperative and Rural Affairs, Water and Power, Economics, and Interior, as well as the executive director of the National Iranian Oil Company and the director of the Plan and Budget Organization and five other "qualified and competent persons" appointed by the chairman and the Shah. [22]

Both the High Council and the Department of the Environment are located within the prime minister's office. This may give both a certain amount of political protection, often lacking for young environmental agencies in other systems. It may also make the department, which is more immediately concerned with the enforcement of protection measures, especially vulnerable to political pressures. Although its 1973 and 1974 mandates are broadly stated, encompassing research; the establishment of air, water, and soil standards; education and beautification programs; and the regulation of hunting and fishing, they also have been deemed rather vague by some local commentators. This can provide an energetic administrator room for discretion and innovation, but it can also allow other ministries or interest groups an effective basis for criticizing an overly energetic environmental official.

Evidently both circumstances were responsible for the dismissal of one of the department's original activists. The head of the department's Human Environment Management Division--the arm that is directly involved in the control of man-made pollution and thus most politically sensitive--was a young Iranian official trained under the American environmentalist Barry Commoner. He reportedly hired a number of bright young people from a variety of countries, a practice common throughout Iranian administration, to work on a variety of projects ranging from DDT to industrial monitoring. His activities aroused antagonism in political circles and led to his departure and to the withering of his projects.

BUREAUCRATICS IN THE POLITICAL CULTURE

Problems of institutional underdevelopment, coupled with the mixed feelings of a governing elite about environmental controls when they seem to jeopardize economic growth are not unique to Iran's Department of Environment. Added to these are strong tendencies in Iranian political behavior that further complicate the task of any environmental administrator. Scholars analyzing Iranian politics have repeatedly noted two characteristics. First is a deep sense of insecurity felt by those in the political arena. This is generated by an often very realistic awareness of just how delicately poised is any person's career in a system that for generations has bred secrecy, policy surveillance, personalized competition, and power jousting within a narrow hierarchical pyramid. Such pervasive feelings of insecurity cannot help but make the average environmental official cautious at best or paralyzed at worst. It certainly does not foster the promulgation of tough air or water standards and the welcoming of confrontation with industries that are known to involve the interests of well-placed Iranians.

The second tendency commonly noted as characteristic of Iranian politics is cynicism. Iranians use the Persian term badbini to refer to the combination of cynicism and pessimism that pervades the political culture. The belief that laws or moral codes are mere charades to be adhered to only by the naive, that only ruthlessness and cunning insure success, that most individuals are, at bottom, concerned only with their own survival and self-aggrandizement--these are the kinds of perceptions that are the hallmark of a cynical polity. It may be that any society in the throes of an economic boom, where money seems to be the currency of social relationships, is prone to such political cynicism. But its visibility in Iran appears to observers to be on a scale that goes beyond merely a "boom mentality."

Marvin Zonis, in his detailed survey of elite attitudes in Iran, traces much of the current cynicism to the role of the monarch. Zonis contends that the Shah has successfully eliminated all opposing power bases and has made himself the sole dispenser of rewards and privileges in the political system. He has mastered the skill of co-optation to the point that there is the widespread belief that he can buy anyone's loyalty or concession.[23]

Consequently, political figures or administrators see nothing unusual in compromising their own convictions and presume that everyone else in the system is behaving likewise. One Iranian with first-hand insight into the modes of governmental behavior likened the society today to a cross between a zoo and a jungle--outer constraints are rigidly defined, but within those boundaries there are

only minimal bonds of trust or security. [24] Ironically, the Shah's
personal drive to clamp down on corruption in 1975 seems only to
have exacerbated the citizens' and officials' suspiciousness and
cynicism, according to long-time Middle East correspondent Eric
Pace. [25]

A Tehran University study of the central government's administrators in 1964 revealed how these tendencies show up in bureau-
crats' behavior. The study concluded that there were nine problems
hindering Iranian administration: (1) absence of cooperation among
administrators; (2) incorrect philosophy behind the entire idea of
administration; (3) bribery; (4) absence of goals or interest in work;
(5) prevalence of influence-wielding; (6) lack of respect for the
people; (7) use of administrative power for personal benefit; (8) con-
tinual absence from work; and (9) misuse of government property. [26]

In this administrative milieu it is especially difficult for an
environmental agency to operate. The environmental department in
any country has to appeal to a certain degree of idealism, as well as
to the necessities of public health and natural resource conservation.
Furthermore, environmental administrators are often in a position
of pressing for controls on growth without definitive or easily under-
stood concrete measures of the dangers that will flow from unbridled development. The "politics of measurement" have to be
coped with by every country's environmental agency, but in a society such as that of contemporary Iran, with its high level of
cynicism and insecurity, the ability to compete effectively within
the politics of measurement becomes particularly crucial.

The Iranian Department of the Environment has not been completely without support, however. While there are no mobilized
interest groups or sophisticated environmental lawyers, there is a
prominent legislator, Senator Jahanshah Saleh, who has attracted
media and public attention to the problems of pollution. Senator
Saleh, a physician, is an appointed member of the Iranian legislature, and thus one cannot presume that his long legislative career,
which has focused on environmental problems, is an indicator of
electoral concern over the issue. Nonetheless, he has had the political security and social status to press for air and water pollution
controls without being accused of opportunism or labeled a potential
threat to the ruling elite. The Department of the Environment has
taken an active part in drafting new legislation, but has needed supporters such as Senator Saleh to get that legislation through, and
here the senator's position on the Senate Committee for the Protection of the Environment, which was created in 1969, is helpful.
Still, in public interviews Senator Saleh is careful to credit the
Shah's sensitivity to the dangers of pollution as a major reason for
the passage of effective new bills. [27]

The phase of development of the Department of the Environment that began in 1975 may have been one of the most difficult politically. It called for the department to design and issue the first of what it hoped would be a series of environmental impact guidelines. Such forms would have to be filled out and submitted to the agency by every company proposing a new plant or facility.

This operation will bring the department into its most direct confrontation with the Iranian government's national development strategy of exploiting its oil resources for the sake of rapid and diversified industrial growth and, in turn, regional hegemony. Moreover, the environmental impact program will intimately involve the agency with not just Iranian entrepreneurs, with their extensive governmental contacts, but with Japanese, U.S., and British multinational corporations, which can threaten to move their investments to other third-world sites if the controls become too burdensome. On the other hand, some of these corporations have much more political experience, given the stress laid on environmental issues in their own countries, in dealing with such environmental stipulations. "Dealing with," of course, can take the form of compliance or tokenism or avoidance. How the department administers the environmental impact guidelines, then, will be a test of the real influence of the agency in a not very hospitable political and cultural milieu. More fundamentally, it will be a test of the Shah's regime in its effort to optimize the short-term advantages of oil demand without undermining the Iranian quality of life and without allowing Iran to be a "pollution haven," vulnerable to foreign investors' own priorities.

ENVIRONMENTAL POLITICS AS THE BOOM FADES

Just how short-term that oil-derived advantage may be is becoming more clear. In 1975 Iranian oil production actually dropped 11 percent from its 1974 level. At the end of the year it was expected that the country's 1975 revenues would be no more than $20 billion, $3 or $4 billion below what government planners had anticipated when they drew up the year's expenditures. The drop in oil production and thus in revenues has saddled Iran with a sizable deficit and negative balance of payments, which was not what the optimistic development strategists for the Shah had foreseen when they issued their ambitious five-year plan. In reaction to the decline, the five-year plan has been revised. Major development programs, especially large "show piece" undertakings such as the new Tehran airport, have been shelved. The Shah has appointed a special unit to monitor development spending. He personally has launched a campaign against profiteering and inflated price fixing.[28]

At first glance this abrupt awareness of the shaky foundations of all-out growth would appear to work in favor of environmental control. It could lead to a greater sensitivity to the need for conservation, a greater reluctance to engage in the consumerist passion for the automobile, a hesitation to plan grandiose projects without consideration of their long-term quantitative and qualitative costs.

On the other hand, a reassessment of government priorities such as is taking place in Iran could limit the efforts at pollution control even more. When budgets are cut and agencies must justify their expenditures in ever more concrete and politically meaningful terms, environmental agencies have been known to come away with less, not more. An editorial in Iran's leading English-language paper was headlined, "Environment Must Join Projects Queue." The editorial went on to note that the director of the Department of the Environment had explained that his organization had not received all the funds it was supposed to receive in order to carry out its new mandate under the stiffened environmental act. The Director was quoted as saying, realistically, "Let's face it, money buys the specialized manpower and facilities needed to implement massive environmental projects."[29]

When the powerful Plan and Budget Organization reconsiders the financial demands of the various ministries and departments, will the environment be deemed a top priority or something that can wait until the Iranian economic boom is rekindled?

The answer to this depends in turn on how the regime, particularly the Shah himself, relates environmental protection to the overall scheme of development. In most third-world nations, those with oil as well as those without, pollution is not an issue of great political importance of its own. Its saliency is usually achieved when it is judged by the governing elite to be a threat to, rather than a product of, economic development and to be a signal that the nation is losing so much of its autonomy that it is becoming unacceptably dependent and vulnerable. In Iran neither condition is totally absent, but each is only in its early formative stage.

NOTES

1. Cynthia H. Enloe, The Politics of Pollution in a Comparative Perspective (New York: David McKay, 1975).

2. Among the interesting studies of environmental politics in third-world nations are Reynaldo M. Lesaca, "Pollution Control Legislation and Experience in a Developing Country: The Philippines," Journal of Developing Areas, July 8, 1974, pp. 537-56; Ross Marlay, "Politics and Administration of Environmental Legislation in the Philippines," paper presented at the Midwest Conference

on Asian Studies, Chicago, November 1974; Roger Mark Selya, "Water and Air Pollution in Taiwan," Journal of Developing Areas, January 9, 1975, pp. 177-202; Conor Reilly, "Environmental Action in Zambia," Environment 17, no. 7 (October 1975): 31-35.

3. For instance, see the Iranian delegate's response to Henry Kissinger at the UN special session, New York Times, September 23, 1975.

4. Quoted in New York Times, September 24, 1975.

5. The Times (London), July 10, 1975.

6. Ibid.

7. Kayhan International (one of two Tehran English-language dailies), June 5, 1975.

8. New York Times, September 20, 1975.

9. Personal communication with the author, July 1975.

10. Reprinted in New York Times, July 26, 1975.

11. Kayhan International, September 13, 1975.

12. New York Times, October 10, 1975.

13. Ann Schulz, "The Politics of Municipal Administration in Iran: A Case-Study of Isfahan," Journal of Administration Overseas, October 1975, p. 233.

14. New York Times, September 6, 1975.

15. Kayhan International, October 4, 1975.

16. Kayhan International, March 6, 1976.

17. Kayhan International, August 2, 1975.

18. Kayhan International, July 19, 1975.

19. Newsweek, May 19, 1975, p. 37.

20. Kayhan International, May 15, 1975.

21. Kayhan Research Associates, A Guide to Iran's Fifth Plan, 1973-1978 (Tehran: Kayhan group, 1975), pp. 37-38.

22. For a description of the organizational and legislative history of the Department of the Environment, see Eskandar Firouz, Environment Iran (Tehran: National Society for the Conservation of Natural Resources and Human Environment, 1974).

23. Marvin Zonis, The Political Elite of Iran (Princeton: Princeton University Press, 1971), pp. 331-32.

24. Personal communication with the author, September 1975.

25. New York Times, February 4, 1976.

26. James A. Bill, The Politics of Iran (Columbus, Ohio: Charles E. Merrill, 1972), p. 110.

27. For an interview with Senator Saleh, see Tehran Journal, May 27, 1975.

28. New York Times, December 9, 1975; Business Week, November 17, 1975, pp. 58-63.

29. Kayhan International, June 3, 1975.

10

CONCLUSION
Donald R. Kelley

When the idea for this study first took shape in the form of a panel at the 1975 International Studies Association meeting, the original participants began their research with a simple assumption based more or less on conventional wisdom. This assumption was that the energy crisis would produce extensive rollbacks in environmental protection measures in both industrial and energy-producing nations. Despite the recent environmental gains won in advanced industrial nations such as the United States, Denmark, and Japan and the beginnings of such awareness in Eastern Europe, the Soviet Union, and developing nations, our collective prognosis was that the political and economic forces animated by real or impending energy shortages or by pressures to reap windfall profits from fuel exports would soon dominate the scene, and important trade-off decisions were reached concerning energy and environmental policies.

To our surprise, our studies produced a much more complex picture of the interaction of energy and environmental policies. This is not to say, of course, that our original expectation that energy development and conservation issues would not weigh heavily against further environmental improvement programs that depended on the utilization of cleaner fuels or on the control of industrial and auto emissions were completely disproven. Pressure for delays in clean air standards or permission to use and develop environmentally risky energy sources did come from energy-related industries and from others who simply regarded the question of adequate energy supplies as a more important national priority. What was surprising was that in most cases environmental and conservationist interests were able to launch strong campaigns against the energy lobbies. While the final picture is far from clear or uniform for the many countries under study, it is significant that in those nations in which environmental interests had already emerged as a viable political force, the efforts of the pro-energy interests were met with considerable resistance. As the earlier chapters suggest, the actual pattern in terms of policy outcomes differed strikingly from country to country. In some cases, such as Japan, environmental protection measures survived largely intact. In others, such as the United States, the record was mixed, producing a still-confusing picture of national and state environmental and energy policies in which no clear victor has emerged. Still other variations have emerged in nations such as the Soviet Union, where no nationally viable environmental program or lobby existed, or in developing and energy-producing nations, where the question of environmental quality has not yet become a salient political issue.

One ambitious goal of this study has been to examine the interaction of energy and environmental policies in a number of nations to see whether common patterns or themes emerged. While the following review is far from exhaustive, it does suggest some surprising results in terms of the technical, social, and political factors that have or have not shaped individual national responses.

At first glance, conventional wisdom would seem to suggest that a nation's status as an energy-rich fuel exporter or as an energy-poor importer would be a vital factor in shaping the emerging balance of energy-related and environmental goals. However, even aside from the consideration that the major energy producers that initiated the crisis are marginally industrialized third-world nations, no completely uniform energy-environment pattern is evident in the industrialized states. Developments in Denmark and Japan, which are probably the most import-dependent of the study, suggest that their status as energy paupers has not led them to permit extensive rollbacks of existing environmental legislation or to rush headlong into the development of alternative technologies.

Nations that are potentially less dependent on imports, such as the United States and the Soviet Union, have made less than adequate attempts to develop known domestic reserves as fully as might be expected, for internal consumption or in order to take advantage of international markets. In the case of the United States, dependency on imported oil has actually increased since the 1973 crisis. This is essentially because conservation programs have lagged and attempts to develop known coal reserves or more sophisticated alternatives such as nuclear energy have been stalemated by technological uncertainties; resistance from environmental groups; and perhaps most importantly, indecision and reluctance on the part of the energy industries themselves to proceed with further investment until the patterns of governmental regulation and economic risks are better known. In the Soviet case, the USSR has found that production from its own admittedly extensive resources has fallen short of current industrial and domestic needs, largely because of delays in the development of new production areas and alternative technologies.

Conventional wisdom would also seem to dictate that the most frantic attempts to deal with real or potential energy shortfalls should occur within the most industrialized states rather than in the emerging nations. Working from the premise that the economic survival of complex industrialized systems is more dependent on continued energy supplies than is the case with only marginally industrialized systems, it would seem logical to argue that environmental concerns would be the first victims of energy shortages in the advanced nations.

This ignores two factors that militate against such a development. The first is the simple fact that the major industrial nations are likely to be in the forefront of environmental protection already. Having become the victims of industrial and automotive pollution, these nations were the first to recognize the danger and to pass environmental legislation. This is not to argue, of course, that the pattern is uniform among the industrial states in our study. Quite to the contrary, some, such as the United States and Denmark, stand out with considerably better track records than Eastern Europe and the Soviet Union. The point is simply that legislative enactments and environmental protection agencies were already in existence by the time of the energy crisis, and in most cases their efforts were supplemented by the presence of environmental or conservationist lobbies of varying strength.

The second factor is that most of the industrial nations simply had more of a technological and economic cushion to fall back on than did third-world consumers. While the crisis seemed painful enough to the man in the street, who viewed it in terms of higher prices and restrictions on consumption, the real challenge came in the form of a rethinking of some overly optimistic assumptions about future economic growth rates and the development of alternative fuel sources. While both questions are certainly critical and unquestionably controversial, neither really implies a fundamental threat to the survival of these nations as major industrial powers, although the short-term adjustments may indeed be traumatic. The real issues facing national policy makers were the necessity of developing acceptable trade-offs between environmental and production goals and assessing the relative economic and social costs within the community.

For marginally developed third-world nations, even if they were energy exporters, the problems were seen in a different light. As Cynthia H. Enloe points out in her chapter on Iran, issues such as the penetration of foreign economic interests and the development of a self-sustaining indigenous industrial infrastructure took precedence over the task of finding a balance between energy and environment.

The fear of being left behind as a permanent pauper nation or of permitting domestic fuel resources to be tapped for the benefit of more industrialized nations has remained a constant factor working against greater recognition of environmental goals.

Although conventional wisdom proved to be of little help in understanding the evolving relationship between energy and environmental policies, some common elements did become apparent. One of these constant factors, at least for the already industrialized nations, was that the energy crisis did not emerge unheralded. While the timing of the 1973 embargo and the subsequent price increases came as a surprise, the basic facts that energy would soon be in short supply and that difficult decisions lay ahead in terms of developing alternative sources were already known to energy experts and environmentalists, if not to the general public. In this case the impact of the crisis was simply to sharpen the issue and to give it immediacy in the public eye. It is true, however, that the experts and governmental leaders had not done their homework before the 1973 embargo; very little long-range planning to deal with impending energy shortfalls was in evidence even in the USSR and Eastern Europe, which pride themselves on their planned economies. What passed for alternative scenarios for energy development and conservation were typically the product of special energy-related or environmental interests within each society, with little effort made on either side to assess the trade-off costs or to work out compromises. The crisis of 1973 merely served to elevate these heretofore limited disputes to the level of public debate.

Another common feature in both the industrialized and the developing nations was the speed with which the energy-environment issue quickly translated into a more fundamental debate about national life styles, images, and aspirations. Perhaps because both the energy-related and the environmental interests sought to mobilize a wider popular audience by describing the dangers of energy starvation or a crippled environment in stark and emotional terms, at least initially the question of energy supply and environmental quality took on the tone of a clash between continued economic viability and environmental devastation. While a more balanced perspective focusing on calculated trade-offs has now emerged in the writing of most analysts, the initial polarization of the issue did much to increase the level of emotionalism.

Another common factor is that commitments to energy and environmental policies are being made in a setting of virtually universal uncertainty about the technological capability of the human race to develop safe energy supplies and protect and manipulate the environment. On the one hand, no one is really certain of the technical feasibility and environmental impact of alternative energy development

schemes. Even the most optimistic proponent of energy development must admit that a host of unanswered technical questions remain about already common procedures, such as strip mining, and
even greater doubts cloud the development of more esoteric sources,
such as nuclear power, to say nothing of their social and environmental impact.

On the other hand, considerable uncertainty also exists about
the parameters of environmental viability, especially in terms of
the limits to which it can be strained and manipulated and still retain its self-regulatory capacity.

Certainly there is agreement that future energy starvation
would fundamentally disrupt modern society as we know it and prevent future economic development in the third-world nations, just
as there is agreement that the environment can bear only a certain
pollution load before it is stretched beyond the breaking point. What
remains unknown is how to calculate just where the energy consumption and environmental survival points converge. What combinations
of energy consumption and environmental protection are possible
without threatening the survival of both the social system and the
environment? How much can energy consumption patterns be altered without causing fundamental economic and social changes, and
how far can the environment be permitted to deteriorate before ir-
replaceable natural cycles and food chains are disrupted?

Even if the technical and economic indicators needed to answer
these questions were clearly enough known so that we could calculate
alternative trade-off plateaus of energy consumption and environmental quality, the political and social issues concerned with the determination of national priorities and the distribution of scarce resources within the community would remain unanswered. Indeed,
it can be argued that, paradoxically, one of the factors that has limited the clash between energy and environmental interests is that the
exact trade-off costs are still vague; no one is yet quite sure ex-
actly how great the cost will be or, perhaps even more importantly,
how it will be distributed.

Still another common point is that there are really two levels
of debate about the interrelationship of energy and environmental
policies. The most immediate deals with stop-gap energy programs
designed to deal with current shortages and the prospects for an immediate rollback of existing environmental protection measures,
such as they may be. In most cases these debates are technologically linked either to the reduction of air quality standards so that more
environmentally destructive fuels can be consumed or to delays or
outright rollbacks of emission controls. This kind of debate has
thrown the proponents of dirtier fuels and the environmentalists into
conflict within the context of the legislative and judicial guidelines

initially set forth before the energy crisis. The general thrust of national policy had already been defined in most cases, creating a situation in which the subsequent conflict resulted in incremental adjustments and short-term compromises. Neither the environmentalists nor the energy interests saw themselves, at least in the short run, as substantially redefining important national goals or making long-term commitments to alternative energy and environmental futures.

Quite the opposite is the case with the second level of debate, which deals with the long-range and more controversial question of future energy development. For the major industrial nations the key issues have become (1) the utilization of more environmentally destructive energy sources, such as high-sulfur oil and coal, over the next several decades and (2) the eventual development of more esoteric replacements, such as nuclear and solar power. For the energy-poor developing nations or the energy producers themselves, the principal questions have centered on access to adequate energy supplies to permit continued development or on the utilization to best advantage of an exhaustible natural resource. In either case, the decisions involved will represent fundamental and essentially irreversible commitments of resources to the development of future energy and environmental profiles. As such, they will undoubtedly generate far more heated debate than decisions about stop-gap measures to deal with immediate energy shortfalls such as the 1973 embargo. Such long-term commitments to the development of alternative energy sources inevitably touch virtually all segments of the community and affect patterns of industrial and domestic consumption that are deeply ingrained in the economic infrastructure and the very life style of each nation.

Finally, the task of developing a coordinated national energy policy is a new and politically uncharted course for most of the nations covered by this study. Except in the Soviet Union and Eastern Europe, energy policy decisions have largely been left to the industries themselves. Even in states such as Japan, in which the central authorities have tried to articulate loosely coordinated national development plans or deal with chronic energy shortfalls, national policy has been directed more toward the technological modernization of industry itself than toward potential shortages. Conservation, as such, or the environmental implications of energy consumption did not emerge as important national goals until about eight to ten years ago.

With the limited exceptions noted above, however, there has been little precedent for the direct regulation of energy production and consumption. This is politically significant for two reasons. First, until recently there has been a general absence of effective

governmental institutions to formulate and enforce energy policy at
the national or regional level. Even though such institutions have
quickly sprung into existence, they remain relative newcomers to
the political scene. In most cases their inexperience and relatively
junior standing in the ministerial pecking order have hampered efforts
to define coherent national environmental policies and defend them
against the attacks of more firmly rooted industrial and energy-
related interests. In this setting the energy industries themselves
have found it easy to penetrate and influence the newly formed planning and regulatory agencies.

Second, it must also be remembered that in most cases the
development of national energy policies leads both legislative and
executive authorities into areas in which policy has in the past been
made piecemeal to suit the needs of special interests or to deal with
short-term problems. Forging a coherent national policy fundamentally changes the nature of the policy-making process from one in
which limited incremental decisions are made on the basis of the involvement of a small number of concerned actors and interests to
one in which wide-ranging policies must be set forth in a more open
and competitive arena. This is not to say, of course, that the
energy-related and industrial interests have been scattered in dis-
array by the advent of the new regulatory agencies or the groundswell
of environmental opposition, but it does mean that new and frequently
skillful political actors in the form of environmental protection groups
and government agencies with policy mandates have taken the stage
in both the energy and the environmental areas.

All of this raises perhaps the most important political point
to emerge in virtually all of the nations under discussion, which is
that the conflict about the interrelationship of energy and environmental policy is really two different but intertwined threads of argument. On the one hand, there has clearly been conflict about the
content of policy itself, that is, where the actual trade-off between
energy consumption and environmental quality will be struck. On
the other hand, there is a second level of conflict about the more
fundamental question of who will make policy in these areas and determine the relative balance. Not only does this conflict include the
predictable line-up of protagonists in the energy and environmental
lobbies, but it also spreads to encompass often-bitter intragovern-
mental power struggles among agencies with conflicting mandates.
In a large number of cases these power struggles often involve the
relationship between central and regional authorities. As Walter
A. Rosenbaum observed in his discussion of the politics of energy
policy in the United States, it is a battle over institutional structures
for policy making. Since in both policy areas new institutions are
being created and traditional institutional patterns of authority and

influence are being remolded or completely restructured, consider-able political conflict is likely to result, not only because of the acknowledged importance of the policies themselves but also, and perhaps more fundamentally, because the recognition and acceptance of energy-related and environmental constraints may merely be the overture to a much more extensive and discordant redefinition of basic social and economic priorities and political prerogatives.

DONALD R. KELLEY is assistant professor of political science at Mississippi State University.

Dr. Kelley has published in the areas of comparative environmental politics and Soviet area studies. He is coauthor of The Economic Superpowers and the Environment: The United States, the Soviet Union, and Japan, and has contributed articles to the American Political Science Review, Journal of Politics, American Behavioral Scientist, Polity, Soviet Studies, and Canadian Slavonic Papers.

Dr. Kelley received his A.B. and M.A. from the University of Pittsburgh and his Ph.D. and Russian Area Certificate from Indiana University.

ROBERT A. BLACK, JR. is associated with the Institute on Western Europe, Columbia University, and is a Research Associate of the Conference Board in New York City. His research and teaching interests have been primarily policies and policy making in advanced industrial societies, especially the European Community. He authored the chapter on energy policy in Policy-Making in the European Communities and is currently completing doctoral research on energy, growth, and pollution in the Nine. He received his B.S. in engineering from the U.S. Naval Academy in 1963, his M.A. in 1974, certificate in European Studies in 1975, and master of philosophy in political science in 1976, from Columbia University.

DAVID HOWARD DAVIS teaches political science at Cornell University. He received his A.B. from Cornell University and his Ph.D. from the Johns Hopkins University, where he held a Woodrow Wilson Foundation Dissertation Fellowship. Professor Davis was on leave from Rutgers in 1973-74 as a National Association of Schools of Public Affairs and Administration (NASPAA) Public Administration Fellow assigned to the U.S. Environmental Protection Agency headquarters in Washington, D.C., where he worked in the Office of Planning and Evaluation and the Office of Legislation. In 1976 he served as a consultant to the National Academy of Sciences Committee on Nuclear and Alternative Energy Systems. He has written two books, How the Bureaucracy Makes Foreign Policy and Energy Politics.

CYNTHIA H. ENLOE is Associate Professor of Government at Clark University, Worcester, Massachusetts. Dr. Enloe has published in the fields of comparative ethnic politics and political development. Among her books are Ethnic Conflict and Political Development and The Politics of Pollution in Comparative Perspective. Dr. Enloe received her B.A. from Connecticut College and her M.A. and Ph.D. from University of California, Berkeley.

THOMAS F. KELSEY is Assistant Professor of Geography at the University of Pittsburgh. He serves as a faculty member of the Department of Geography and the Center for Latin American Studies. Dr. Kelsey is a Brazilianist whose research interests include food supply systems, economic and social development processes, and competition for utilization of basic (natural) resources in developing nations. Dr. Kelsey holds a B.A. (1964) and an M.A. (1966) in geography from the University of Michigan, a Ph.D. certificate in Latin American studies, a Ph.D. certificate in tropical agriculture, and a Ph.D. degree in geography (1972) from the University of Florida.

GEORGE KLEIN is a professor of political science at Western Michigan University.
Dr. Klein specialized in East European politics and has been a frequent contributor to scholarly works in the field. Various contributions have appeared in Studies in Comparative Communism, The Changing Face of Communism in Eastern Europe, ed. Peter A. Toma; Ethnic Dynamics, ed. C. L. Hunt and Lewis Walker; and From Cold War to Detente, ed. Peter J. Potichnyj and Jane P. Shapiro (New York: Praeger, 1976). Dr. Klein received his A.B., M.A., and Ph.D. from the University of Illinois.

MARGARET A. McKEAN is Assistant Professor of Political Science at Duke University, Durham, North Carolina. Her publications have dealt with environmental protest and changing political values in Japan. Her reviews have appeared in the Journal of Asian Studies and the Journal of Politics. Dr. McKean holds a B.A. and Ph.D. from the University of California at Berkeley and an M.A. from Harvard University.

WALTER A. ROSENBAUM is a professor of political science at the University of Florida. He has been a staff member, and is now a consultant, with the U.S. Environmental Protection Agency. He has published articles and other papers on various aspects of environmental protection. Presently he is completing the second edition of his book, Politics of Environmental Concern (New York: Praeger, forthcoming).

JOANNE S. WYMAN is an energy and environment consultant with Booz, Allen and Hamilton, Bethesda, Maryland. Previously she was a community planner with the Federal Aviation Administration, Washington, D.C.

Ms. Wyman has written in the area of Scandinavian environmental politics. She is guest editor of a forthcoming issue of the Scandinavian Review.

Ms. Wyman holds B.A. and M.A. degrees from Clark University, Worcester, Massachusetts, and is a Ph.D. candidate at Brandeis University, Waltham, Massachusetts.

LAW AND OFFSHORE DEVELOPMENT:
The North Sea Experience
David B. Keto

ENERGY, ECONOMIC GROWTH, AND EQUITY
IN THE U.S.
Narasimhan P. Kannan

CLEANING UP: The Cost of Refinery Pollution Control
Council on Economic Priorities
and Joan Norris Boothe

ENERGY POLICY IN THE UNITED STATES
edited by Seymour Warkov

COAL AND CRISIS: Political Dilemmas of Energy
Management
Walter A. Rosenbaum